Making sense

A Student's Guide to Research and Writing

ENGINEERING
AND THE
TECHNICAL SCIENCES

Margot Northey   Judi Jewinski

OXFORD
UNIVERSITY PRESS

1904 ❧ 2004

100 YEARS OF
CANADIAN PUBLISHING

OXFORD
UNIVERSITY PRESS

70 Wynford Drive, Don Mills, Ontario M3C 1J9
www.oup.com/ca

Oxford University Press is a department of the University of Oxford.
It furthers the University's objective of excellence in research, scholarship,
and education by publishing worldwide in

Oxford New York

Auckland Bangkok Buenos Aires Cape Town Chennai
Dar es Salaam Delhi Hong Kong Istanbul Karachi Kolkata
Kuala Lumpur Madrid Melbourne Mexico City Mumbai Nairobi
São Paulo Shanghai Taipei Tokyo Toronto

Oxford is a trade mark of Oxford University Press
in the UK and in certain other countries

Published in Canada
by Oxford University Press

Library and Archives Canada Cataloguing in Publication

Northey, Margot, 1940–
Making sense : a student's guide to research and writing :
engineering & technical sciences / Margot Northey, Judi Jewinski.

Includes index.
ISBN 0-19-541693-7

1. Technical writing. 2. English language—Rhetoric. 3. Report
writing. I. Jewinski, Judi, 1952– II. Title.

T11.N67 2004   808'.06662   C2004-904796-5

Cover and text design: Brett J. Miller

1 2 3 4 – 05 04 03 02
This book is printed on permanent (acid-free) paper ∞.
Printed in Canada

TABLE OF CONTENTS

Acknowledgements

As a teacher of writing to engineers, both students and professionals, I am grateful for the willingness of so many people to allow their work to provide examples for this book. The following deserve special mention: Mehdi Ansari, Maria Castro, Jessada Jitjareonchai, Andrew Milne, Claudia Mueller, Caroline Page, Insop Song, Alireza Tassoudi, Adrien Wolff, Yu Ping. Kate Hoye was especially helpful in developing definitions for the glossary, and Harikla Zafiris did a tremendous amount of photocopying. Both Ed Jewinski and Eric Sinkins were wonderful editors and proofreaders. I am also very fortunate to have had the support and help of several of my colleagues at the University of Waterloo, particularly Susan Bryant, John Crossley, Hsaio d'Ailly, Ed Jernigan, Keith Hipel, and Mary Merikle. Librarian Doug Morton was a source of good advice on research techniques. Above all, however, I am indebted to my longtime friend Peter Roe, one of the founders of the Department of Systems Design Engineering at the University of Waterloo, for his sensitive reading of the manuscript and his always expert and apt advice.

A NOTE TO THE STUDENT

This book has been developed for students of the engineering and technological sciences. Its purpose is to provide a framework for conducting research and writing clearly and comprehensively about it.

Engineering is a blend of science, industry, technology, mathematics, and business; the assignments you complete as part of your studies require you to bring together theory and practice not just accurately but intelligibly and convincingly. This book will show you how to refine your research and writing skills so that you can present your ideas professionally on paper as well as in person.

Contrary to what many people believe, good writing does not come naturally. Even for the best writers, it's mostly hard work, following the formula of "one per cent inspiration and ninety-nine per cent perspiration" famously set out by Thomas Edison.

Writing in university or college is not fundamentally different from writing elsewhere. Yet each piece of writing has its own special purposes, and these are what determine its shape and tone. *Making Sense in Engineering and the Technical Sciences* examines both the general precepts for effective writing and the special requirements of academic work in engineering and related fields (especially the reporting of research, experiments, studies, projects, or other investigations in papers, reports, and summaries). It also points out some of the most common errors made by inexperienced writers and suggests how to avoid or correct problems. Written mostly in the form of guidelines rather than strict rules—since no rules are perfect—this book should help you escape some common pitfalls and develop confidence through an understanding of basic principles and a mastery of sound techniques.

The structure of this book follows a standard developmental process from design to prototype to product. Above all, it is intended to be a clear, concise, and readable guide that will help you do well in all your courses—and eventually in your professional career.

SYMBOLS FOR COMMON ERRORS

NOTE: If a marker uses any of the following short forms in assessing an assignment or report, consult Chapters 12, 13, 14, 16, or the Glossary for help.

agr	agreement of subject and verb
amb	ambiguity
awk	awkwardness
cap	capitalization
cs	comma splice
dm	dangling modifier
D	diction
gr	grammar or idiom
mm	misplaced modifier
¶	new paragraph
ref	pronoun reference
p	punctuation
quot	quotation marks
rep	redundancy or repetition
RO	run-on sentence
frag	sentence fragment
sp	spelling
T	tense
trans.	transition missing
⌣	transpose
wdy	wordy
ww	wrong word

CHAPTER 1

WRITING AND THINKING

You are not likely to produce clear writing unless you have first done some clear thinking, and thinking can't be hurried. It follows that the most important step you can take before beginning to write is to leave yourself enough time to get organized.

Start by considering writing very much as a process—that of recording ideas for yourself in notes and of preparing to share those ideas with others in some written form. Whether you are communicating formally or informally, there are three steps to this process: the planning, the drafting, and the refining. The planning stage calls for you to assess the various requirements of the job at hand, such as the format, the purpose, the audience, and the approach. If the time you take planning, researching, and preparing to write is well spent, the final two stages—the drafting and refining—will be a lot easier.

INITIAL STRATEGIES

Developing a project calls for you to make choices about what ideas you want to present and how you want to present them. Practice makes the decisions easier to come by, but no matter how comfortable you become, you will have to make choices with every project you take on.

You can narrow the field initially by acknowledging that you are *not* doing work for just anyone, anywhere, for no particular reason. With every project you undertake, it's sound strategy to ask yourself two basic questions:

- What is the purpose of this?
- Who is the reader?

The obvious reaction may be, "Well, I'm writing for my lab instructor to fulfill a course requirement," but that's simply not sufficient. The people who will be assessing your work expect you to recognize the demands of the context, to demonstrate that you can imagine—and write to suit—the professional setting for your work, even though you might not graduate for another three or four years.

THINK ABOUT THE PURPOSE

Course work is intended to confirm that you understand the concepts presented in class and have learned to apply them. Depending upon the assignment, your purpose may be any one or more of the following:

- to record and present data from tests and experiments that you have performed
- to show that you understand and can apply certain principles, concepts, or theories
- to show that you can do independent research
- to confirm your ability to solve problems and share convincing solutions
- to demonstrate that you can think critically
- to demonstrate that you can think creatively
- to confirm your professionalism
- to show your ability to synthesize ideas and present evidence
- to record stages in the development and completion of a project
- to confirm what you know and show that you can apply it to specific situations.

A lab assignment in which you must show that you have understood and confirmed a hypothesis calls for an approach that's different from the one you would take to write a proposal to solve a problem. In the first, your approach is straightforward, with an emphasis on the accurate recording and reporting of a process. In the second, you must provide convincing support for your recommendations, and you achieve that goal by anticipating and overcoming potential objections.

You may also want to bear in mind the weight of an assignment within the context of the overall marking scheme. A project that is worth 50 per cent of your final grade merits an equivalent amount of time and effort. For assignments that may not be weighted so heavily, consider their successful completion as just another step towards your professional career.

While your primary purpose will differ from one type of writing to the next, your secondary purpose will always be the same: to confirm that you not only understand what's expected but are capable of demonstrating it.

THINK ABOUT THE READER

Thinking about the reader means recognizing that there may be others besides your instructor involved in evaluating your assignment. Eventually, there may be both primary and secondary readers. This will almost certainly be the case when you are writing in a professional context, particularly if you are completing an apprenticeship or co-op placement as part of your studies. Your primary readers (your professors or your supervisors) will be experts in the field, and you can expect them to be knowledgeable about the subject. A secondary reader, on the other hand, may not even be an engineer, so you have to consider how much special explanation will be necessary.

Writing for multiple readers is a skill all professionals must develop. Start by imagining how you might describe a concept like desalination to a lab technician, to your aunt, or to your friend who's in economics. Each reader has different needs and expectations. Before you turn in a project, consider whether you should add an executive summary—just so your message is clear to a nontechnical reader who wants only to know the results.

THINK ABOUT THE RESEARCH QUESTION

Before you set out to explore any subject, you need to have a pretty clear idea of what you are looking for. If you take the time to put your thoughts into a sentence, you will find it falling somewhere between a *statement of purpose* and a *thesis*. This sentence, or *research question*, will become the controlling idea for your research, and once you've done the background work, you can come back to it and adjust it for your results. (Of course, if you begin with a hypothesis that your results eventually disprove, you nevertheless present these findings fairly and revisit your hypothesis for your next project.) The research question is the central statement in the writing that you do to share your findings with others.

You may recognize the pattern: the development of this statement comes at the beginning of the approach known as the *scientific method*, which involves the following steps:

1. formulating and delineating the problem
2. thoroughly reviewing related literature
3. developing a theoretical framework
4. formulating hypotheses
5. selecting a research design
6. specifying the object or population for study
7. developing a plan for collecting data
8. conducting a pilot study and making revisions
9. selecting the sample
10. collecting the data
11. preparing the data for analysis
12. analyzing the data
13. interpreting the results
14. sharing the findings with others

The last step of this process—the formal writing up of results—will highlight the controlling idea in the introduction, perhaps phrased as a question, and confirm the answer in the conclusion. Take the time to frame your thesis carefully at the start of your project by asking the right question: *what? how? why? where? when? who?* Note how each response suggests a way of developing and organizing the content. The following examples illustrate this progress from question to answer to structure:

- *What* are the best turbo-coding algorithms?
  - *The best ones are A and B.*

- *How* much fertilizer will produce optimum crop yields of barley?
  - *The optimal amount is X.*

- *Why* do rechargeable lithium-ion cells store energy best?
  - *Lithium-ion cells are the best for three reasons.*

- *Where* is the best location for emergency water supplies in Red Deer?
  - *The two best locations for emergency water are P and Q.*

- *When* is the critical maintenance time point for the King Street Bridge?
  - *The King Street Bridge needs maintenance work completed by mid-2006.*

- *Who* stands to benefit most from Bluetooth technology?
  - *Bluetooth technology holds particular promise for two groups of people.*

The answers—which take more or less work to come up with—are nevertheless limited and precise. Use this question-and-answer structure to provide a focal point both for you in your project and, more usefully, for your eventual reader.

THINK ABOUT THE STRUCTURE

A number of blueprints exist for the formal presentation of written material. These are all variations on the basic introduction–body–conclusion structure you've been working with since your very first composition. What you may not have known is that this same arrangement reflects the process of reasoning common to all empirical sciences. One of the most common applications of the scientific method is the technical report, which objectively presents the results of experiments and tests (see Chapter 4). Of course, the analysis done in such writing is largely theoretical. That's a common complaint of work done in academic contexts, far from what many refer to as the "real world." But theoretical analysis is an important first step. The practical writing you learn to do on the job refines the principles of academic writing to develop discussions that people can read and use as a basis for making sensible decisions. This practical application is generally associated with problem solving.

The step-by-step system for arriving at results can also guide you as you develop a plan for writing. For one thing, it provides a means of sorting or classifying information into concrete observations and the generalizations that can be made about them. If you come to a conclusion based on what you have observed, it's called *inductive* reasoning, or *induction*. When you begin with a hypothesis and proceed to test it according to evidence you uncover, it's called *deductive* reasoning, or *deduction*. Archimedes' discovery of the laws of buoyancy (said to have occurred when Archimedes stepped into a full bath, causing it to overflow), however accidental, is the model for this organizational approach, which is represented in Fig. 1.1.

Whether you start with the evidence and come to a conclusion about it, or start with a hypothesis and discover the evidence to support or reject it, this pattern blends general and specific content. Take advantage of its value as a pattern for any writing you do—in a course or on the job.

Here is a basic model to follow:

$$\boxed{\text{statement}} + \boxed{\text{specifics}} + \boxed{\text{summary}}$$

For every main point, some kind of development is always necessary. If it's a one-paragraph answer to a question on a test or a section in an extensive project, your organization imitates this fundamental pattern. You will find this model especially useful as you develop skills for writing summaries—of your own work and of the work of others (see Chapter 3). In fact, it enables you, quite methodically and mechanically, to take advantage of complementary organizational patterns. There are generally two such patterns: one organized by time, such as you might find in a technical report, and one organized by priority, such

FIG. 1.1   INDUCTIVE AND DEDUCTIVE REASONING

as you might find in a proposal or in a paper addressing a specific problem. Once you have done the background work, you approach a writing project the same way you'd tackle any problem-solving or design exercise, by selecting the most promising organization for each section in light of what you want to say about your hypothesis or research question.

The following are traditional models based on a pattern of enumeration. Note how each general statement (**G**) anticipates the *several* points that follow. These are listed point by point in a predictable order of importance: *first, second, third,* and so on, to *finally*. (When you adapt such models to your own context, of course, you not only fill in the missing topic but also replace the word *several* with the appropriate number.)

- **Process** (time order). This model shows how something works or has worked. Whether used for a list of instructions or a record of observations, it subdivides material into a series of stages or steps:

  (**G**) There are *several* steps in the development of _____.

- **Cause/effect** (time order). This model is used to represent an applied process. Beyond merely showing the order of events, it emphasizes their interrelationship. When using this model, be careful to distinguish between a direct cause (*A produces B*), a contributing cause (*A helps produce B*), a condition (*If A, then B*), and a coincidence (*A and B both exist*).

  (**G**) _____ has *several* causes.
  (**G**) _____ has *several* effects.

- **Description** (space order). This model identifies the composition of something, from a piece of equipment to a site, by listing distinguishing details and characteristics. The arrangement follows a logical progression, say from left to right, and is usually supplemented by a diagram or map. This pattern is typical of engineering specifications.

  (**G**) _____ has *several* features.
  (**G**) _____ has *several* constraints.

- **Classification** (space order). This model is a method of dividing something into components according to a principle of selection which you define.

  (**G**) There are *several* types of _____.
  (**G**) There are *several* criteria for _____.

Communications devices, for example, may be classified according to brand name, construction materials, cost, or practicality—and each classification would have different members. It's also possible to classify people. Students, for example, may be full-time or part-time, regular or co-op, engineers or other. There are two strict rules to follow when classifying groups:

1. You must be able to account for all members of a class. If any are left over, you must adjust your categories or add to them.
2. You can divide categories into two or more subcategories as long as there are significant differences within one grouping. The standard classification of rocks into three types—metamorphic, igneous, and sedimentary—calls for an examination of subcategories too.

- **Comparison** (space order). This is a way of considering two members of the same class with respect to both similarities and differences. Although it is possible simply to follow descriptive order, characterizing the first item and then the second, comparisons are more effective if you do a point-by-point examination, considering the two items together, feature by feature.

(G) Although they share certain characteristics, A is different from B.

- **Contrast** (space order). This is a comparison that considers only the differences.

(G) A and B are different.

- **Problem/Solution** (time order). This model generally depends on cause/effect order to identify something as a problem to be solved, then on process order to identify the methodology. Comparison offers a useful structure if more than one solution is possible.

As you develop an outline for your writing, you can save yourself organizational time by identifying which of these patterns will govern your overall arrangement of material, paragraph by paragraph and section by section.

THINK ABOUT THE FORMAT

Take time to think about what the final product involves in terms of appearance, layout, length, and style. Attention to format means understanding your faculty's expectations as well as those of the discipline. What works for an engineering project won't necessarily work elsewhere. If you were taking an elective course in classics, for example, you would have to become familiar with and follow the conventions of the Modern Languages Association (see Chapter 15). Before you begin, then, consider what it is you are preparing. Are you writing product specifications, a technical report, a letter, a position paper, an article, a progress report, an analysis, a lab report, a proposal, or an abstract? Examine examples and models carefully, including those in this handbook, so that you understand the conventions. Understanding expectations is the first step to meeting them.

THINK ABOUT THE LENGTH

A very basic rule in professional writing is that it should be "no longer than it needs to be." Before you even start the planning phase, recognize potential restrictions on the length of the assignment. If you have been asked to develop your own project, trust someone with experience to guide you. Consult with your instructor, professor, or supervisor, and refer to examples of similar assignments available in the library or on course home pages to give you an idea of how to limit your focus. Of course, there are often strict length requirements associated with engineering assignments. (An abstract must be kept to fewer than 250 words, a cover letter kept to a page, and so on.)

THINK ABOUT THE TONE

Tone essentially refers to a writer's use of language. The words friends use together may be casual, and may include a lot of slang, but the words used in a professional setting—whether at school or on the job—are usually formal and specific. The language in a piece of writing reflects the familiarity between the writer and the audience. Two friends are close; students and professors are less so. When you e-mail friends or colleagues, a casual tone is both natural and appropriate. An e-mail to a professor or a personnel committee, however, will take a much more formal tone. As Fig. 1.2 points out, just how formal you need to be depends both on the assignment and on the instructions you have been given. In some cases—for example, if your fluid mechanics instructor expects you to turn in your lab notes—you may be able to write in point form. When you write instructions for someone, you can comfortably refer to the reader as "you." This style of address is clearly more personal than the conventional, more formal tone of most projects, reports, and papers. Choosing the appropriate register and maintaining a consistent approach throughout your work is one of your most important responsibilities as a writer. Begin to determine what's appropriate by identifying where your writing fits on the following scale:

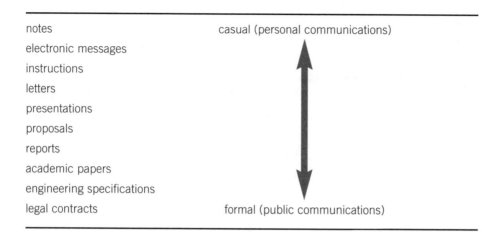

notes

electronic messages

instructions

letters

presentations

proposals

reports

academic papers

engineering specifications

legal contracts

casual (personal communications)

formal (public communications)

FIG. 1.2 THE SCALE OF FORMALITY

Depending on the type of assignment, your purpose, and your reader, your writing will contain features that move it one way or the other along the scale of formality. For example, the tone of this handbook is fairly informal, because its purpose is instructional. We address you personally, we talk to rather than write at you, and we keep the words simple. Most engineering contexts, however, call for more businesslike formality. Thus you will want to recognize—and minimize—features of your style and tone that make your writing too casual for the academic or professional situation. At the same time, you need to be careful of sounding unnaturally formal, with language that belongs in another century. The following features will make your writing less formal.

Colloquial language or slang

The language you use every day comes to you naturally enough, but it belongs to casual contexts like e-mails. Using informal language in the wrong context suggests that you don't recognize or appreciate the important distance between yourself and your reader. Consider the language you choose to be like the clothes you wear. Do you wear the same clothing to a movie with friends that you would wear to an interview with a prospective employer? Indeed, if you use words like "This needs to get fixed" for "this needs repairing," your language seems to be wearing denims rather than a suit. On the other hand, you don't want your language to appear overdressed ("exaggerated" is perhaps a better way to put it). A tuxedo is fine attire for a wedding, but inappropriate for the office. Similarly, it is more comfortable and fitting to write "the tool was repaired" than to write the somewhat artificial "the contrivance underwent reparations." Make

sure that the language you use in writing shows appropriate respect for the situation. Don't use slang, but don't develop an overblown vocabulary either.

Short forms and abbreviations
Even though it's quick and easy to rely on popular instant messaging abbreviations
(CY, BTW?), they are never appropriate in the writing you do for someone you
hope to impress, especially someone who may be giving you a job or a grade. Even
if you are e-mailing a teaching assistant a question about homework, use standard
unabbreviated language that proves you are not in too much of a hurry to be polite.

Contractions
Contractions such as *can't*, *it's*, *won't*, and *we'll* are not suitable for formal academic
writing, although they are common and natural in letters or, for that matter, any
writing that's intended to be read aloud, like a paper designed for an in-class presentation. If you want to use contractions, remember that they make writing sound
chatty and informal. If that's your purpose, then the contraction is justified.
Remember, however, that there are readers who will never accept the casualness
of contractions. You are wise to spell things out in all your professional writing.

Point form
Bullets are becoming more and more common in formal writing because they
simplify lists for the reader. If you use them, follow conventions of presentation
to distinguish between formal and informal types. A complete sentence ending
with a colon (:) precedes formal bullets, which have their own conventions:

1. They use punctuated numbers instead of dots or dashes or diamonds.
2. They include appropriate punctuation at the end of each entry.
3. They are grammatically complete and use parallel wording.

Informal bullets use point form without punctuation, except perhaps for
periods if each one is a complete sentence. Choose the bullet format to suit your
situation.

Personal pronouns
In personal communication, whether spoken or written, it's natural to use personal pronouns such as *I*, *you*, or *we*. In fact, it's impossible to address anyone
directly without them. The objective nature of scientific and technical writing,
however, emphasizes evidence, results, and recommendations rather than the
people responsible for them. In fact, many readers object that a dependence on
I reveals a lack of certainty or conviction, definitely not an impression you want
to convey in your assignments:

✗   I feel the concept behind this software is sound.

✗   In my opinion, the concept behind the software is sound.

✓   The concept behind the software is sound.

At the same time, there needs to be a way to avoid reconstructing sentences with awkward passive constructions (for example, "It can reasonably be concluded, based on the evidence that has been presented, that . . ."). Technical writing does permit the substitution of *we* for *I*, especially when reporting the results of a team investigation. Substituting *the team* for the sometimes controversial first-person pronouns is another option:

✗   It was determined that the prototype that had been developed by the team would be too expensive to produce.

✓   We discovered that our prototype would be too expensive to produce.

✓   The team recommended abandoning the prototype, for it would be too expensive to produce.

Try to reserve *I* and *you* for less formal situations, like letters and oral presentations. (A hint: when you do use *I*, it will be less obtrusive if you place it in the middle of the sentence, rather than at the beginning—a point to bear in mind for cover letters, especially the one accompanying your résumé.)

Good writers simply write well—either formally or informally. More importantly, they know what a situation calls for and keep both their tone and register consistent—whatever approach they've decided is appropriate. You can learn a lot about appropriateness from the people you are studying with. The best writers keep to a level and approach that is inconsequential—no one notices the language they use because it is so fitting. Refer to Chapter 12 for further help keeping your language both suitable and readable, whether your context and the audience call for you to be formal, informal, or somewhere between.

GUIDELINES FOR WRITING

Whenever you embark upon a writing project, keep the following guidelines in mind:

- Be clear about your subject and your purpose, what it is you expect to achieve.
- Think about your audience, the reader or readers of your writing.
- State your purpose clearly.

- Define your terms.
- Make sure you are accurate in all of your statements, in your analysis and presentation of data, and in your documentation of sources.
- Arrange your material logically.
- Include only relevant material. Don't pad your writing to achieve a certain length.
- Draw conclusions that are based on the evidence.
- Be simple, clear, and consistent in expressing your ideas.
- Choose and maintain an appropriate tone and level of formality throughout.
- Allow yourself plenty of time to work on drafts before completing the final copy of major and minor projects.
- Edit and proofread carefully.

Consider the flowchart in Fig. 1.3 a framework for the various stages of a writing project—from conception to publication. At a number of points, you revisit stages already completed, modifying as necessary, so that you end up with a professional piece of work that will satisfy everyone's expectations.

The chapters that follow address each of these guidelines in detail.

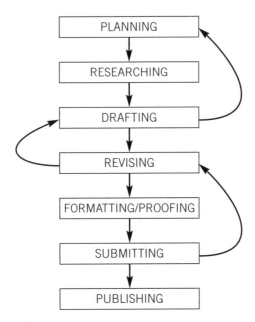

FIG. 1.3 THE WRITING PROCESS: FROM CONCEPTION TO PUBLICATION

cHApter 2

KEEPING NOTES AND DOING RESEARCH

One of the most important skills you develop as an engineer is the ability to keep extensive and efficient notes. A carefully cross-referenced file of articles, references, data, ideas (inspired or not!), sketches, and so on is a permanent record you add to throughout your career. Ultimately, your notes and files establish a foundation for everything you will write. It's important, therefore, that they be thorough and exact.

Develop the habit of carrying a notebook at all times, preferably one with sewn-in pages, so you won't be tempted to tear pages out if you aren't happy with what you've scribbled. More often than not, you will return to such entries later, grateful for the record they provide even if it seemed unsatisfactory at the time. In fact, if you want to delete material from your notes, put a clear X through the selection so that its contents can still be read even if you want them to be ignored. Don't use whiteout or otherwise obliterate what you've written. Your engineer's notebook, with every entry dated, will help you trace the chronology of your work on an enterprise and, when corroborated by an independent third party, even serve as proof of authenticity in case of legal disputes. What better proof of ownership of intellectual property than a series of meticulously dated notes? Indeed, even if you are not working on a sensitive project, it is good to have an independent person confirm with a signature that the work is your own.

In addition to the records you keep in this personal notebook, you will find good note-taking skills invaluable in three common situations: in the classroom, in the lab, and in the library.

LECTURE NOTES

Learning to recognize the classroom manner of your professors and lecturers will help you take the most efficient notes in their classes. Some instructors rely heavily on textbooks, class notes (either bound or to be downloaded from the course website), and handouts. Add your own comments to these directly, highlighting important points and expanding on them in margin notes throughout the lecture.

Other instructors assign a textbook as supplemental reading and spend class time on applications. In these classes, be prepared to take more substantial notes: record everything the professor or lecturer writes on the board or overheads, keep track of page references and web addresses, use headings and subheadings as a chronological record of what was covered in class, and copy all equations and formulas accurately.

Whatever the lecture style, take advantage of some time-honoured techniques for making the most of your classes.

- For each course you take, keep a separate binder, large enough to include your own notes as well as additional material like handouts and photocopies of supplemental readings. Spiral-bound notebooks are not as bulky as binders, and they are useful in classes where there are few or no handouts.

- Be prepared for class. Note-taking is much easier if you know beforehand what the topics of discussion will be. Keep your course outline at the front of your binder so that you know what to expect. Do assigned problems or readings before class, and review your notes from the previous class.

- Start a fresh page for each class, writing the date at the top right-hand corner. Listen and take note of any organizational overview of the course material, recording main points and summarizing examples. Develop your own shorthand, building on the following abbreviations:

$=$	is, are, equals	**w**	with
$\neq$	does not equal / differs from	**w/o**	without
$\approx$	is like, approximately	**+**	and
$\Rightarrow$	leads to, produces	**/**	or
$\varnothing$	nothing	**¶**	new paragraph
$>$	greater than	**!*°**	important
$<$	less than	**? or Q**	query, question
$\Uparrow$	increases	**A**	answer
$\Downarrow$	decreases	**±**	plus or minus
cf	compare with, see also	**@**	at
$\because$	since	**p**	page
$\therefore$	therefore	**x**	times
$\forall$	in all cases, for all	**Iff**	If and only if

- Leave a wide margin on the right-hand side of each page so that you can elaborate on key concepts later on and have room to add a summary or cross-reference when you are studying for exams. Mark important points with an asterisk. Put a question mark next to points you will want to reconsider and clarify after class—either with classmates or with the course instructor.

- Use columns to record comparisons.
- Record all key terms, including names, numbers, and nomenclature. Write out all definitions.
- Copy all diagrams, sketches, charts, and graphs.
- Record and highlight all assignments and due dates. (If you don't carry a personal organizer, transfer these dates to your calendar as soon as you get home.)
- Take time, as soon as possible after class, to review and refine your notes, using the right margin to set down questions that might show up on an exam. If you have recorded references to external material (the textbook, web pages, course notes, etc.), read these now and add summaries as necessary.

SHARING CLASS NOTES

You will naturally develop close relationships with classmates during the term. Whether or not you establish study groups with them, make sure you develop reliable contacts early on in case one of you has to miss a class. Don't abuse a friend's willingness to share notes, and always be prepared to return the favour. If you have to borrow notes, don't just photocopy them. Instead, take the time to work through them and summarize them for inclusion in your own binder.

LAB NOTES

When you take notes in class, you must adjust to the pace of your instructor. In the lab, however, you control both the process and the timing. It is up to you how much time you need to take to keep accurate and complete records.

Success lies in your thorough preparation for the experiment and any pre-lab work, so that you are well organized and ready to record your results.

- Most courses with labs have detailed specifications for your lab book. Because you will likely be handing it in for grading, make sure you keep your lab book independent of your class notes. The best lab books have hard covers and sewn-in pages of graph paper. Number the pages and reserve three or four sheets at the front for a title page and general table of contents (so that you can, later, add the title, date, and page numbers for each lab the book includes).

- Write in ink. If you are working with a lab partner, consider having each of you write in different coloured ink so that you can tell your contributions apart.
- Complete all required pre-lab exercises in the book so that you are well prepared. Review and record the context, the methodology, and the apparatus for the experiment. Many professors recommend that you note the specifics of the equipment you will be using (brand names and serial numbers, for example), in case disparate results later need to be justified.
- As necessary, prepare simple data grids to be filled in during the experiment. Whatever you can do to simplify the recording of data during the lab will make the job of analyzing the data later on outside the lab easier. It will also minimize the risk of misreading your data.
- If your data is complicated and calls for computer manipulation, paste the printout carefully into your lab book. Write the file name and disk title directly into your book so that you won't waste time if you have to retrieve it later.
- Be systematic and thorough in recording calculations and equations. Be sure to identify all terms.
- Make sure you include the date and the name or title of the experiment at the beginning of each entry. As you work page by page through the book, put each day's date at the top of the page, just below the page number.
- Keep your conclusions simple and precise. Before you turn in your lab book, make sure that you have answered all the questions.

Remember that lab work is essentially a process. By recording it carefully and chronologically, you make it easy for a reader to retrace your steps, follow your reasoning, even duplicate your results.

RESEARCH NOTES

You do research to keep up to date with scientific trends, to verify what other work is being done in your field, and to spark or develop ideas for projects. When you are not in class or in the lab, your life as a student likely puts you in front of a monitor. This is a good place to start identifying materials for your research, and you might as well be systematic about your approach. Use your note-taking skills to keep track of your sources as well as to record the information you find.

EXPLORE YOUR LIBRARY

The importance of getting to know your way around a library can't be stressed enough. You may find its vast collections intimidating initially, but everything you need to know is very close at hand. It's worthwhile to take part in orientation seminars at the beginning of term and to get to know the people at the information desk. You will quickly learn how to use the catalogue and reserve system. Librarians are glad to show you the bibliographies, indexes, online databases, CDs, journal abstracts, and other reference tools for your particular field. Once you are familiar with these basic resources, you will be able to check systematically for available material.

Never underestimate the serendipitous potential of a visit to the stacks, for you may well discover valuable sources during a random search. Take the time to look up works listed in the bibliographies and references of your course textbooks. You might come across related material that would be difficult to find otherwise.

Every academic library now has its catalogue in computer form, and access to these catalogues is generally available on the Internet. Computerized databases can simplify your search for relevant sources of information, which are often scattered across a number of journals and books in different locations. You will find that most libraries subscribe to a range of databases, some of them designed for specialized fields and others more general in their application. All you need to do, in fact, is start at your library's homepage. The convenience of links means that everything you need is only a few clicks of the mouse away.

If you are having trouble finding what you want, however, don't hesitate to ask for help from a librarian. These professionals are intimately familiar with the library's holdings and the various means for unearthing information. They are well prepared to give you guidance and direction or to walk you through a search. More and more college and university libraries now offer information services with names like "Ask a Librarian" or "Virtual Library." Without leaving your computer, you can connect with a librarian—either by going online (or telephoning) during designated hours or by sending queries by e-mail. Whenever you are preparing a major project, don't forget in your acknowledgements to thank your librarian for help.

The principles for conducting an online search are fairly standard. For any database, you enter certain keywords that describe your topic, and the computer searches for those words in all the titles and abstracts in the database. You are then provided with a list of the titles, references, and abstracts for each article or book. In some cases, the full text is also available.

If a computerized search is not available or practical, you can still conduct thorough research by turning to the bibliographies and collections of abstracts on hand at the library itself. Just remember that since printed bibliographies may not be as up to date as computer databases, you must always check to make sure you have covered recent source material.

EXPLORE THE INTERNET

With Internet access you can find a wealth of current information. Among the most useful features of web browsers is the function that allows you to store a site's uniform resource locator (URL)—its network address. When you find a website you plan to return to, save the URL so that you can call the site up again without having to type in what might be a very long address or to retrace your search steps. One of the very first URLs to store is that of your school's library. Other useful starting points for research in engineering appear below:

- *Natural Sciences and Engineering Research Council of Canada* <http://www.nserc.ca>
- *Gateway to Authoritative Science Information provided by US government agencies* <http://www.science.gov>
- *Thomson Institute for Scientific Information* <http://isi6.isiknowledge.com>
- *Directory of Open Access Journals* <http://www.doaj.org>
- *Council of Science Editors* <http://councilscienceeditors.org>
- *Elsevier Science's science-specific search engine* <http://www.scirus.com>
- *SciCentral Scientific Research News Source* <http://216.65.16.34>
- *Techtarget's Information Technology Resource Link* <http://www.whatis.com>

Storing the addresses of favourite websites is easy and convenient. However, you may soon find your list so long that you have trouble remembering which site you're looking for. Don't forget that most web browsers allow you to create folders and to sort sites so that they are meaningful to you. You may find it helpful to keep a separate folder of relevant websites for each course you're taking or for each project you're working on. Take advantage of such opportunities to keep yourself organized.

Search the World Wide Web

If you are doing a web search, you want to strike a balance between not missing relevant information and being overwhelmed with lists of web pages that have nothing to do with your topic. The process for conducting the search may vary depending on the web browser, but you can take advantage of onsite help files that offer necessary instructions. Generally speaking, you can narrow a search by enclosing phrases in quotation marks to reduce the number of hits. Use AND, OR, and NOT to refine a search further. For example, to find information on voice identification, type in "voice identification" AND "security systems". To exclude Walkerton from a search on e-coli in Canada, key in "e-coli" NOT Walkerton. On some sites, the plus sign (+) substitutes for AND, and the minus sign (–) for NOT. (The absence of such operators is interpreted by the sites as OR.) Thus, you search for artificial vision in robots by typing in +vision +robots.

Not all web browsers will produce the same list of sites from the same set of keywords. Some are case-sensitive, which means that you have to enter upper- and lowercase variations to maximize your search. Some may have trouble interpreting numbers and unusual characters. Another reason for discrepancies is that a search engine locates only sites registered with it. Although registration is a simple procedure, some organizations or content providers do not sign on with all search engines. In addition, some Internet service providers limit the range of sites you may visit. For example, some colleges and universities now block access to sites from which students might download illegal materials, and other providers may block on the basis of content. If you can't find exactly what you're looking for, try a different browser.

Evaluate your online sources

Everyone can publish on the Internet, regardless of their credentials (or lack of them), so consider online sources with special care. When judging whether a website is reliable or legitimate, apply the following criteria:

- **Credibility.** Who is the author, and what organization is sponsoring the site? Many sites are affiliated with an educational or professional organization, and sites hosted by an individual should provide you with information about that person's qualifications. Recognize the differences between—and the motivation of—commercial enterprises (ending in .com in North America and .co in the UK) and not-for-profit organizations (ending in .org). Is the sponsoring organization a professional or scholarly society? Is it a government department or educational institution? If you have any doubts about the authenticity of any material or site, investigate further before relying on it.
- **Comprehensiveness.** How extensive is the coverage? Is the documentation thorough? What links exist to and from the site? How thorough and reliable are these links? Answers to such questions will help you determine if you have found a useful source.
- **Currency.** When was the site last updated? Check the homepage and the source for the date, and be skeptical if the date is not recent or is missing altogether. There should be a contact e-mail address for questions. Check thoroughly so that you do not base research on information that is out of date or simply wrong.

If you think about it, these are the same questions that you should ask about anything you read. Developing a critical eye is just one more step to becoming a professional engineer.

SYSTEMIZE YOUR RESEARCH

More important, perhaps, than finding research material is taking notes that are comprehensive, dependable, and easy to use. With time you will develop your own best method, but for a start you might try index cards. This system has you record each new source, idea, or piece of evidence on a separate card. When you've finished with your note-taking, you arrange the cards in a useful order— by subject, by date, or by author.

You may prefer to create computer files containing information you have discovered in the library or on the Net. It's then easy to cut and paste your notes to arrange them logically. But be especially careful to do this *only* with material that you have prepared yourself. If you begin cutting and pasting with online sources, it soon becomes impossible to tell where each piece of information has come from. You don't want to risk accusations of plagiarism just because you have cut and pasted enthusiastically.

Whatever method you follow, remember that exact records are essential for proper references. The following are some guidelines for taking good notes:

- For every source, prepare one main entry that includes all bibliographical details eventually required for your reference list: the name of the author(s), the full title of the source, the place and date of publication, the journal volume and issue numbers, as well as the relevant page numbers. If it's material from a library, be sure to record the call number. If it's an online source, copy the URL accurately and completely (even if you have it somewhere else), the date you accessed the material, and the date the website or page was last updated. Nothing is more frustrating than wanting to use a piece of information in a paper only to find that you aren't sure where it came from. But if you don't know the source, you can't use the reference. To save yourself a frantic last-minute rush to the library or search of the Net, be thorough the first time.
- Record bibliographic details in the citation format required for your paper. That way, when you're preparing your list of references later on, you can copy or paste in the source directly.
- If you're using index cards, put the main bibliographic details about the author and work on one card, and then use separate cards for each special reference, idea, quotation, or theory. Assign a code or abbrevi-

ation for the source so that you save time recording information on subsequent cards. Keep all cards from the same source together (with a rubber band or paper clip) until you have made sure they're fully referenced and indexed.

- Be sure to quote accurately when you copy material directly from a source, and use quotation marks to indicate that these are not your words. Do the same for equations. More usually, your notes will be a paraphrase or summary of the material in the source, and it's useful to remind yourself of this by labelling the card either "sum" or "para" when you first write it.

- Include your own comment cards on which you present your own assessment of the material and its value to your project. Remember to include full source references for the material you're commenting on.

- Include page numbers for every reference, even if you paraphrase or summarize the idea rather than copying it word for word. If you are referring to a website, use paragraph or section numbers if these are available.

- Keep collections of notes together cross-indexed by project and by course. If you are careful and well organized, you will be establishing a solid bank of reference material that will be useful throughout your professional career.

A WARNING ABOUT PLAGIARISM

When you present something as your own work, you guarantee that you are its author except for material specifically identified as coming from elsewhere. If you haven't cited your sources fully and completely, you could be accused of plagiarism.

Plagiarism is a form of stealing. As with other offences against the law, ignorance is no excuse. Within academic institutions, penalties for plagiarism range from a zero grade for the work to outright expulsion, so it makes sense to familiarize yourself with your school's regulations as set out in the calendar or on the website. It is not worth jeopardizing a career just because you have neglected to give credit where credit is due.

It's considered plagiarism if you do one or more of the following:

- You quote someone else's material without acknowledgement, especially when you don't use quotation marks.
- You paraphrase someone else's material without acknowledgement.

- You present someone else's ideas or examples as if they were your own.
- You follow the general organization or overall plan of another source, even if your subject is different.

Since research papers and projects depend on support from materials from various sources and experts, you increase your own credibility and reputation for thoroughness when you cite experts in the field. A thoroughly documented paper including accurately cited material shows skill, selectivity, and thoroughness—so it makes sense to be complete and specific about material used to back up and document ideas, arguments, proposals, and conclusions.

The most obvious type of plagiarism is the deliberate misrepresentation of a source as your own. Consider the following excerpt:

> In designing, the two processes that must be understood are *system analysis* and *system synthesis*. Designing is a process by which new systems are made; these new systems may incorporate many components and subsystems, and it is the object of the designer to produce the best system for certain missions. Therefore, he or she must be able to analyze the operation of the components and the overall system; he or she must also be able to devise or synthesize systems of given components. *Analysis* is the process of breaking down the system into parts and discovering whether or not it will fulfill a mission. *Synthesis*, on the other hand, is the process of building up parts into an organized whole that can fulfill a mission.

As you might guess, it is outright plagiarism to take selections, whether sentences or parts of sentences or simple phrases, from this source and include them in your own text pretending that they were your own. But it is also plagiarism if you use only a phrase or paraphrase of the original without properly documenting it. In the sample passage above, the scrupulous distinction between *analysis*, "the breaking down [of] the system into parts," and *synthesis*, "the building up of parts into an organized whole," is appropriately acknowledged only by the quotation marks that identify the exact phrasing of the original. If you were to leave out the quotation marks, even if you credited the original source in an endnote, you would still be faulted for plagiarism. The rule is simple: if the words or the points aren't yours, identify them with quotation marks and a citation note.

There is a third form of borrowing that is often not recognized as plagiarism. You might think that you could generalize from your readings to say the following: *Analysis is easily distinguished from synthesis because the former concentrates on breaking down a system while the latter builds it up.* After all, you haven't actually used phrases from the original. Still, one glance at the source reveals that the central idea has been taken unfairly. Such a borrowing, without acknowledgement, is as much plagiarism as the word-for-word citation without quotation marks. It is simple and fair to acknowledge your borrowing with an introductory statement like this:

> Roe, Soulis, and Handa in *The Discipline of Design* suggest that the fundamental distinction between analysis and synthesis depends on the distinction between separating a system into sections and unifying it into a whole [1].

Here the authors receive full credit as the source of the comparison, and you receive full credit for concisely summarizing the key distinctions. Writing experts say that the only way to write a summary (see Chapter 3) is to distance yourself from the original so that you don't unintentionally echo its phrasing. Even when you represent an excerpt entirely in your own words, it is plagiarism without a reference to the source. Consider the following paragraph from *The Discipline of Design*:

> It is worth noting that the classification of the inputs, outputs, and mission of a given system may vary from application to application. Consider a fire: the inputs are usually fuel and air, while the outputs consist of a flickering light, heat, ashes, smoke, and various gases. When the fire is confined to a fireplace in an ordinary North American home, the mission is to provide an ornamental light, the satisfactory output is the flickering light, and all the remaining outputs are incidental. However, in a home in the United Kingdom, where central heating is not common, the mission is to heat the house, the satisfactory output is the heat, and the remainder are incidental. If now, in either location, the fire is not successfully confined to the fireplace, the situation is drastically changed. The mission is to cease burning, the outputs are all spurious, and the inputs are all interfering ones [1].

Now compare it with the following:

> One example of varying missions, outputs, and inputs comes from considering the differences between North America and Britain when it comes to home heating. Fireplaces perform very different functions in both places: in North America they are aesthetically pleasing, and in Britain they are used for warmth. Thus their missions and outputs

> differ, even though the inputs are the same. Of course, if the houses
> catch fire, the missions become the same—to put out the fire—no
> matter what the country.

Even though the writer clearly did not copy the original, the ideas and the examples have been presented as if they were the writer's own. Unless the writer introduces the explanation with an acknowledgement of the source and provides bibliographical information in a note, such writing is plagiarism. To avoid it, include an introductory sentence that fairly introduces the paraphrase:

> To clarify variations in inputs, outputs, and missions, Roe et al. offer
> the example of fireplaces in two different countries [1].

Plagiarism sometimes occurs by accident, but more often it is the result of unfair, unethical borrowing. With so much material available in libraries and on the Internet, dishonest people think no one will suspect that their work is not their own. They are usually mistaken. Readers who are experts in the field already know the best sources and can recognize material that has been copied. At the same time, the writer who borrows indiscriminately is usually caught because the style of some sections is clearly inconsistent with the rest of the writing—a sure indicator that there is more than one writer at work (and that at least one of them is a professional). Experienced readers recognize such discrepancies instantly, to the detriment of the devious copier. To avoid any such suspicion, you should always to do the following:

- Acknowledge any and all sources in notes and/or a bibliography.
- Use quotation marks around all direct quotations.

If you are using anyone else's ideas, acknowledge that fact, even if you have just summarized the main points. Whether or not you name the author directly in the text ("As Porter confirms, . . ."), be sure to include the reference number in square brackets and give full documentation information in your list of references. Don't be afraid that your work will seem weaker if you acknowledge the ideas of others. On the contrary, it will be all the more convincing: serious academic treatises are almost always built on the work of preceding scholars, with credit duly given to the earlier work.

Where should you draw the line on acknowledgements? As a rule, you don't need to give credit for anything that's common knowledge. You wouldn't footnote Einstein's $E = mc^2$, for example, but you should acknowledge any clever turn of phrase that is neither well known nor your own. And always document any fact or claim—statistical or otherwise—that is unfamiliar or open to question.

Remember, too, that information you find on the Internet must also be properly acknowledged. Even though websites are instantly accessible, they are in fact the property of the individual or organization that publishes them and are protected by copyright in the same way that printed material is. Now that academic institutions are using software to detect plagiarism from the Internet, you must be very careful never to put yourself in a position in which you are open to charges of wrongdoing.

Whether on the job or at school, you will often collaborate on projects or assignments. Always list every contributor's name on the title page and give credit for special help in acknowledgements at the front of the paper. But bear in mind that if an academic situation calls for independent work, it is considered plagiarism to copy another person's assignment and present it under your own name, even if you worked on it together. While consultation is permitted, even encouraged, copying is never allowed. Given the penalties, letting someone copy your work is asking for trouble, too. Collaborating with classmates is acceptable and may even be encouraged, but be sure to produce your own independent write-ups.

In any situation, your careful selection and documentation of material confirms your ability to capitalize on, while fully acknowledging, someone else's research. Above all, remember that anything you put in writing is there to encourage your reader—especially someone who is going to give you a grade— to appreciate how methodical, precise, and professional you are.

NOTE

[1] P.H. Roe, G.N. Soulis, and V. K. Handa, *The Discipline of Design*. Boston: Allyn and Bacon, 1972, p 54.

chapter 3

WRITING SUMMARIES AND ABSTRACTS

One of the most valuable writing skills that you can develop as an engineer is the ability to strip something to its essence—to reduce something quite complicated to a few paragraphs or even words. You develop this skill through all the practice you get taking notes. You can also develop it quite deliberately through the exercise of learning to write an effective summary.

Some professors still reminisce about learning the art of précis writing when they were at university. (Writing a précis was the exercise of reducing a passage to exactly one third of its original length.) This rather unnatural assignment helped teach people to make every word count, and many excellent writers still attribute their talents to what they learned from working on the précis. Today we teach students how to prepare a summary, and its function is not purely academic. From the abstract of a scientific paper to the executive summary prepared for the non-technical reader of a proposal or report, all summaries are designed to save time—not for the writer preparing them, perhaps, but certainly for the reader. A good summary lets a busy decision-maker know immediately whether the original, sometimes lengthy document is worth reading. If you are the writer responsible for such a project, it makes sense to master the technique.

As a writer with important information to convey, you have good reason to make your summaries concise, accurate, and well focused. Following the suggestions in this chapter will make the task of writing succinct, informative summaries easier.

DEFINITION

Every summary is compact. Its purpose is to present, in the fewest, most precise words, the essential content of a piece of writing. In an academic paper, the summary is called an *abstract*, and you write it for inclusion in a library database or similar index. Its key feature is its length: almost all abstracts are expected to be shorter than 250 words (or one page of double-spaced text). You probably already depend on abstracts to help you decide which papers, articles, or dissertations you will look to for support in your research. In learning to compose an abstract for an academic project or a summary for your own engineering proposals or reports, you become better prepared to join the academic and professional community.

SUMMARIZING YOUR WORK

A summary is not the introduction to a paper. It is a self-contained composition of one or two paragraphs that can be read independently and still make sense. The following seven rules are key to writing an effective summary:

1. **Always prepare the summary or abstract after you have completed, and edited, your document.** Not only will you be working with a polished product, but you can be confident that the content will not change. Put the final version of the summary at the front of your report or paper, before the table of contents.

2. **Remember to consider the needs of the reader.** Most readers will have the technical expertise to understand your subject, but there may be other readers who will not. If you know your audience, you will be able to choose language that is suitable. Non-technical readers depend on the summary to answer two questions: *what is this?* and *what am I supposed to do with it?* Often such readers will read only the summary, so it's especially important that it be simple yet precise.

3. **Keep to the specified length.** Depending on the project, your summary or abstract may be strictly limited to a specific number of words, in which case you must meet those requirements exactly, or risk having your work rejected. It makes sense to check requirements carefully before you begin. If you have not been given a word limit, match your summary to the context. Most summaries should not be longer than a page of double-spaced text (maximum 250 words), but the executive summary for a major project may well be longer.

    Some professors assign extended summaries as part of a major coursework project. Here's a rule of thumb for preparing these: using your section titles as headings, produce a brief paragraph or two for each one. Include graphs or charts as long as you keep to the page limits for the assignment.

4. **Stress important findings.** Highlight specific discoveries or other new material you present in the complete text of your report or paper. If you use your summary to make your reader aware of these innovations, he or she will have good reason to read beyond the summary.

5. **Avoid generic statements about contents.** It's very tempting to use the summary as a roadmap for the paper, a sort of table of contents in prose. You must not, however, waste the reader's time by writing something like the following: "Findings are discussed extensively, and recommendations for further research are included." Readers expect your paper to present findings and recommendations. They want to be guided to the specifics, not be told the obvious. Unless you provide them with a summary of the details, they are not going to want to read further.

6. **Take advantage of conventional structures to make the writing easier.** Though your table of contents should not be the focus of your summary, it will serve as the best first outline for it, since it points you to the subjects that you must account for. One of the following models and sets of questions will help you stay on track.

- **the chronological summary**

PAST	Where did it begin? How was it done?
PRESENT	What can we see now?
FUTURE	What lies ahead?

- **the experiment summary**

PURPOSE	What is the hypothesis?
METHOD	In what order were operations performed?
RESULTS	What happened?
CONCLUSIONS	What does it all mean?

- **the problem statement summary**

CONTEXT	What is the background of the problem?
DEFINITION	What are the complications?
OPTIONS	What are the alternatives?
RECOMMENDATIONS	What action should be taken?

- **the proposal summary**

CONTEXT	What is the background of the situation?
CONSIDERATIONS	What basic requirements/specifications are being addressed?
NEEDS	What time/money/effort is involved?
IMPLEMENTATION	What are the next steps?

Choose the formula that's most appropriate for your context. If your summary answers each of the questions in a sentence or two, it will be well organized. More importantly, it will meet the reader's needs exactly.

The following summary of a 17-page project report is organized in chronological order:

> In November 2004, the XYZ Film Lab in Toronto commissioned the design of a machine for chipping motion picture film for recycling. The aim was to conceptualize an alternative to the equipment currently used. The team developed a 2 cubic-metre prototype with a cylindrical blade like that of a push lawn mower. Stabilized on a drafting table, the prototype handled up to 10 rolls of film simultaneously, requiring sharpening after at most 28 hours of operation. With its efficient size, safety features, and low power requirements, the new film chipper outperformed the existing equipment. Proposed research will lead to improvements in blade life, dust control, and noise reduction. (108 words)

7. **Do not include references to other works.** Use your summary to point to the work you have done in your paper or report.

The place for references to the work done by others is in the text of your document and in your bibliography. If you have room at the end of a report, you may include a sentence or two of description to orient your reader to the contents of the other material. But be sure you say something worthwhile. It's a waste of a reader's time just to turn the title of the work into a sentence. The following is a good example of a sentence explanation that follows a reference to a website: "This site discusses the protocols, available and proposed, to interwork LAN and WAN networks."

SUMMARIZING THE WORK OF OTHERS

Sometimes you will be required to produce a summary of someone else's work, either as an academic exercise or, on the job, as a backgrounder for a busy colleague. This summary isn't like a review: it is not intended to evaluate, comment, or criticize.

Your summary of someone else's work simply records, as accurately as possible and in as few words as possible, your understanding of what the author has written. Whether you like what you have read is not the issue. Your job is to get to the heart of things—to separate what is important from what is not.

1. **Determine the author's purpose.** Every author writes for a reason: to cast some new light on a subject, to propose a theory, or to bring together the existing knowledge in a field. Whatever the purpose, you have to discover

it if you want to understand what guided the author's selection and arrangement of material. The best way to discover the author's intention is to check the preface, the introduction, and—if there is one—the author's own summary or abstract. If such a comprehensive summary exists, be careful of borrowing too liberally from it in a course assignment. If you're on the job, don't reinvent the wheel: tell the person who commissioned the summary that a good one already exists. A quick overview of headings and subheadings, titles and subtitles will show you what the author considers most important and what kind of evidence he or she presents. The details will be much more understandable once you know the direction of the discussion.

2. **Read carefully and take notes.** A second reading will be the basis of your note-taking. Since you have already determined the relative importance that the author gives to various ideas, you can be selective and avoid getting bogged down in less important details. Just be sure that you don't neglect any crucial passages or controversial claims.

   When taking notes, try to condense the ideas. Don't take them down word for word, and don't simply paraphrase them. You will have a much firmer grasp of the material if you resist the temptation to quote. Force yourself to summarize. This approach will also help you be concise. Remember: you want to be brief as well as clear. Condensing the material as you take notes will ensure that your report is a true summary, not just a string of quotations or paraphrases.

3. **Follow the same order of presentation as the original.** It's usually safer to follow the author's lead. That way your summary will be a clear indication of what's in the original.

4. **Discriminate between primary and secondary ideas.** Give the same relative emphasis to each area that the author does. Don't just list heading or chapter titles or reiterate conclusions.

5. **Include the key evidence supporting the author's arguments.** Include supporting details. Without them, your reader will have no way of assessing the strength of the author's conclusions.

EDITING FOR ECONOMY AND PRECISION

Whether you are writing a summary of your work or someone else's, it is essential to leave time for thorough editing. These two final guidelines are key:

1. **Reread and revise your summary to make sure it's coherent.** Summaries can often seem choppy or disconnected because so much of the original is missing. Use linking words and phrases (see pp. 75–6) to help create a flow and give the writing a sense of logical development. Careful paragraph division will also help to frame the various sections of the summary.

2. **Revise to make every word count.** You may find that you have to edit your work a number of times to eliminate unnecessary words and get your summary down to the required length. Be ruthless about eliminating deadwood (see Chapter 12) and avoid passive sentences. If you find it impossible to reduce the length any further, try starting over rather than picking at words. It may be easier to generate another set of answers to the model questions than to be constrained by a bulky first draft.

cHApter 4

WRITING A LAB REPORT

A major part of the work you do as a student involves learning the fundamentals of research and analysis. This is one reason that you are expected to attend labs and prepare reports to turn in for credit. When you graduate to an engineering career, knowing how to write and interpret technical reports will be essential to the work you do. You will have plenty of opportunity for practice at college or university.

All lab assignments demand accuracy and objectivity in recording and presenting what has been done. Engineers are interested in exact information and the orderly presentation of supporting evidence. Although you may wish to make a case for a particular hypothesis, professionalism obliges you to separate the facts you are reporting from your own speculations about them. Never allow preconceived opinions or expectations to interfere with the way you collect or present your data; if you do, you risk distorting your results. Conduct your experiment as objectively as possible, and present the results so that anyone reading your report or attempting to duplicate your procedures will likely reach the same conclusions you did.

PURPOSE

As a student in a lab, you prepare reports to demonstrate that you can apply a theory or know how to test a certain hypothesis. The person who marks your work already knows the methodology and the nomenclature. But while there is no need for you to explain your terms, you must still make it clear that you understand them. Your reader will be on the lookout for any weaknesses in method or analysis and any omissions of important data. Usually you will be expected to give details of your calculations, but even when you have been asked to provide only the results of these calculations, you should still identify and justify irregularities that might affect their accuracy.

FORMAT

Whether your report is handwritten or printed, it will be organized into separate sections, each with a heading. By convention, most lab reports follow a standard order:

1. title page
2. *Abstract* (or *Summary*)
3. *Contents* (for extended reports)
4. *Introduction* (or *Purpose* or *Objectives*)
5. *Materials* (or *Equipment*)
6. *Method* (or *Procedure*)
7. *Results* (or *Observations*)
8. *Discussion* (or *Analysis*)
9. *Conclusions*
10. *References*
11. *Appendices*

The order of these sections is always the same, although some sections may be combined or given slightly different names, depending on how much information there is in each one. Some instructors expect lab work to be recorded in a bound notebook turned in periodically for grading. These handwritten assignments may not include all the formal sections demanded of a technical report, but they still call for answers to specific questions and require data to be recorded accurately and analyzed in the context of the course. Different departments also have slightly different rules, but the following will give you an overview of what should go into each section of a lab report.

TITLE PAGE

The first page of the report should include your name, the title of the experiment, the date it was performed, and the date you turn in the report. For practical purposes, it should also include the name of your course and instructor. If you are using a bound lab book, course information will occupy the top half of the first page in the book, followed by a few blank pages on which you will record titles and dates of labs (and their page numbers) as you complete these.

Titles should be brief—no more than ten or twelve words—but informative, and you should make sure they clearly describe the topic and scope of the experiment. Avoid meaningless phrases, such as "A study of . . ." or "Observations on . . ." Simply state what it is you are studying, such as "Flow Rate Tests for 6V Pumps."

ABSTRACT

The *Abstract* appears alone on the page following the title page (or on the lines following the title in a lab book). An abstract, as explained in Chapter 3, is a brief but comprehensive summary of your report that stands alone. Anyone should be able to read it and know exactly what the experiment was about, as well as what the results were and how you interpreted them. Remember that economy and precision count: for a simple experiment, keep the summary under 75 words; for a complex one, make the maximum length 150 words. Of course, to achieve these limits you will need to avoid vague or wordy phrases, such as "The reason for conducting the experiments in this study of X was to examine . . .," when "The study of X examined . . ." is only one third as long.

CONTENTS

If the report is lengthy, extending over several pages and including attachments as appendices, provide a *Contents* page that lists section numbers, titles, and page numbers. In formal extended reports, you also include a *List of Figures* and a *List of Tables* on separate pages following the *Contents*. If you are writing in a bound notebook, it is especially important to put a table of contents at the beginning, so that the person marking your lab can find it.

INTRODUCTION

In the *Introduction* you will give a detailed statement of purpose for the experiment you have undertaken. Describe the problem you are studying, your reasons for studying it, and your research strategy for obtaining data. If, as is often the case, your purpose is to test a hypothesis, state both the nature of the problem and your expectations of the findings. The introduction should also include the theory underlying the experiment and any pertinent background data or equations. Although you may refer to outside sources—especially if you want to add legitimacy to an experiment you've developed yourself—you should still put the emphasis on your own work and its context. If you are completing the experiment as part of a course, your introduction will be a statement of purpose that's only a sentence or two long.

MATERIALS

The *Materials* section presents a description of the materials and equipment you used and provides some explanation of how you set up the experiment. Often you can include this section as part of your discussion of procedures in the *Method* section. If you did any manipulating of the equipment at different points in the experiment, give a full list of equipment here, and describe each separate arrangement.

A simple diagram or two—produced by computer or by hand—will help the reader visualize your arrangement of the equipment. If a diagram is too complicated to fit a regular page, include it as an appropriately labelled attachment at the back of the report and direct the reader to it with a reference.

Even if the apparatus or materials you are using are standard, commercially available items, note the name of the manufacturer, the model number (if applicable), and the name of the source or supplier: for example, "spectroscopic-grade carbon tetrachloride (99 per cent pure) supplied by B.D.H. Chemicals in St. John's."

METHOD

The *Method* section is a step-by-step description of how you carried out the experiment, with procedures presented in the order you performed them. If your experiment consisted of a number of tests, begin this section with a summary identifying how many tests you ran. This way, your reader is prepared for the numbering of your series. When you describe the tests later on in the report, use the same numbering system to prevent confusion.

Write this part of the report with enough detail that anyone can duplicate the experiment in all its details. If you are following instructions in a lab manual, include page references. Summarize the instructions in your own words rather than copying directly. Verify conventions for acknowledging such sources with your lab instructor.

Although you should be concise in your description of the experimental method, make sure that you don't omit essential details. If you heated the contents of a test tube, for example, be sure to report at what temperature you heated them and for how long. If you performed a chromatography or other process at a faster or slower rate than usual, it's important to indicate the rate. Readers need to know exactly what controls to apply if they try to perform the experiment themselves.

When reporting the results of experiments, it is standard practice to use the past tense. However, scientists regularly debate whether to use the active or passive voice (e.g. "*I tested* the sample" versus "The sample *was tested*"). Traditionally, the passive voice was preferred because its detachment seemed appropriate for scientific contexts (see pp. 115–16). More recently, writers have tended to use the active voice because it is less likely to produce convoluted sentences. Ask an instructor about your department's preferences, but use your own judgment about what sounds best. Your goal, whichever voice you use, is to be clear, concise, and objective. When people write well, readers don't take exception to their phrasing.

RESULTS

The *Results* section is the section of most interest and value to experts, and they depend on its accuracy. It usually presents a blend of data and description. It may also contain statistical calculations.

Find out from your instructor whether you are expected to give the details of your calculations or only the results of those calculations. (You may be required to include extensive calculations in an appendix.) Take time to double-check your numbers. You should also make sure where possible that the calculated values you report include any "uncertainty." For example, you might report that the calculated volume of a hollow sphere is 23.45 ± .05 cc (where ± .05 is the uncertainty in the volume measurement). When reporting any calculations or measurements, check to see if you need to include the standard deviation, the standard error of the mean, or the coefficient of variation.

The format of your *Results* section depends on the type of experiment you have performed. Generally it begins with your main findings and then deals with secondary ones. Whenever practical, summarize your results in a graph or table. (Graphs and charts generally have greater visual impact than a table, but the table is more useful if you have made several measurements.) Whatever graphics you use, label them clearly. Make sure that you refer to and explain each figure or table. You cannot expect such material to speak for itself.

Pay attention to the following guidelines when you are creating charts or graphs for your lab report (see Chapter 9 for additional information):

- Use a scale that will allow you to distribute your data points as widely as possible on the page.
- Use large and distinctive symbols, with different symbols for each line on the graph.
- Put error bars (±) on data points, where necessary.
- Label the axes clearly, and always include the units of measurement used so that the reader knows exactly what you have plotted on the graph. Always include a legend to identify the units or to explain what different symbols represent.
- Label the graph (for example, "Fig. 1") so that you can refer to it by number in your report. If you have more than a couple of these, include a *List of Figures* after the table of contents at the beginning of your report.

DISCUSSION

The *Discussion,* or *Analysis,* section of the lab report allows you the greatest input, since it is here that you will analyze and interpret the test results and comment on their significance. You will want to show how the test produced its outcome—whether expected or unexpected—and to discuss elements that influenced the results. In determining what details to include in the *Discussion* section, you might address the following questions:

- Do the results reflect the objective of the experiment?
- Do these results agree with previous findings, as reported in the literature on the subject? If not, how can you account for the discrepancy between your data and those accepted or obtained by other students and researchers?
- What may have gone wrong during your experiment, and why? Can you propose a source of error?
- Could the results have another explanation?
- Did the procedures you used make sense in light of what you hoped to accomplish? Does your experience suggest a better approach for next time?

For a good discussion, remember to think critically about how your own work relates to previous work that you have read about or done yourself.

CONCLUSIONS

The *Conclusions* section briefly lists the conclusions that may be drawn from the experiment. You don't necessarily need a separate section for these—they may also appear in a short paragraph at the end of the *Discussion* section.

REFERENCES

List references to any outside sources named in your experiment, including the course textbook, on a separate page before the *Appendices*. For details on documentation format, see Chapter 15.

APPENDICES

If you have extensive detailed results, particularly computer-generated ones that fill more than a page or two, include these at the end of your report. If you have more than one section, number them *Appendix 1*, *Appendix 2*, and so on. Make sure each has a title that identifies its contents (for example, *Appendix 2: MATH-CAD Worksheet*), and list them, including the titles, in your *Contents*. In a lab book, you will simply paste these data or calculations in where they fit naturally (as suggested in Chapter 2).

chapter 5

WRITING PROPOSALS AND PROJECT REPORTS

Much of professional engineering work is straight problem solving. Whether you are working independently or collaborating as a member of a team, your professional life will often require you to prepare full-scale reports on work that has been done—or on work that you want to be allowed to do.

As a student, you will have opportunities to develop your writing and research skills in preparing reports on major research or design projects on campus. If you are involved in work/study projects as a co-op or internship student, you will soon gain experience in writing on the job. The guidelines presented in this chapter offer general strategies and techniques for writing effective proposals and reports, in school or on the job.

BEFORE YOU BEGIN

Remember that people with demands on their time want to know as quickly as possible the central point of anything they are reading. They also expect to be able to trust its accuracy. There are three basic principles to keep in mind at all times:

1. **Whatever you are writing, put the most important information up front.** You should always include a summary, of course, but a business context may call for a cover letter in addition. Adopting different phrasing from the summary (to make reading each one worthwhile), you use the cover letter both to establish the context for your document and to highlight the action you are recommending.

2. **Be concise.** Everything you write should say as much as possible in as little space as possible.

3. **Be objective.** Readers must be confident that the information you are providing is professionally justified and free of any bias or ulterior motive.

PLANNING

What you will be writing varies according to where you are in the problem-solving process. The following kinds of reports suit different stages of this process:

Problem statement

A problem statement can be a fairly extensive discussion to introduce and document a problem you have identified. An academic context can require you to examine four separate considerations: context, definition, constraints, and criteria. In your engineering courses, a problem statement may be an independently evaluated assignment. More likely, however, it will find a place at the front of your final project report.

Proposal

Once you have a firm definition of the problem, you need to identify solutions, evaluate alternatives, and determine the process you want to follow. Your aim at this stage is to get the go-ahead to embark on the project. You now have to develop an extensive, detailed proposal that lays out, section by section, the process you will follow, the equipment and staff you will require, the timelines and costs for the project, and, most importantly, the results you are predicting. In the academic context, a research proposal generally establishes the theoretical context for the work and includes a tentative outline for the final write-up.

In the professional world, the emphasis is on results. Proposals are accepted only when they are deemed to meet the needs of the organization better than any other proposal. It is essential, therefore, that the proposal identify and address all issues of concern to the company.

There are two separate contexts in which you might prepare a proposal for business. If you have been invited to present a proposal, look to the organization of the RFP (request for proposal) to spell out the detailed content and arrangement of material you are expected to supply. If, on the other hand, you are developing a proposal independently, you will have to make an even stronger case. A company that sends out an RFP or RFB (request for bid) already knows that there is work to be done. But when you are the one making contact, with an unsolicited proposal, your problem statement and solutions must make it obvious that the work is worth doing. In any case, if you want your proposal approved, your writing must be clear and convincing—and your format professional.

Progress report

Once a proposal has been accepted and a project begins, you will be expected to keep people informed of your progress. These regular updates may be informal (for example, you might send them by e-mail), but they are important enough to spend time on writing them well. Use them to emphasize not just what work has been completed, but also where the project stands with respect to the approved plan. If there are any deviations from the original, you must account for these immediately.

If schedules or budgets have to be revised, you must report the situation thoroughly and responsibly. Even when everything is going according to plan, it is your responsibility to keep your supervisor informed. There's no need for an extensive discussion in this situation—a quick message will do to prevent your reader from worrying why he or she hasn't heard from you for a while. Whether your progress report is extensive or brief, therefore, depends on its message.

Final project report
Once a project is complete and all the assigned work is done, you must prepare a final comprehensive report as a permanent record. Make sure you allow time in your original project schedule for the production, editing, and distribution of this final report.

DEFINING YOUR TASK: THE FOUR R'S
Taking time to organize your thoughts and to devise strategies is well worth the effort. Wherever you are in a project, define your task precisely by asking questions about four aspects: *reason, reader, restrictions,* and *research.*

What is the *reason?*
Why are you writing? What goal are you trying to achieve? Broadly speaking, you write for one of two basic purposes: to provide information or to recommend some course of action. Many informational reports (like progress reports, production reports, and monthly sales reports) are designed to pass along facts and data as they accumulate. So that they don't strike the reader as bureaucratic busywork, you must make sure they focus on exceptional rather than routine matters. On the other hand, reports written to make specific recommendations—to help someone make a decision or to propose an alternative—usually receive close attention from both writer and reader. Examples are a feasibility study, a proposal for a new product design, or a suggestion for making a process more efficient. This kind of writing provides the most opportunity for you to show your analytic ability and creativity—clear evidence of professional competence.

Determining the reason underlying what you are writing means establishing both a purpose and an expected outcome. If an important decision rests on the document, you will have to consider exactly what information is needed to make that decision and precisely how you will support any recommendations.

Who is the *reader?*
Although several people may read your report, you usually have only one primary reader. Knowing who this reader is helps you organize and present your

material so that it's likely to be well received. If the project is assigned in a course, your reader will probably be your professor or supervisor, but there may also be a committee, or even an outside reader if you are doing graduate work. In professional, non-academic contexts, the reader might be a department head, a CEO, or even a board of directors.

You can always expect your primary reader to be professional, demanding, and highly motivated. The more you can identify his or her priorities, the better you will be able to meet them. When there are secondary readers involved, you can count on your primary reader for advice on writing for them. Among the details you should consider are these:

- **What is your relationship to the reader?** Is the reader your boss or a colleague? How has he or she reacted to past communications with you? If you are writing for someone in a position higher than yours, your tone and approach should be more formal than they would be for an associate you talk to often. Always remember to keep things readable though. (See Chapter 12.)

- **Has the reader asked for the report?** If you are writing a proposal in response to a request, you may not need to fill in much detail about the purpose. If what you are writing is unsolicited, you must establish a compelling context for your recommendations.

- **What is the reader's area of expertise or responsibility?** You will need to go into more detail about an area that is your reader's specialty than you will for one in which he or she is less interested or involved. In business, top management will want an overview, whereas a specialist will require all the particulars. Remember that your report might be going to several different kinds of readers—to a plant supervisor as well as to your boss, for instance. If so, you prepare the complete analysis for the supervisor while sending management only the executive summary.

- **How is the reader likely to respond?** Consider the reader's situation and the expectations and concerns that he or she is likely to have. Are you delivering good news or bad news? If you can anticipate objections or concerns and answer them in your writing, your solutions will be much more convincing.

- **How might the reader benefit from the report?** Your suggestions will always be more persuasive if you can point out their advantages for the reader. The benefit could be significant: giving the reader a competitive edge, for example, or saving the business money. Even if the benefit is a more general one, such as improving the reader's ability to anticipate future problems, you should point it out.

What are the *restrictions*?

From the outset, consider the practical restrictions on your own writing. For example, how much time do you have? How much help is available for typing the final report and for producing illustrations, photographs, or prototypes?

Other restrictions will apply to the subject of the report. If you are asked to choose your own project, be sure to narrow it to a manageable size. On the job, however, you will likely be given a predetermined project, one on which you may be the chief consultant, but still one with clear limitations. Since it's always better to do a thorough job on a narrow subject than a superficial job on a broad one, invest the time to limit your topic to manageable proportions.

What *research* is required?

In deciding what information to gather, you should weigh the time and money required to do the research against its usefulness to the report. In other words, you must determine what is essential.

It is especially useful to determine how much your reader already knows; in many cases your reader will need no background information at all. If you must provide some, remember that too much detail may draw attention away from more important matters. One solution to this problem is to put distracting details in appendices at the end of the report.

Once you have decided on the information you need, ask yourself what cross-checking you have to do. Are your sources reliable? What facts or figures do you need to verify? Use your engineering expertise to determine the degree of accuracy or precision required for any figures you supply. Indicating the margin of error will show the reader that you are thorough and objective.

If you are on the job, the facts and figures you need can usually be obtained either by questioning people or by researching company documents. If you find that an earlier report covers some of the same material you are working on, it's important to refer to it, updating facts and figures as necessary. If more extensive research is required, you may consult government documents, company reports, or academic publications available at the library or on the Internet. Most companies today have websites that give you easy access to annual reports, corporate information, product announcements, and financial information. Just remember that, even in a non-academic context, you must always be sure to acknowledge all your sources and give proper references. (See Chapter 15 for instructions on documenting your sources correctly.)

If you obtain your own data—through experiments, tests, or surveys, for example—make sure that any results are based on an appropriate sample. If you aren't familiar with proper sampling methods yourself, consult someone who is. Nothing weakens credibility more than providing outdated, unreliable, or invalid statistical information.

DEVELOPING YOUR DISCUSSION: THREE COMMON PATTERNS

The way you develop ideas depends on your purpose and the order in which you decide to present them. The origins of a problem, for example, are often presented in chronological order. When you want to convince a reader to accept your recommendations, however, most of your content will follow patterns for *defining, listing,* or *comparing.* Here are some suggestions for taking advantage of these three patterns.

DEFINING

Sometimes you want to explain the meaning of a term that is complicated, controversial, or simply important to your field of study: for example, *bias* in measurements, *ergonomics* in design, *dendrites* in geology, *fidelity* in electronics. Often, all it takes is a single sentence, even a quick definition in parentheses. But sometimes, a definition becomes a separate assignment or a question on an exam. It's worth recognizing the requirements.

If you decide a definition is necessary for your context, perhaps because you are preparing a problem statement, begin with a general statement to introduce the term. Then make your definition more exact: it should be broad enough to include all the things that belong in the category but narrow enough to exclude things that don't belong. A good definition builds a kind of verbal fence around a word, herding together all the members of the class and cutting off all outsiders.

For anything beyond a bare definition, include illustrations or examples. Depending on the nature of your discussion, these could vary in length from one or two sentences to several paragraphs. If you are defining *cybernetics,* for instance, you may want to discuss at some length the various so-called sciences of complexity, including neural networks and artificial intelligence.

In an extended definition, it's also useful to point out the differences between the term you're defining and any others that may be connected or confused with it. For instance, if you are defining *deciles* in statistics, you will want to distinguish them from *quartiles*; if you are defining *precision*, you should distinguish it from *accuracy*; if you are defining *trademarks*, you may want to distinguish them from *patents* or *logos*.

LISTING

One way to organize material persuasively is to follow the current trend of "prioritizing" information, arranging things in their order of importance. At the heart of this structure is the bullet list, which can introduce any lineup of details: causes, effects, criteria, constraints, objectives, advantages, disadvantages, costs, findings, or recommendations. The attraction of this approach, which also governs what appears in the executive summary, is that readers recognize priorities right away. There's no time wasted.

Whenever you can simplify material by listing it, do so. A list, like a heading, is an aid to a quick understanding of any sequence of three items or more. If you will be referring to the items in the list later, number each one; otherwise you may simply use a dash (–) or a bullet (•). Whenever you list items, make sure all of your points are consistent and parallel. For example, if you phrase one point as a complete sentence, make all of your points complete sentences. Or if some of your points begin with verbs, make all of them begin with verbs. If your list is introduced with an incomplete sentence, make sure each point in the list properly completes the sentence. (See Chapter 13 for additional information.)

The principle of "important things first" also applies to the arrangement of points within each section. In the *Recommendations* section especially, it's a good idea to put your most important point first, followed by the remaining points in descending order of importance.

Still, you should always keep in mind your purpose and reader. For example, if you are trying to persuade a hostile or skeptical reader, you may find it better to begin with the point—major or minor—that will get the most favourable reaction.

COMPARING

When you are presenting information and recommending a choice, you should organize your material in a way that will help the reader understand the options. For example, suppose that you have been asked to recommend one of three LAN models. The comparisons will be clearer for your reader and an assessment easier to make if, instead of describing each model in turn, you use a single paragraph to define the criteria—processor speed, memory, connectivity, and price—and then assess all three models together with respect to each criterion. This kind of comparison is represented most logically and concisely in a table, which you supplement with a paragraph or two justifying your recommendation. In other words, after defining the criteria, you present the results of the comparison explaining the advantages of each choice and concluding with your recommendation.

Whichever way you choose to arrange the details, remember to be systematic and consistent. In addition, if you include a chart or table to illustrate the points of comparison, make sure you add a summary paragraph of explanation. You can never expect graphics to speak for themselves.

ORGANIZING THE PARTS

Normal proposals and reports include a number of conventional parts, whether the context is academic or professional. You determine which parts to include according to the extent of your project, its purpose, and the expectations of your audience. Most academic institutions and professional organizations have specific expectations of the written work you will do for them, so it makes sense, right from the start, to confirm what these are. Many companies and organizations have templates and software to help you create standard documents from memos to project reports. These make it wonderfully easy to structure and format work consistently. It would be silly not to take advantage.

A progress report may be nothing more than an e-mail message or printed memo with a line or two of copy. More formal documents, however, call for some or all of the following elements.

FRONT MATTER
The following material appears at the beginning of any formal document, from an extended project report to a Ph.D. dissertation. Unless you are formatting your work for electronic submission or publication, use lower-case roman numerals to indicate the page number at the bottom of the pages of front matter. You don't need to number the first page (which likely features the executive summary). Be sure not to include the title page or the letter of transmittal in your numbering.

Letter of transmittal
The letter of transmittal is a standard letter or memo addressed to the intended reader. It is usually attached to the front of the document, but it may also be placed after the title page, before the *Summary*.

As is true of most business correspondence, this letter has four parts. It opens with a sentence establishing the context for the proposal, paper, or report; in the next paragraph, it highlights the main contents. You reserve the third paragraph to acknowledge the contributions of people who helped you with the work. (If you are preparing such a letter to accompany a student project, you may also need to include a statement asserting that you are the sole author.) The final paragraph ends politely and conventionally, with a specific request for action, if called for. Here is an illustration:

> In September, you asked the Engineering Students Association to investigate campus security. We are pleased to enclose our report.
>
> Our main recommendation is that the Student Council, with the co-operation of the Student Volunteer Bureau, establish an evening escort service to safeguard students walking across isolated areas of the campus at night. This service would benefit not only part-time and extension students going home from classes but also students who need to work late in the library or computer rooms.
>
> We are grateful for the support of your administrative assistant, Felicia Penofsky, whose suggestions were extremely helpful to us in conducting our investigation.
>
> When you have had the time to consider our recommendations, we would welcome the chance to discuss them with you.

Title page

The front page features the title of the document, the name of the company or organization for whom the work was done, the names of the person or people who prepared the document, the academic affiliation, and the date of submission. If you're writing a course assignment, don't forget to include the necessary information, such as course name or number. In introductory courses, it's always best to include your student number as well.

Abstract/summary

Place your summary on a separate page directly after your title page. In formal academic papers this will be called an *Abstract*, but you can use the designation *Summary* for most situations.

Key words

If you are preparing an academic article for a journal, you will probably be asked to provide an alphabetical list of up to ten terms that will enable someone doing a search to find your paper. You may be asked to include a similar list in major projects at college or university. (The website of the Institute for Electrical and Electronics Engineers provides a link to 55 pages of standard key words referred to in its publications. You can find this link at <http://www.ieee.org/portal/index.jsp?pageID=home>.)

Table of contents
Readers look to the table of contents for immediate guidance to specific information. Formats may vary. To make yours as clear as possible, number each section and subsection of your document, and record these numbers together with their titles in the table. Indent subheadings, and place the page numbers for all sections and subsections in a corresponding column on the right-hand side of the page.

List of tables/list of figures
If your project contains tables or illustrations, or both, include a separate table of contents for each list. If there are not many of these, the two lists may share a page; otherwise, keep each on its own page.

List of symbols
If you have used symbols that are not common enough to be recognized or understood by your colleagues, list them on a separate page here.

Definitions/nomenclature
Sometimes you will want to include a list of definitions of key terms. You can insert such a list here, or you can put it at the end of your work, in which case you will call it a glossary.

Preface/acknowledgements
In longer documents, and especially for projects that have received financial backing, it's appropriate for you to acknowledge any assistance you have received in a few sentences or paragraphs at the beginning of the document. This acknowledgement goes in a section entitled *Preface* or *Acknowledgements*. Although sometimes you will use the preface to put your investigation into a historical context, the preface does not fill the entire role of an introduction and cannot replace it.

MAIN BODY
Introduction
This section may include a statement of purpose, a discussion of the background or reason for the report, and/or an explanation of the method used to gather the information.

Problem statement

If you are writing a proposal or an investigative report, your reader might find it useful if you present a short summary of the problem, along with a discussion of the *constraints* (the limitations imposed on the solution) and the *criteria* (the features or characteristics required of the solution). Sometimes the constraints and criteria have been provided in project specifications or an RFP, in which case you might include them in an appendix instead of repeating them here.

Discussion

By far the most extensive part of your proposal or report, this section contains the specifics of your investigation and is generally referred to as "the body." In it, you lay out detailed information, section by section, according to your project plan. Give each part a meaningful, yet brief, title: *Overview*, *Methodology*, *Site Visits*, *Design*, *Test Case*, *Results*, *Refinements*, and so on.

If you are preparing a problem-solving proposal, you will include all the specifics of your timelines and budgets in addition to your objectives and the procedures you expect to follow. Remember that a proposal is written before a project is undertaken; you will look efficient if you prepare for as many contingencies as possible. On the other hand, a final project report is submitted after all the work has been completed, whether or not things took place according to plan. Part of your discussion in a final project report will consider how well the results met the original requirements set out in the proposal. Details of failures as well as successes are expected. In fact, the discussion section often contains, near the end, a part entitled *Findings*, in which you discuss the details of your results, both expected and unexpected.

Conclusions/recommendations

Conclusions are the inferences you have drawn from the findings, and recommendations are suggestions about what actions to take. Depending on your reasons for writing, you may have conclusions or recommendations or both in this section, so the title you give this section will vary accordingly.

BACK MATTER

After the main body, you include one or more of the following sections, as called for.

References

The *References* section should document all material, published or unpublished, that you have cited in the report. You have several options for formatting this section, as outlined in Chapter 15. You are, however, expected to follow the conventions of your organization or academic institution: check with your instructor or employer to find out if there is a particular method of documentation you are required to use.

Bibliography

If you want to recommend books, articles, and other materials that you have consulted but not cited or referred to in the report, the place to do so is here. Follow the same format you used for your references, but here you can also add a sentence or two summarizing the contribution of each work (see Chapter 3).

Appendix/appendices

An appendix contains any material that substantiates claims made in the body of your document but that you have not, for various reasons, included there. Appendices might include additional tables, questionnaires from a survey, summaries of raw data, parts of other reports that are pertinent to your findings, or any other information that would slow the reader down unnecessarily if it appeared in the main text. Keep separate appendices for each different type of material, and be sure to give each one a name and a place in your table of contents. More importantly, you must be sure to make reference somewhere in the text of your discussion to the material in the appendices. If you don't somehow refer to an appendix, your reader can reasonably suspect you of padding your work with unessential bulk.

FINALIZING YOUR WORK

INCLUDE ILLUSTRATIONS

Tables, charts, and other illustrations—especially those that analyze a quantity of data—are common and useful in any kind of report. Such visual aids help the reader grasp information that would take many words to explain. Use visual aids wherever you can to summarize or pull together information—but not simply to repeat what you have said in words. (See Chapter 9 for guidelines on using effective visual aids.)

When determining the best place for your tables and figures, begin by identifying the importance of the information you are trying to present. If a chart or table contains supplementary information, it belongs in an appendix. If the information is germane to the discussion, position the illustration soon after you first mention it. Number and label it appropriately. At the same time, be sure that you refer in your text both to the illustration and to the point it makes: for example, "As Fig. 2 shows, costs have decreased for each of the last five years."

NUMBER EACH SECTION

Numbering helps readers understand each section's relative importance. Here are the three basic systems:

Decimal	Alphanumeric	Roman numeral
1.0	A	I
1.1	1.	A.
1.11	a.	1.
1.12	b.	2.
1.2	2.	B.
2.0	B	II

Increasingly, technical reports use the decimal system. Whichever method you choose, be sure to use equivalent symbols for sections of equivalent importance.

Here are some other suggestions for producing a report that is as appealing to the eye as it is to the mind:

• Leave a generous amount of room around the text to create an impression of space; wide margins and spaces between sections help break up an imposing mass of type, especially when it's single-spaced. (If you are preparing an assignment for a college or university course, you should ask if your instructor prefers double-spaced text; many academic readers refuse to mark any paper that's not written on every other line.)

• Make headings stand out by using bold or uppercase letters. But don't go overboard by using colour or fancy typefaces that will only distract the reader from the essential content you are trying to present.

• Use different alignment and font sizes for different levels of headings. Systems for formatting headings vary, but the following is one convention that's widely used for technical papers:

SECTION HEADING
CENTRED AND IN UPPERCASE 14-POINT LETTERS

Secondary Heading at Left Margin

The heading is 13-point bold type. The initial letter of the first and other important words is in uppercase, and the text begins on a new line.

Third-level heading. The heading is in 12-point italics, and only the first letter of the first word is in uppercase. The text follows on the same line.

No matter what style you decide on, remember that the watchwords for headings with visual appeal are clarity and consistency.

Have your work bound professionally

In business, formal presentations call for professionally bound proposals or reports. Make sure you leave enough time to have this work done. Extended academic projects look better bound as well, but you should check with your instructor before you go to unnecessary expense. Some professors want assignments turned in with only a simple staple at the top left-hand corner. It's the reader, as always, who governs what you do. Whatever written work you submit, make sure it meets the expectations of the person who will be judging it.

cHApter 6

WORKING COLLABORATIVELY

As you know, a large part of engineering depends on teamwork. It makes sense, therefore, to have a straightforward plan for collaborating with others in the design and execution of work that you do together as a team.

If you don't already know each other, it's a good idea to spend time in the initial meeting getting to know the other members of your workgroup and discovering your strengths and weaknesses. One of you might be a good problem solver; another might be a confident writer and editor. Everyone on a team has different abilities, so it's worth identifying these right from the start.

Begin by designating one person to head the team, ideally someone who is both a good organizer and a natural leader. This person acts essentially as team coach and captain. He or she will coordinate the team's efforts, help assign tasks, assess progress, and generally oversee the presentation of the final product. Even if your team is being supervised by a faculty member, you still must select someone for the role of project manager. The adviser may offer suggestions, but you are ultimately responsible for the work you do as a team.

One of the greatest worries associated with collaborative work is that a team will end up with one member who doesn't pull his or her weight. You need to make it clear at the very first meeting that although the project leader has overall authority for maintaining the momentum of the project, each person has responsibilities, too. Decide as a group what to do if someone misses a deadline or doesn't measure up. This is the time to establish the ground rules for contributions.

Whether or not your project will be presented in person—in class, at a conference, or in a boardroom—you will likely produce a written copy. Here are the steps to take to prepare and present work involving several people.

GETTING ORGANIZED

Your first official group meeting (either the "get to know you" session or the one immediately afterward) is a critical part of the process. Use it as a brainstorming session to accomplish the following:

- assigning roles and responsibilities. Recognizing that everyone has a role to play is a key to successful teamwork. Whether it is a position, such as "project manager," or a responsibility, such as keeping a list of expenses, make sure everyone knows and feels comfortable with what is expected. Be sure to appoint someone as a secretary to be in charge of the project logbook; this person's job begins immediately.

- defining the nature and limits of your project
- organizing your project, both in terms of what has to be done (the plan) and when it has to be done (the schedule). Determine the optimal order of activities and decide which team members will be accountable for these. (If you have already studied the Critical Path Method in your engineering courses, use it to plan the project.) It also makes sense to prepare a Gantt chart to confirm timelines and responsibilities (see Fig. 6.1). The horizontal axis divides into the days, weeks, or months for the project; the vertical axis lays out the project stages and names the team member each involves.
- Establish an agenda for the next meeting that calls for everyone to give a progress report.

Your good engineering textbook will give you strategies for undertaking the project. What is important here is how you chronicle your team's progress and manage the schedule. Be sure to allow enough time at the end for a full write-up, including plenty of time for the drafting of sections and the overall editing, proofreading, and formatting called for in a formal report. If you build this schedule into your Gantt chart and designate a project editor, you will prepare everyone to contribute to the writing right from the beginning of the project. Two essential parts of this process are the *project logbook* and the *planning sheets*.

Activities	Week 1	Week 2	Week 3	Week 4	Week 5
Project Definition (All)	▬	▬			
Research (Mo, Andy)	▬▬				
Review Meetings (All)	▪		▪	▪	▪	▪
Prototype Development/ Testing (Kim, Faye)			▬▬▬		
Report Writing (Kim, Andy)				▬▬	
Preparation for Presentation (All)					▬

FIG. 6.1 GANTT PLANNING CHART

MAINTAINING THE PROJECT LOGBOOK

Like the official minutes of board meetings, material included in your engineering project logbook [1] establishes a legal record. In keeping track of the ideas you've had and progress you've made, the logbook offers proof of originality (intellectual property) and helps others retrace your steps. That's why it's so important to have members of your team corroborate its contents by initialing and dating each entry.

The logbook is a version of the engineer's notebook that you read about at the beginning of Chapter 2. It, too, should have a hard cover and sewn-in pages. If the pages aren't already numbered, do this at your initial meeting, when you designate someone on your project team to be the keeper of the log. Of course, anyone in your group can make an entry, but it's a good idea to have one person responsible for overseeing what gets recorded.

For legal reasons, it's important to write in non-erasable ink (never pencil) and to use a colour that photocopies well, like black or red. The following are additional conventions that help you legitimize the contents of your logbook:

- Use the logbook to record, in chronological order, all your activities as a team—your meetings, discussions, ideas, decisions, sketches, designs, calculations, solutions. For each entry, record the date and time as well as the names of everyone in attendance. If you haven't worked on the project for a while, it's still important to make an entry about the pause in activity, stating the reason and having the entry initialed by team members.

- Use the regular space available on each page to make your entries without leaving spaces or extraordinary margins. You don't want to leave yourselves open to the accusation that you are planning to add to an old entry at a later date. It's normal to fill all pages, but if you decide to start each new entry on a fresh page, draw a diagonal line neatly through the space so that it cannot be used again.

- It is best to keep the order of entries chronological and dated. If you want to add to an earlier entry, it is standard practice to add the material at the end of your entries and make clear cross-references to the earlier pages and dates. Initial all of your cross-references well. Of course, if the addition is not much more than a phrase, you can add it to the original entry in a different colour of ink—just be sure to date and initial it.

- If you want to include photographs, computer printouts, or other pieces of paper, glue them in carefully, initial them, and date them.

- Be as objective and accurate as possible in recording discussions among team members. Always give reasons for decisions, and use wording that cannot be misinterpreted by anyone reading the logbook.
- If you want to delete something, either because it is a mistake or because it is not relevant, cross it out with a single tidy line, so that you can still read what it says. If you tear out pages, erase entries, or use whiteout, you reduce the value of your project notebook, and your team loses credibility.

These precautions are nothing less than standard practice in the engineering world, so it's worth getting used to following them while you are still a student. In fact, if you are working on a groundbreaking project, your logbook takes on even more importance. As a permanent historical record of all the work your team has done, it may be required as evidence in court. To add to its authenticity, your group may decide to have it regularly corroborated by independent witnesses—especially if your work is precedent-setting.

As you can imagine, it's hard to find knowledgeable people willing to read and sign every entry in a logbook. They must also be disinterested third parties with no reason to make false attestations about your work. Still, if your team is serious about proving ownership of original material, getting professional corroboration is worth the effort. Have your witnesses verify each entry within hours of its writing. Use the following wording, and be sure your project leader signs as well.

The preceding entry was made by _____ on this ____ day of
_____, 200__.

Project leader: _____

Witnessed and understood by _____ on this ____ day of _____,
200__ and by _____ on this ____ day of _____, 200__.

FIG. 6.2 LOGBOOK TESTIMONIALS

PREPARING THE PROJECT REPORT

As you learned in Chapter 5, the report is the printed culmination of your work on a project. When you are working as a member of a team, the preparation of this document takes on new dimensions, since the contributions of several people will have to be synthesized in a coherent document. It's a good idea to start by assigning the job of master compiler/editor to one of the team members. This role should be assigned to the person who is the most comfortable with and knowledgeable about writing, not necessarily the project leader.

Arrange to have everyone on the team get together at a strategy meeting near the end of your project. Try to leave yourselves as much time as a week for preparing the final report. Even if you have ample material to draw from, you should never underestimate the effort it will take to write it up. Take a few minutes at the beginning of the meeting to make sure everyone will be using the same template and format throughout. This is time well spent, for it will save the master editor a lot of grief when standardizing the final draft.

Together, use your project logbook to establish a comprehensive table of contents outline for the final report, and assign writing responsibilities to team members according to their expertise in the project. This work will be much easier if you prepare *planning sheets* (or *charts*) in advance. Use the model below and have team members fill out one sheet for every section or subsection that they are responsible for, including appendices. It will be the job of the project editor to check these sheets against the outline to ensure that all parts of the project have been assigned and there are no gaps in the organization.

Section/subsection number: _____ [position in Table of Contents]

Heading: _____ [title or subtitle]

Team member: _____ [name of person responsible for the draft]

e-mail: _____

Purpose: _____

Organizational Pattern: _____

Key points:

-
-
-
-

Graphics, support [tables, graphs, diagrams, equations etc.]:

-
-
-

FIG. 6.3 STORYBOARD PLANNING CHART

Drawing up planning sheets is essentially the same work that story developers do in preparing scripts for production. It's their way of making sure that there are no gaps in the plot.

If you are the designated editor, here's how you use the storyboarding method to prepare the final draft of your group's project:

- Set firm deadlines for submissions. Ask for material to be supplied on disk or as an e-mail attachment so that it is easier to collate.
- Photocopy the planning sheets to create a master copy against which you will check the completeness of all submissions. This is the best way for you to know what material, if any, is outstanding. (Be sure to let your contributors know right away if anything is missing.) More importantly, you will know which sections are complete, so that you can start your editing work there.
- Use the format rules for the project as guidelines for editing and standardizing the text.
- Set aside enough time to do one last thorough editing in a single sitting. By working your way from beginning to end of the draft, you will be more likely to discover and eliminate inconsistencies. By the end of this session, you should be confident that
  - the style is consistent throughout,
  - the text is readable,
  - the grammar and punctuation are accurate, and
  - the charts and graphs are consistent and understandable.
- Once you are satisfied with your editing, prepare the abstract or executive summary that will be included at the beginning of the report. It will also be your responsibility as editor to write the transmittal letter.

Now you are ready to call one last project meeting. Make sure it is at least a day before the final polished report is due. Give everyone on the team a copy of the report and its cover letter to proofread and edit independently. The more people proofreading, the more likely it is that someone will catch errors. As the editor, you are in charge of collating last-minute changes or corrections, but it's still valuable to share the overall responsibility for spotting them.

If your team is going to present the report to an audience, cut and paste the final draft of the paper to make a script for each member of the group. Take the time to rehearse at least twice so that you can verify and refine the timing. You will find additional guidelines for presenters in the following chapter.

chApter 7

Giving an Oral Presentation

Engineers are expected to be able to present research, solutions, creative ideas, and proposals not just on paper but also in person. To help you prepare for professional life, many of your courses will thus include class presentations as part of their requirements. Whether you are asked to report on work in progress or to present a finished project, the key to success is careful planning. Even if public speaking is not one of your natural talents, you can still present material confidently as long as you are both well prepared and well organized.

Consider the characteristics of classes or seminars you have enjoyed. What made them so good was probably the confidence, know-how, and enthusiasm of the speaker. Most audiences prefer presenters who seem well prepared, who speak without reading directly from their notes, who use a range of visual aids, and who look animated and interested in what they are talking about. Still, it's never easy to stand up in front of a group of people, no matter how well prepared you might be. To make the best impression, follow these guidelines.

PREPARING YOUR PRESENTATION

UNDERSTAND YOUR PURPOSE

When preparing for any presentation, remember that you probably know more about your specific topic than anyone else in the room (including your supervisor). Your aim is to convince your audience that you know what you're talking about and that your grasp of the subject matter goes beyond what you are including in your presentation. Prepare yourself for questions by doing all the necessary background reading. (For example, you need to be familiar with all the resources you list in your bibliography.) If you are presenting a report on work in progress, develop questions to ask your audience so that you can take advantage of their ideas. If you are delivering a final project report, be ready to justify your recommendations by producing support and evidence from other, similar projects.

CONSIDER YOUR AUDIENCE

As always, your primary consideration must be your audience. To appreciate their information needs, you should identify exactly who will be attending your presentation. Faculty members? Fellow students? Your project supervisor? A potential employer? Knowing how large your audience is and whom it will include will also help you determine both your approach and your tone. After all, there are distinct advantages to addressing people in person:

- You can establish a rapport with your audience by personalizing your focus with references to *you*, to *I*, and to *we*. Your language and approach will be more casual and comfortable than what you use in a formal paper.
- You can count on your audience to give you immediate feedback. If people look puzzled or unconvinced, take the time to restate your ideas or expand upon them in a way that is not possible in writing.
- You don't have to worry about such conventions as spelling, formatting, and punctuation (except as they apply to your visual aids) because you are speaking, not writing.
- You can use your voice, facial expressions, and body language to add energy to what you have to say.

Your audience will appreciate receiving a one-page outline of your presentation—as long as you make it more specific than just *1. Introduction 2. Discussion 3. Conclusions* and so on. Put your name, title, date, and course number at the top of the page, and include a bibliography and additional references at the end. If possible, leave space so that your listeners can write as you talk. They will also be grateful if you provide definitions of terminology that might not be common knowledge.

PLAN YOUR PRESENTATION

Except for very formal presentations of conference papers, you should never simply read a prepared text out loud. (Unless you are a skilled reader, it is easy for such a presentation to sound awkward and monotonous.) That isn't to say that you shouldn't write it all out first—doing so will help you be better organized and perhaps less nervous. But if you have the full text in front of you at the presentation, the temptation to read from it can be overpowering. It's better to present from an outline instead.

Take advantage of your visual aids to help you get organized. As you design your series of transparencies or slides, you are essentially planning the overall presentation. Take note of the special demands for each section and produce visuals to match:

1. **Introduction.** Establish the context for your presentation by relating it to topics you and your classmates or colleagues have already discussed as a

group. Start by posing a question to be answered, or by making a provocative statement to catch the audience's attention and to identify your subject.

2. **Discussion.** Follow an obvious organization, just as you would in writing. Take full advantage of words that help your audience see where you are heading: *first, next, on the other hand, then, finally* are always helpful signals.

3. **Conclusion.** Use the final minutes of the presentation to summarize and reinforce your main points. Bring the presentation to a satisfying conclusion for your audience by referring to the question or issue raised in your introduction.

While you do your planning, keep in mind how much time you have been allotted. It's essential to stay within the time limits. (You can probably recall an occasion on which you've been annoyed watching someone else go on longer than expected.) Ideally, you should plan to make your talk a little shorter than the amount of time you have available so that you have some leeway to answer questions. As a rough guide, it takes a minute or two to read a page of double-spaced text, so you can time yourself accordingly by rehearsing with a written-out copy of your presentation. Use your text to prepare index cards listing the details of your presentation. Key these to your visuals so that you can deliver everything in the right order.

USE EFFECTIVE VISUAL AIDS

There are good reasons to take advantage of visual aids like blackboards, whiteboards, flip charts, transparencies, slides, and even PowerPoint technology if you have a laptop and access to a projector. First, they attract and focus the audience's attention. If you become self-conscious in front of a group, you will be more at ease when the eyes are on your visual aids rather than on you. Second, they allow you the flexibility to present your information in a variety of ways, for maximum effect.

With the availability of graphic presentation software, as well as laptop computers and video projectors, your ability to use visual aids in a presentation is limited only by your own ingenuity and your instructor's willingness to let you use the technology in class. You must be absolutely sure, however, that your visuals do not take away from your content. Novice presenters can get so carried away by the potential of technology that they defeat their purpose. No matter how appealing the bells and whistles seem, you must remember that you are making a presentation, not a cartoon.

A PowerPoint presentation that includes video clips and sound as well as animated diagrams is effective only if these elements are necessary and appropriate. Instructors commonly complain that the time taken to design extravagant visuals would have been better spent on research. Don't leave yourself open to this criticism: use graphic presentation software to make professional slides that enhance the content rather than call attention to their excesses.

Even if you won't have access to a computer or video monitor during your presentation, you can still print your main points and photocopy them onto transparencies to display on an overhead projector along with any charts or diagrams. Most seminar rooms are equipped with screens and plugs, as well as black or white boards to write on in case of questions. Make sure you confirm that there will be an overhead projector for the day of your presentation. If you have blank transparencies and coloured markers, you can use fresh overheads instead of the board to write things down during your question period.

The following suggestions apply to any material you might want to display during a presentation.

Keep things plain and simple

The demand for simplicity governs every aspect of visual aids. It is better to put too little on a visual than too much. Your aids should help you make your point, not detract from it. The following suggestions will help you keep it simple:

- **Use a plain font.** Any word-processing or graphics package gives you lots of font options. Stay with the clean and simple ones like Courier, Times New Roman, or Arial, even **Comic Sans**. Avoid all fancy fonts, including italics; use bold type instead if you want to emphasize something.
- **Choose an appropriate font size.** Verify that your slides or overheads can be read from the back of the room in which you will be giving the presentation. Remember that the size of any type you have used will depend on how far your projector is from the screen, not on the font size you used to prepare the slide. If you're in doubt about the size, make a trial transparency with fonts of different sizes, and try it out in the room where you'll be making your presentation.
- **Use a simple background.** If you're using PowerPoint, choose a plain background and use the same one on every slide.
- **Don't overuse colour or other effects.** Using two colours can provide effective contrast; using more than two is overkill. Avoid multi-coloured slides and other flashy effects, which get tiresome for the audience because they are so busy. This warning does not apply to colour photographs, of course, though it's worth noting that a picture in black and white often gets much more attention than one in colour.

- **Don't put too much information on one visual.** If you treat your visuals as a script, then you'll be tempted to read directly from them. If instead you use bullets for an outline, expanding on each point as you talk, your presentation will sound much more professional. If you have a table, diagram, or graph, use the simplest version possible and explain it thoroughly to your audience.
- **Don't use too many visuals.** The number of visuals you use will depend to some degree on your topic and the kind of material you are presenting. A rule of thumb for determining how many to use during your presentation is to have no more than one per minute. You'll go through some quickly, but you'll need to take more time with others.
- **Use simple transitions.** PowerPoint offers the option of introducing text in a variety of ways, even letter by letter. Don't be tempted by the possibilities. Consider your laptop a glorified overhead projector. Display everything that relates to a single point at the same time. It is annoying for an audience to have information displayed in tiny portions. No one wants to be kept in suspense.

Keep things organized

The second rule for visual aids is to make sure your material is well organized. If you follow a consistent pattern of presentation, the audience will become used to it and will be able to follow along more easily. At the same time, you will be more comfortable in your presentation. The following suggestions will help you keep your visual aids—and your presentation—organized.

- **Begin with a title slide.** Like the outline you distribute to your audience, a title slide orients the audience. It should contain the title of the presentation, your name, the date, and the name of the course. Have your title slide on the screen as people enter. Wait for everyone to be seated before you begin to speak.
- **Have an overview slide.** Put an overview of your presentation on the screen as you introduce your topic and pass out your outline.
- **Use headings and subheadings.** Most of your slides should be in point form, using numbers or bullets, with headings and subheadings. If you do this, the audience will be able to tell which are your main points and which are elaborations. Remember to be consistent: if you're using numbers, don't switch needlessly between Arabic and roman numerals; if you're using bullets, use the same style of bullets throughout.

- **Consider section breaks.** If you are giving an extended presentation that lasts thirty minutes or more, consider dividing your presentation into sections, with separate title pages for each section. Anything that helps the audience to see the structure of your presentation is worthwhile.
- **End with a summary and/or conclusions slide.** If you have been discussing an ongoing project, list the questions you want to pose to the audience at the end. If you are making a proposal, your final slide should identify *next steps* (your suggestions for follow-up or future planning).
- **Keep your overheads in order.** If you are using photographic slides or overhead transparencies, always make sure that they are in the right order—and facing the right direction—when you start. Be careful to keep them in an ordered pile as you work through them. You may need to go back to one later, and you don't want to be forced to shuffle through a disorganized pile in search of the one you want.

REHEARSE YOUR PRESENTATION

Once you have prepared your outline and your visual aids, take the time to run through your presentation at least once. Perhaps it's possible to use the actual seminar room after hours. If so, take the opportunity to check the equipment and the readability of your visual aids while you get used to standing at the front. It's best if you can rehearse with someone whose opinions you trust. Take advantage of his or her feedback to improve your delivery. A couple of dry runs will show you any weak points in your presentation and let you know if you are keeping to your time limit. Keep the following points in mind as you rehearse.

- **Speak slowly and deliberately.** Make sure your voice can be heard at the back of the room. Remember that a room full of people will muffle sound, so you will have to talk even louder at the actual presentation.
- **Practise looking around the room as you talk.** Choose three focal points where you will direct your gaze during your presentation—left, right, and centre. By looking from one place to the next, you will appear to include everyone. That way you will seem less wooden and more comfortable addressing your audience.
- **Time your delivery accurately.** Be prepared to cut out sections if you go over time. In fact, as you rehearse, it's a good idea to note places where you could skip over material in case time gets tight during the actual presentation.

MAKING YOUR PRESENTATION

Dress comfortably

Dressing comfortably means dressing for the occasion, not overdressing. Don't wear anything that you feel awkward in, including new shoes. There's no need for a business suit unless you know the rest of the audience will be wearing one too. Something that's clean, neat, and casual sets the right tone.

Leave yourself plenty of time to get there

Don't arrive at the last minute. Leave yourself time to set things up and make sure all your equipment works. There's nothing more disconcerting for you or your audience than to have an overhead fail or a laptop lose power. In fact, it is wise to check that the projector you will be using has a working replacement light before you get started. If the projector is not your own, make sure it's compatible with your laptop so that you're not searching for an adapter cable at the last minute. If everything is ready before you're scheduled to begin, you will have time to relax. Best of all, you won't get flustered rushing to set things up with your audience looking on.

Speak in a calm, clear voice

When you speak, be sure you're loud enough that everyone in the classroom can hear you. Also, try to put some energy into what you are saying. It is difficult to remain attentive to even the most interesting presentation delivered in a monotone.

Don't apologize

Never start with excuses: "You'll have to forgive me. I'm really nervous about this," or "I sure hope this projector is going to work properly." An audience will be more receptive if you focus on your topic rather than on your nervousness. After all, you don't want to suggest that you are unsure of your material. Most of your audience won't even recognize your discomfort—as long as you don't draw attention to yourself by apologizing.

If you are someone who who finds it difficult to stand up in front of a crowd, consider options for confronting your discomfort. Many colleges and universities offer courses in public speaking, and some local organizations even have regular monthly meetings of Toastmasters International. If your future involves regular presentations and you are naturally reticent, consider getting some off-campus practice to make yourself more comfortable. Start by checking with the career services department on campus.

Maintain eye contact with your audience

Look around the room as you speak, shifting your gaze from one to the other of your focal points. When you look at people, you involve them in what you are saying. As you scan the faces in front of you, you can watch for signs that your audience is following. If you sense confusion, adjust your talk accordingly by explaining a difficult point or slowing the pace of your discussion.

Work with your visual aids

Take advantage of your visual aids (while remembering that the visual material should enhance your presentation, not deliver it for you). Here are some guidelines for using visual aids effectively:

- When you are referring to a point on an overhead, use different words to elaborate on what appears there. Use your slide or overhead as a set of notes to expand on. Don't simply read the words.
- Be sure to leave your audience enough time to make sense of each visual. There is nothing more frustrating than watching images, overheads, or slides flash by without having a chance to take them in. It is better to skip a visual than to rush it by your audience.
- Explain your figures. If it's a graph, make it clear what the x- and y-axes represent, then explain what the graph shows. If it's a diagram, take the audience through it step by step. Remember that you are much more familiar with the material than your audience is. Never take for granted that anything is so obvious that it doesn't need to be explained.
- During your presentation, move around periodically so that you are not permanently blocking anyone from seeing your visual aids. Don't put yourself between the overhead projector and the screen, and make sure the material on transparencies is properly projected and centred.

Pace yourself

As you speak, adjust your speed to your content. If you're discussing background information that everyone knows from class, you can go a little faster. If you're describing something complex or new, slow down. It often helps to explain a complicated point a couple of times in slightly different ways. Don't be afraid to ask your audience if they understand. Almost certainly, someone will speak up if there is a problem. But don't let this rattle you. A one-sentence answer will allow you to continue on schedule.

Monitor your time

Position yourself so that you can see a clock throughout your presentation, but don't make too big a deal of removing your watch at the beginning. (Many of those who make a dramatic statement with the watch go over time anyway.) If you've carefully rehearsed your presentation, you should know roughly how long it will take. Always leave extra time for questions that people might ask.

End confidently

Bring your presentation to a strong finish by summarizing the main points you have made and drawing conclusions. Remember to have these available on a flipchart or overhead so that they can be left there for the ensuing discussion. If you raise questions in your conclusions, you can use them to help structure the question period to follow.

Be prepared for questions

The question period is the time when you can really make a good impression. It is an opportunity for you to demonstrate your thorough understanding of the topic and even to reinforce one or two points that you think you may have missed. If you know your material well, you should have no problem dealing with the content of the questions, but the way you answer these questions is important, too:

- Don't introduce the question period with a hurried "Any questions?" This abrupt approach will make you seem anxious to rush through or altogether dodge the process. You will appear eager to accept questions if you phrase your request slowly this way: "What questions would you like to ask?"
- It's a good idea to repeat a question if you are in a large room where everyone may not have heard it. Repeating the question can clarify it for you and give you extra moments to think before answering.
- If you didn't hear or didn't understand a question, don't be afraid to ask the person who asked it to repeat or clarify it.
- Keep answers short and to the point. Rambling is neither helpful nor convincing. Long answers often confuse the audience, so it's best to start briefly and then elaborate if necessary.
- If you don't have an answer, say so. It's okay to ask your audience for suggestions or refer the question to the course instructor. Certainly, it's better to admit that you don't know an answer than to guess or to make up a response that everyone will know is not correct.

cHApter 8

WRITING IN OTHER CONTEXTS

Not all the writing you do will be scientifically oriented. In addition to the summaries and reports you prepare in technical contexts, you may find yourself required to write essays, discussion papers, or reviews. Fortunately, your engineering training will help you adapt traditional organizational approaches to these different writing projects.

PREPARING TO WRITE

If you are one of the many students who dread writing, you will find that following careful steps in planning and organizing will make the task easier—and the result better.

Some students claim they can write essays without any planning at all. On the rare occasions when they succeed, their writing is usually not as spontaneous as it seems; in fact, they have thought or talked a good deal about the subject in advance and have come to the task with some ready-made ideas. More often, students who try to write a lengthy essay without planning just end up frustrated. They get stuck in the middle and don't know how to finish, or they suddenly realize that they're rambling.

Most writers agree that the planning stage is the most important part of the whole process. Certainly the evidence shows that poor planning usually leads to disorganized writing. In much student writing, the single greatest improvement would not be better research or better grammar but better organization.

This insistence on planning doesn't rule out exploratory writing (see p. 72). Many people find that the act of writing itself is the best way to generate ideas or overcome writer's block; the hard decisions about organization come after they've put something down on the page. Whether you organize before or after you begin to write, however, at some point you need to plan.

NARROW YOUR FOCUS

Some instructors provide a range of topics to choose from; others consider it the student's responsibility to limit and develop a subject. If you don't have a ready-made subject, begin by identifying an area that you know something about, that you like, and that you don't mind writing about. Ask questions that will help you gain some focus. Your aim at this point is to frame the single-sentence statement—the thesis—that will set the stage for the discussion in your paper.

One scheme for applying systematic question strategies is the three-C approach. It makes you look at a subject from three different perspectives, asking basic questions about *components, change,* and *context*:

Components
- What parts or categories can the subject be broken down into?
- Can the main divisions be subdivided?

Change
- What features have changed?
- Is there a trend?
- What caused the change?
- What are the results of the change?

Context
- What is the larger issue surrounding the subject?
- To what tradition or school of thought does the subject belong?
- How is the subject similar to, and different from, related subjects?

What are the *components* of the subject?

In other words, how might you break the subject down into smaller elements? This question relates to *classification* as a method of development. It forces you to look closely at the subject while avoiding oversimplification or easy generalization.

Suppose that your assignment is to discuss ATM networks. After asking yourself about components, you might decide to split the subject into (1) public networks and (2) private networks. Alternatively, you might divide it into (1) local area networks, (2) wide area networks, and (3) public telephone service networks. If these components seem too broad, you might break them down further, perhaps according to individual providers.

Similarly, if video games were a topic, you could ask, "What are the different types?" (for example, driving simulations, adventure games, and strategy games). Or you could sort video games according to their origins by asking, "What are the sources of these games?" (for instance, board games, puzzles, or cards). If you were interested in looking at stock market analysis, you might ask, "What relative risk is associated with each of three common trend predictors?"

Approaching your subject this way helps you appreciate its complexity while avoiding broad generalizations. Asking questions about the components of your subject may help you find one element that is not too large to explore in detail.

What features of the subject suggest *change*?

This question helps you to think about trends. Consider it an extension of the traditional chronological order you are used to in engineering. It points to antecedents or causes of an occurrence as well as the likely results or implications of a change.

Suppose you have decided to focus on communications systems. You might consider whether privatization of phone companies has had an effect on spending for research and development. You might look at increases in traffic congestion on company networks.

For a paper on video games, you might examine increases or decreases in popularity of a type of game, or trace improvements and developments in general. You could even track or account for complaints of how preoccupation with games destroys people's social skills.

In terms of the stock market, you might ask, "Have there been changes or trends in the rate of criminal offences committed?" or "Have there been changes in the nature or definition of insider trading?" Then ask, "What are the causes or results of these changes?"

What is the *context* of this subject?

Into what particular school of thought or tradition does the subject fit? What are the similarities and differences between this subject and related ones? The following are typical context questions:

- How do Internet Explorer and Netscape Navigator compare?
- What are the essential differences between two databases?
- What characteristics do the most popular video games share?
- How predictable is a typical buy–sell algorithm in a bull or bear market?

All these questions lead to better questions—and answers—from which you refine your topic and determine your controlling idea.

DEVELOP THE THESIS

All writing needs a controlling idea around which the material can be organized. This central idea is usually called a *thesis*, though in expository writing you may prefer to think of it as a *theme*. Consider these statements:

THEME: There are three standard techniques for treating contaminated groundwater.

THESIS: Governments should force polluters to use bioremediation to treat contaminated groundwater.

The first is a straightforward statement of fact. A paper centred on such a theme would follow a classification structure, describing the three remediation techniques one at a time. By contrast, the second statement is one with which readers might well disagree. A paper based on this thesis would have to present a convincing argument. The expository approach leads to an informative and interesting paper, but the argumentative approach is more likely to produce strong writing—as long as there's solid support for the argument. The key thing to remember about the theme or thesis, however, is that it must be stated in a single sentence that is restricted, unified, and precise [1]. Ideally, this sentence should prepare the reader for the argument to follow. It is, in other words, what holds a paper together.

CREATE AN OUTLINE

Individual writers differ in their need for a formal plan. Some say they never have an outline; others maintain they can't write without one. Most fall somewhere in between. Since organization is so vital to the success of a paper, it's worth knowing how to draw up an effective plan. Of course, the exact form it takes will depend on the pattern you use to develop your ideas—whether you are describing, classifying, or comparing, for example (see pp. 6–7).

For most students, an informal but well-organized outline in point form is the most useful model. As you've seen in earlier chapters, your table of contents will sometimes be all you need before you start to write.

The following is an example of an outline:

INTRODUCTION: Definition
THESIS: Virtual environment technologies have tremendous potential in the health care field.

I. Tools for Virtual Environment Applications
    A. Head-Mounted Displays
    B. Instrumented Clothing
    C. Spatialized Sound
    D. Other Interface Technology
        1. Virtual balance sensors
        2. Virtual eyes

II. Virtual Environment Applications in Medicine
    A. The Virtual Medical Classroom
    B. Virtual Reality–Assisted Surgery

      1. Preview
      2. Simulation and rehearsal
      3. Operation
   C. Virtual Rehabilitation

CONCLUSION: Design Implications

You can take advantage of the same formula to organize yourself. The guidelines for such an outline are straightforward:

- **Code your categories.** Use different sets of markings to establish the relative importance of your entries. Most computer outlining programs provide default coding but permit alternatives.
- **Categorize according to importance.** Make sure that only items of equal value are put in equivalent categories. Give major points more weight than minor ones.
- **Use parallel wording.** Phrase each entry in a similar way to make it easier to be consistent in your presentation.
- **Check lines of connection.** Make sure that each of the main categories is directly linked to the central thesis; then see that each subcategory is directly linked to the larger category that contains it. Checking these lines of connection is the best way of confirming that your paper is well organized.
- **Be consistent.** In arranging your points, avoid discrepancies or contradictions. You may choose to move from the most important point to the least important, or vice versa, as long as you follow the same order every time.
- **Be logical.** In addition to checking for lines of connection and organizational consistency, make sure that the overall development of your work is logical. Does each heading/idea/discussion flow into the next, leading your reader through the material in the most logical manner?

Be prepared to adapt the structure at any time in the writing process. Your initial outline is not meant to put an iron clamp on your thinking but to relieve anxiety about where you're heading. A careful outline prevents frustration and dead ends—the feeling of "I'm stuck, and where do I go from here?" But since the very act of writing will usually generate new ideas, you should be ready to modify your original plan. Just remember that any modifications must have the consistency and clear connections required to maintain unity.

WRITING AN ESSAY

One major difference between reports and essays is the format. Reports are organized around headings and subheadings, which help orient both the writer and the reader. Papers and essays, on the other hand, depend entirely on the writing to provide unity and coherence. Essay writing sometimes seems complicated to do without signposts.

Many essay writers find it easier to compose a first draft as quickly as possible and do extensive revisions later. However you begin, never expect the first draft to be the final copy. You already know that revising is a necessary part of the writing process and that careful revisions make the difference between mediocre writing and good writing.

If you ever face writer's block, remember that you don't need to write all parts of your essay in order. In fact, many students find the introduction the hardest part to write. If you face the first blank page with a growing sense of paralysis, leave the introduction until later and start somewhere in the middle with a subtopic you know well. Once the body of the essay is fleshed out, your introduction will be easier to write. Many experienced writers—not only those with writer's block—find this a productive way to proceed.

DEVELOP THE INTRODUCTION

The beginning of an essay has a dual purpose: to indicate your topic and approach and to whet your reader's interest in what you have to say. One effective way of introducing a topic is to place it in a context—to supply a kind of backdrop that puts it in perspective. Your structure can follow the **GEST** pattern below:

GENERAL STATEMENT (**G**): N is the larger subject.

EVIDENCE (**E**): Here are some applications/examples.

SUMMARY STATEMENT (**S**): These applications/examples include X.

THESIS (**T**): X is the focus of this essay.

Sheridan Baker [2] calls this the funnel approach because it works its way from broad to narrow in a few short sentences. The funnel introduction works for almost any kind of essay. The following example sets the stage for a discussion of needs analysis in design work:

> (**G**) Most products or structures eventually wear out or become obsolete. (**E**) Sometimes they can be converted to other uses (the horse barn becomes a garage and the icebox becomes a storage cabinet), or they are scrapped and the materials reused. (**S**) In each case, the environment in which a design must be converted or scrapped has a

serious effect on the problem statement. By analyzing this salvage or conversion environment, the designer can determine the effective life for new products and structures. **(T)** This is the exercise known as a needs analysis.

In an essay, you try to catch your reader's interest right from the start. The following variations on the funnel pattern can help you do so:

- **The quotation.** This approach works especially well when the quotation is taken from the person or work that you will be discussing.
- **The question.** A thought-provoking question can make a strong opening. Just be sure that you do actually answer it by the end of your essay.
- **The anecdote.** This is the kind of concrete lead that journalists often use to grab their readers' attention. Save this approach for your least formal essays—and remember that the incident must really highlight the ideas you are going to discuss.

However you choose to start a paper, your introduction must relate to your topic. Never sacrifice relevance for originality. Finally, whether your introduction is one paragraph or several, make sure that by the end of it your reader knows exactly what to expect from the paper that follows.

DEVELOP THE BODY

In an essay, it takes several paragraphs to develop an idea fully, and each new paragraph signals a change in the way you approach that idea. Skilled skim-readers know that they can get the general drift of a piece of writing simply by reading the first sentence of each paragraph. The reason is that most paragraphs begin by stating the central idea to be developed. If you are writing your essay from a formal plan, you will probably find that each section and subsection contains a topic sentence that indicates how the paragraph relates to the idea being developed.

Like the thesis statement for the essay as a whole, the topic sentence is not obligatory: in some paragraphs, the controlling idea is stated near the middle or even the end; in others, it is merely implied. It's still a good idea to think out a topic sentence for every paragraph. That way you'll be sure that each paragraph has a readily graspable point and is clearly connected to what comes before and after. When revising, check that each paragraph has a topic sentence, either stated or implied. If you find that you can't formulate one, you should probably rework the paragraph.

Maintain focus

A clear paragraph should contain only details that are in some way related to the central idea. Try structuring it so that the details are also seen to be related. One way of establishing these relations is to keep the same grammatical subject in most of the sentences that make up the paragraph. When the grammatical subject keeps shifting, a paragraph loses focus, as in the following example [3]:

orig.   The speed of computer systems nowadays has led to many innovations. Artificial intelligence (AI) is an interdisciplinary sector of computer science. A lot of research is being done to recreate the cognitive processes of humans with computer software. You can already find some special applications with a limited number of possible decisions. Modern cameras use artificial intelligence to select the appropriate display window from three to ten choices for focusing the picture. People get a lot of entertainment and challenge out of computer games, where the artificial player has to make all the right decisions in order to beat the human.

In the example above, the grammatical subject (underlined) changes from sentence to sentence. Notice how much stronger the focus becomes when all the sentences have the same grammatical subject—either the same noun, a synonym, or a related pronoun:

rev.   Artificial intelligence (AI) is an interdisciplinary sector of computer science. It deals with methods for recreating the cognitive processes of humans with computer software. To date, artificial intelligence has been used for applications with a limited number of possible decisions. In modern cameras, for example, artificial intelligence selects the appropriate display window from three to ten choices for focusing the picture. One of the most complicated AI applications is the computer game, where the artificial player has to make all the right decisions in order to beat the human.

Naturally it's not always possible to retain the same grammatical subject throughout a paragraph. If you were comparing two computer games, for example, you would have to switch from one to the other as your grammatical subject, just as you would when shifting between two ideas.

Avoid monotony
If most or all of the sentences in your paragraph have the same grammatical subject, how do you avoid sounding boring? Here are two ways:

1. **Use stand-in words.** Pronouns, either personal (*I, we, you, he, she, it, they*) or demonstrative (*this, that, these, those*), can stand in for the subject, as can synonyms (words or phrases that mean the same thing). The revised paragraph on artificial intelligence, for example, uses the pronouns *it* and

one as well as the acronym AI to avoid too much repetition. Most well-written paragraphs have a liberal sprinkling of these stand-in words.

2. **"Bury" the subject by putting something in front of it.** When the subject is placed in the middle of the sentence rather than at the beginning, it's less obvious to the reader. If you take another look at the revised paragraph, you'll see that in several sentences there is a word or phrase in front of the subject. Even a single word, such as *first, then, lately,* or *moreover,* will do the trick.

Link your ideas

To create coherent paragraphs, you need to link your ideas clearly. Linking words are those connectors—conjunctions and conjunctive adverbs—that show the relations between one sentence, or part of a sentence, and another; they're also known as "transition words," because they form a bridge from one thought to another. Make a habit of using linking words when you shift from one grammatical subject or idea to the next, whether the shift occurs within a single paragraph or as you move from one paragraph to another. The following are some of the most common connectors and the logical relations they indicate:

Linking Word	Logical Relation
and	
also	
again	
furthermore	
in addition	addition to previous idea
likewise	
moreover	
similarly	
alternatively	
although	
but	
by contrast	
despite, in spite of	
even so	change from previous idea
however	
nevertheless	
on the other hand	
rather	
yet	

accordingly
as a result
consequently
hence
for this reason $\Big\}$ summary or conclusion
so
therefore
thus

Enumerators such as *first*, *second*, *third*, *next*, and *finally* also work well as links.

Vary the length, but avoid extremes

Ideally, academic writing will have a balance of long and short paragraphs. However, it's best to avoid the extremes—especially the one-sentence paragraph, which can only state an idea without explaining or developing it. A series of very short paragraphs is usually a sign that you have not developed your ideas in enough detail, or that you have started new paragraphs unnecessarily. On the other hand, a succession of long paragraphs can be tiring and difficult to read. In deciding when to start a new paragraph, remember always to consider what is clearest and most helpful for the reader.

WRITE A CONVINCING CONCLUSION

Endings can be painful—sometimes for the reader as much as for the writer. Too often, the feeling that one ought to say something profound and memorable produces a pretentious or affected ending. You know the sort of thing:

> The field of broadband multimedia networking is burgeoning. In the years to come, the communications system is destined for dramatic changes thanks to the monumental enhancements provided by electrical engineers.

This ending is too packed with clichés to be meaningful. The writer seems only relieved to get to the end.

Experienced editors say that many articles and essays would be better without their final paragraphs: in other words, when you have finished saying what you have to say, the best thing to do is stop. This advice may work for short essays, where you need to keep the central point firmly in the foreground and don't need to remind the reader of it. However, for longer pieces, where you have developed a number of ideas or a complex line of argument, you should provide a sense of closure. Readers welcome an ending that helps to tie the ideas together; they don't like to feel as though they've been left dangling. And since the final impression is often the most lasting, it's in your interest to finish strongly. The following are two of the most convenient options.

The inverse funnel

The simplest conclusion is one that restates the thesis (**T**) in different words and discusses its implications (**I**). Sheridan Baker calls this the inverse funnel to contrast it with the funnel in the opening paragraph [2]. The discussion of the needs analysis, cited earlier for its funnel opening (p. 72), concludes with an "inverse funnel":

> (**T**) Having relied on a needs analysis to develop a problem statement, the designer is now ready to develop alternatives as solutions. (**I**) At the same time, he or she must appreciate the uncertain and iterative nature of the process and be prepared to rework, adjust, or even radically change the approach if necessary.

One danger in moving to a wider perspective is that you may try to embrace too much. When a conclusion expands too far it tends to lose focus. It's always better to discuss specific implications than to trail off into generalities in an attempt to sound profound.

The full circle

If you began your paper by posing a question or citing a startling fact, you can complete the circle by referring to it again in your conclusion, relating it to some of the insights revealed in the main body of your essay. This technique provides a solid sense of closure for the reader.

EDIT CAREFULLY

Editing doesn't mean simply checking your work for errors in grammar or spelling. It means looking at the piece as a whole to see if the ideas are well organized, well documented, and well expressed. It may mean making changes to the structure of the essay by adding some paragraphs or sentences, deleting others, and moving others around. Experienced writers may be able to check several aspects of their work at the same time, but if you are inexperienced or in doubt about your writing, it's best to look at the organization of the ideas before you tackle sentence structure, diction, style, and documentation.

Below is a checklist of questions to ask yourself as you begin editing. Far from all-inclusive, it focuses on the first step: examining the organization of your work. Since you probably won't want to check through your work separately for each question, you can group some together and overlook others, depending on your own strengths and weaknesses as a writer.

- Is my title concise and informative?
- Are the purpose and approach of this essay evident from the beginning?
- Are all sections of the paper relevant to the topic?
- Is the organization logical?
- Are the ideas sufficiently developed? Is there enough evidence, explanation, and illustration?
- Would an educated person who hasn't read the primary material understand everything I'm saying? Should I clarify some parts or add any explanatory material?
- In presenting my argument, do I take into account opposing arguments or evidence?
- Do my paragraph divisions make my ideas more coherent? Have I used them to keep similar ideas together and signal movement from one idea to another?
- Do any parts of the essay seem disjointed? Should I add more transitional words or logical indicators to make the sequence of ideas easier to follow?
- Do my conclusions accurately reflect my argument in the body of the work?

An additional approach is to devise your own checklist based on comments you have received on previous assignments. This is particularly useful when you move from an overview of organization to the close focus on sentence structure, diction, punctuation, spelling, and style. If you have a particular weak area— for example, wordiness or run-on sentences—give it special attention. Keeping a personal checklist will save you from repeating the same old mistakes.

THE BOOK REPORT

The book report is usually more than a summary of a book's contents, yet not the sophisticated literary review you might expect to read in a newspaper. If you are required to prepare something for a course, it will likely be an analytic report containing some evaluation. The following guidelines should help.

Approach a book report the same way you would approach an essay, by writing an outline. Begin with an introduction, then follow with a summary and an evaluation. Publication details are usually listed at the beginning but can also be placed at the end.

PREPARE AN INTRODUCTION

In your introduction you should provide all the background information necessary for a reader who is not familiar with the book. Here are some of the questions you might consider:

- What is the book about? Is the title pertinent and useful as a guide to the book's contents?
- What is the author's purpose? What kind of audience is he or she writing for? How is the topic limited? Is the central theme or argument stated or only implied?
- How does this book relate to others in the same field of interest?
- What are the author's background and reputation? What other books or articles has he or she written?
- Are there any special circumstances connected with the writing of this book? For example, was it written with the co-operation of particular scholars or institutions? Does the subject have special significance for the author?
- What kind of evidence does the author present to support his or her ideas? Is it reliable and up to date?

Not all of these questions will apply to every book, but an introduction that answers some of them will put your reader in a much better position to appreciate what you have to say in your evaluation.

INCLUDE A SUMMARY

You cannot analyze a book without discussing its contents. You may choose to present a condensed version of the book's contents as a separate section, to be followed by your evaluation; or you may prefer to integrate the two, assessing the author's arguments as you present them.

FOCUS ON THE EVALUATION

In evaluating the book, you will want to consider some of the following questions:

- How is the book organized? Does the author focus too much on some areas and too little on others? Has anything been left out?
- How has the author divided the work into chapters? Are the divisions valid? Do the chapter titles accurately reflect each chapter's contents?
- What kind of assumptions does the author make in presenting the material? Are they stated or implied? Are they valid?

- Does the author accomplish what he or she sets out to do? Does the author's position change in the course of the book? Are there any contradictions or weak spots in the arguments? Does the author recognize those weaknesses or omissions?
- What documentation does the author provide to support the central theme or argument? Is it reliable and current? Is any of the evidence distorted or misinterpreted? Could the same evidence be used to support a different case? Does the author leave out any important evidence that might weaken his or her case? Is the author's position convincing?
- Does the author agree or disagree with other writers who have dealt with the same material or problem? In what respects?
- Is the book clearly written and interesting to read? Is the writing repetitious? Too detailed? Not detailed enough? Is the style clear? Or is it plodding, "jargonish," or flippant?
- Does the book raise issues that need further exploration? Does it present any challenges or leave unfinished business for the author or other scholars to pick up?
- If the book has an index, how good is it?
- Are there illustrations? Are they helpful?
- To what extent would you recommend this book? What effect has it had on you?

Remember that your job is not to interpret the content of the book but to indicate its strengths and weaknesses. Also, be sure that you review the book the author actually wrote, not the one you wish he or she had written. In short, be fair.

NOTES

[1] For a more detailed discussion of heuristic procedures, see Richard E. Young, Alton L. Becker, and Kenneth Pike, *Rhetoric, Discovery and Change* New York: Harcourt Brace Jovanovich, 1970, pp. 119–36.

[2] Sheridan Baker and Laurence B. Gamache, *The Canadian Practical Stylist*, 4th ed. Don Mills, ON: Addison-Wesley, 1998, pp. 55–6.

[3] Joseph F. Trimmer, *Writing with a Purpose*, 12th ed. Boston: Houghton Mifflin, 1998, pp. 62–3.

cHApter 9

FOLLOWING CONVENTIONS FOR FORMATTING AND GRAPHICS

Our reliance on the visual reflects the need to communicate ideas quickly with images and symbols that transcend linguistic and cultural barriers. Illustrations capture in a picture concepts that are difficult to express in words.

Before you begin to write a report or an essay, consider what information you will be able to represent graphically. Computer programs make it easy to create, format, and annotate visuals to illustrate important points, but you must still be sure to follow conventions. Here are the most important guidelines for using visual aids effectively:

- Information in an illustration should complement rather than duplicate the text.
- Simple illustrations are better than cluttered ones. The easier it is for the reader to grasp the information quickly and accurately, the better. Do not include visuals unless they have a clear purpose.
- Make the caption of the visual reflect the point of the illustration, not just the topic. The heading appears in capital letters above a table; for figures, the heading is placed below. There is room, with figures, for a sentence or two of explanation within the caption. For tables, additional information may be included directly below the table in a footnote.
- Introduce every visual in the text before its insertion, explaining why you have included it and what it represents. Number each table or figure so that you can make a clear reference to it in your discussion. Some style manuals, like that of the IEEE (the manual of the Institute of Electrical and Electronics Engineers), recommend abbreviating *Figure* as *Fig.* Note, however, that *Table* is never abbreviated.

  As Fig. 1 shows, . . .

  (See Table 2 for a comparison of nozzle types.)

- Prepare a list of tables and figures to include after the table of contents at the beginning of a major report.

TABLES

A table can convey a large amount of information, both numerical and verbal, without losing detail. There is no simpler system for expressing comparisons.

If you are giving specific information in numerical form, a table allows you to show precise data more clearly than a graph does. This makes a table the sensible choice for data too detailed or too complex to be clearly illustrated in a graph, for example when small differences are critical, or when some or all of the information is verbal. If you have a qualification to make about one entry in a table, do so in a footnote by using superscript letters starting with [a].

Table 9.1 illustrates the type of information that is best represented in a table. You list all information in a chart format, with horizontal lines to separate headings and footnotes from the table itself, but with no vertical lines. Do not put a box around the table either.

TABLE 9.1   A COMPARISON OF WIRELESS 2-WAY MESSAGING COMMUNICATORS

Model	Style	Weight	Encryption security	Memory	Price
Smithson TP211	Clamshell chassis with 4-line backlit display	5.0 oz	No[a]	5.0 MB	$499
PSI 492	Large chassis, 16- to 20-line LCD graphical interface	7.4 oz	Yes	4.0 MB	$589
Ajax Timesport	Large chassis, 9-line backlit LCD screen with full PIM functions	6.7 oz	Yes	4.5 MB	$549
Ace Series 420	2.5 × 1.5 in. 256-colour display with microphone	5.4 oz	Yes	4.0 MB	$609

[a]planned for 2005

EQUATIONS

Use standard equation formats, like the Microsoft equation editor or Mathtype, to produce equations, which will appear in italics. Unless you have only one in your text, number your equations consecutively by putting the number in parentheses flush against your right margin. You will use this number to refer to the equation in the text of your discussion:

Equation (2) reveals 3 parameters.

If the reference does not come at the beginning of the sentence, however, use the number alone as follows:

There are three parameters for the Black-Sholes equation as shown in (2):

$$\theta + rS\Delta + \tfrac{1}{2}\sigma^2\,S^2\Gamma = rf \qquad (2)$$

Where r is the risk-free state of interest, f is the future price of the stock, S is the current price of the stock, σ is the volatility of the stock, and θ is the time rate of change of the portfolio, Δ is the weighted sum of the individual time derivatives of the stocks, and Γ is the rate of change of the portfolio's Δ with respect to the underlying asset [1].

FIGURES

There are many situations in engineering where figures help readers visualize the writer's meaning. Whether you include a photograph, a drawing, a diagram, a site map, a flowchart, a pie chart, or a graph, all these visuals will be classified as figures. You will need to be careful to label the relevant parts of these visuals (as we have done in Fig. 9.1 below), and make sure that you explain their purpose clearly in your text. (For labelled figures, it is usually best to use drawings rather than photographs and to prefer black and white to colour.) Make any drawings or diagrams as clean as possible. In the example below, a clip-art drawing of a computer might have produced a more consistent picture:

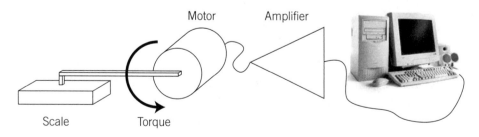

FIG. 9.1   SETUP OF MODEL

GRAPHS

Although they don't permit the combination of words and numerical data as well as tables, graphs blend analysis and presentation. In traditional organizational fashion, they represent either process or comparison. Computer programs allow for a wide variety of types, but you will probably limit yourself to using only line graphs or bar graphs.

Line graphs

A line graph (see Fig. 9.2) is best used to represent change over a period of time or space. (If it measures time, it's called a *histogram*.) It's often used to point out trends or fluctuations in trends.

In devising a line graph, you put the independent variable along the horizontal axis (the *abscissa*) and the dependent variable along the vertical axis (the *ordinate*). Never distort your graph to emphasize a point—for instance, by shortening the horizontal axis and lengthening the vertical axis to make a gradual rise look more dramatic. Doing so will only reduce your credibility and cause your reader to question the reliability of your information and the validity of your arguments—in a word, your professionalism. If your variables are dramatically different, you will probably want to use a logarithmic scale, in which you con-

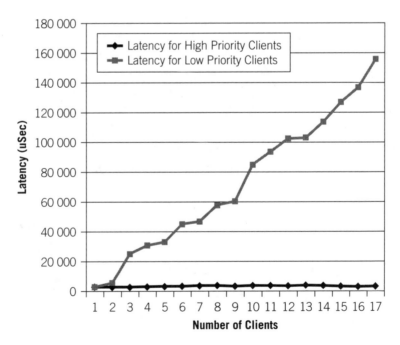

FIG. 9.2　LINE GRAPH REPRESENTATION OF RT-CORBA
CLIENT-PROPAGATED PRIORITY MODEL
PERFORMANCE TEST RESULT [2]

vert your data values into their logarithms and plot these on the graph. This will expand the low end of the scale and compress the high end. If you are using a log scale, remember that your measurement units cannot begin at zero. Also, be sure to label clearly whichever set of variables you have converted so that your reader is aware that the graph represents log and not linear values.

Remember to include a legend as an inset, either with a border or not, and label the axes clearly.

Bar graphs and pie charts

A bar graph is used to compare elements at fixed points in time. For example, a business report might use a bar graph to show the profits made by each department in a company in a particular year, or the changes in a company's sales from one year to the next. The bars can be horizontal or vertical, depending on the range of data, and they can be segmented to show different parts of the whole. For example, a bar used to show a company's sales for a given year could be segmented to show what part of the total is domestic sales and what part is foreign sales. Bars can also be clustered or grouped to compare one category with another, as in Fig. 9.3.

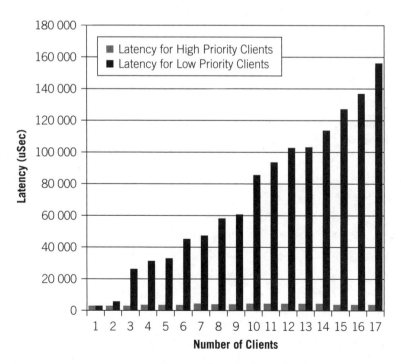

FIG. 9.3 BAR CHART REPRESENTATION OF RT-CORBA CLIENT-PROPAGATED PRIORITY MODEL PERFORMANCE TEST RESULT [2]

Bar graphs and pie charts are more usually found in business contexts—often in presentations (as overheads or PowerPoint slides)—because they look impressive. But because bar graphs and especially pie charts lack the precision of tables or line graphs, engineers rarely use them. Even though a word processor can instantly devise a pie chart, it's usually worth taking the time to produce a histogram, which is more professional.

FORMATTING YOUR WORK

We say that no one should judge a book by its cover, but readers do so all the time. An attractive paper helps make a receptive reader. Good looks won't substitute for good thinking, but they certainly enhance it. Unless you are presenting your work in a professional context, always double-space it and use margins of at least 1 inch to frame the text. Make judicious use of formatting features such as bold and italics for emphasis, and choose appropriate typefaces.

The kinds of tables and figures discussed in this chapter are easy to create with most word-processing software. But as you have seen, while computers can help you add visual impact to your written material, they can also make it tempting to add so much detail that you obscure the basic data. Be sure that the designs you are creating are not too elaborate for your purpose. And remember that any illustration, even if it is created on a computer, can distort information. For instance, the slope of a graph line can be made to look steep or shallow, even with the same data; trend lines can begin at a time that omits unfavourable periods. Although line and bar graphs are the most susceptible to distortion, the shapes and proportions of other diagrams can also give a false picture. Be careful to present as accurate a picture as possible so that your illustrations add to the credibility of your text. Visuals are meant not to dazzle but to make your content clearer and easier to understand. Use the simplest and most accurate means available to make your point.

WORKING WITH WORD PROCESSORS

Word processors have often functions for making the best final product possible, but you must be careful not to trust them too far. For example, your word-processing software will catch typing as well as spelling mistakes, but it can't point out actual words that are wrongly used (such as "there" when you need "their," or "trail" when you thought you typed "trial"). A spell-checker is a useful first check, never a final one. Similarly, grammar checkers, despite over twenty-five years of improvements, are still in their infancy. They may pick up on some grammar and stylistic problems, but they regularly make mistakes. They will never match the judgment of a good human editor.

For final editing, most experienced writers suggest working from the printed page rather than from the computer screen. Print one draft to read and edit before you produce your final copy. Your eye will get a better sense of the text by visualizing a page at a time than by scrolling down a screen.

When you are preparing the final document, resist the temptation to use colour, fancy fonts, or unnecessary clip-art. Keep in mind that while a computer can make your work look good, fancy graphics and a slick presentation will never replace intelligent thinking. Read over your work with a critical eye, in the knowledge that you can easily change something that is unsatisfactory. Remember that your computer is a tool for you to use—no more.

PROTECT YOUR WORK

Lost files are the nightmare of the computer age. Keeping adequate copies of your work will protect you from losing it as a result of a computer or disk problem. The following practices will ensure that your work is adequately saved:

- Save regularly to protect against a computer failure.
- Always create a backup file so that you have at least one copy in addition to the one you keep on your hard drive.
- Keep a copy of your file at least until you receive your grade for the course.
- Print an extra copy just to be on the safe side.

Getting into the habit of following these steps is a good investment in both time and security.

NOTES

[1] T. Chou, R. Gupta, J. Macintyre. "Financial Modelling and Optimization" in *Fourth Year Workshop Symposium 1999*. University of Waterloo, p.10.

[2] I. Song, F. Karray, and F. Guedea. "A Distributed Real-Time System Framework Design for Multi-Robot-Cooperative Systems using Real-Time CORBA" in *Proceedings of the 2003 IEEE International Symposium on Intelligent Control*. Houston, Texas, 2003, pp. 793–798.

chapter 10

WRITING TESTS AND EXAMINATIONS

Most students feel nervous before tests and exams. It's not surprising. Writing an essay exam—even if you are allowed to bring a cheat sheet or a textbook—imposes special pressures because both the time and the questions are restricted. With some exams being worth 50 per cent or more of the grade for a course, you want to be prepared to answer every question thoroughly and accurately. On the surface, objective tests may look easy because you don't have to develop extended answers, but they force you to be decisive about your answers. To do your best, you need to feel calm—but how? The following general guidelines should help you approach any test or exam with confidence.

PREPARING FOR THE EXAM

Review regularly

Exam preparation begins long before the exam period itself. A daily or weekly review of lecture notes and texts will help you remember important material and relate new information to old. If you don't review regularly, at the end of the term you'll be faced with relearning rather than remembering.

Set memory triggers

As you review, condense and focus your material by writing down in the margin key words or phrases that will trigger whole sets of details in your mind. The trigger might be a concept word that names or points to an important theory or definition, or it might be a quantitative phrase such as "four elements of a feasibility analysis" or "six types of intellectual property."

Sometimes you can create an acronym or other memory device that will trigger an otherwise hard-to-remember set of facts—remember how useful BEDMAS was when you were first learning to do calculations? Since the difficulty of memorizing increases with the number of items you are trying to remember, any method that will reduce this number will increase your effectiveness.

Ask questions: try the three-C approach

Think of questions that will get to the heart of the material and force you to examine the relations between various subjects or issues; then think about how you would answer them. The three-C approach, discussed in Chapter 8, may help. For example, reviewing the **components** of the subject could mean focusing on the main parts of an issue or on the definitions of major terms or theories. When reviewing processes, you might ask yourself what the causes or results of those **changes** are. To review **context** you might consider how certain aspects of the subject—issues, theories, actions, results—compare with others in the course. Essentially, the three-C approach forces you to look at material from different perspectives.

Copies of exams used previously in the course are useful both for seeing the types of questions you are likely to be asked and for checking the thoroughness of your preparation. Your professor will normally tell you where to find old exams—check your departmental library or course web pages for ideas. It's also a good idea to get together with friends who are taking the same course and work on problem sets. Just remember that the most useful review questions are not the ones that require you to recall facts and formulas but the ones that force you to analyze, synthesize, and apply what you have learned.

Allow extra time

Give yourself lots of time to get to the exam. Nothing is more nerve-wracking than the fear of being late. If you have to travel by car or public transit, don't forget that traffic can jam, as can alarm clocks. Always allow for a good margin of error. Of course, if the inconceivable does take place and you are late for or miss an exam, document the situation as best you can (for example, with a police report or emergency-room record). Let your professor and the department know the situation immediately, so that alternative arrangements may be made.

WRITING AN EXAM

Read the exam

Much as time seems an issue, an exam is not a hundred-metre dash. Instead of starting to write immediately, take time at the beginning to read through the questions and create a plan. A few minutes spent thinking and organizing at the outset will bring better results than the same time spent scribbling furiously. It's even more important to read each question carefully, to be sure you understand exactly what's being asked. Nothing is more frustrating than comparing notes with a classmate afterwards and discovering that you did not do what you were supposed to do.

Apportion your time

Read the instructions carefully to find out how many questions you must answer and to see what choices you have, if any. Subtract five minutes or so for planning, and then divide the time you have left by the number of questions you have. If possible, allow for time at the end to review your answers. If the instructions on the exam indicate that not all questions are of equal value, apportion your time accordingly.

Choose your questions

Decide on the questions that you will do and the order in which you will do them. You never have to do an exam in the same order as the questions. Tackle first the questions you can answer fastest and best, to save time for those you need to work hard at answering well. That way you will be sure to get the maximum marks.

Keep calm

If your first reaction on reading the exam is panic, force yourself to be calm, take slow, deep breaths to relax, and then decide which question you can answer best. Even if the exam seems impossible at first, there's always one question that looks manageable. That's the one to begin with, to get you rolling and increase your confidence. By the time you have finished the first answer, you will probably find that your mind has automatically begun to consider the next question.

Read each question carefully

As you consider each question, read it carefully and underline key words. The wording will specify the direction your answer should take. Be sure that you don't overlook or misinterpret anything (an easy mistake when people are nervous). If you are required to complete the exam on the test paper itself, pay attention to the amount of space allotted for each answer. It will tell you better than anything else how much detail your answer should contain.

Note the difference between questions and instructions in the phrasing. Questions beginning *Do*, *Does*, *Is*, or *Are* call for a straightforward answer of *yes* or *no* or some similar choice. The *why*, *how*, and *what* questions call for justification, explanation, and details—all expressed as short answers, preferably in sentences. It's easy to recognize exam questions in this category by their end punctuation (?).

Other exam questions are worded as instructions, which must be followed precisely. You will recognize, for example, the standard verbs that direct you to do calculations in order to solve problems: *calculate*, *compute*, *determine*, *estimate*, *find*, and *solve*. Others require some kind of illustration or graph: *chart*, *draft, draw, diagram, highlight, plot, sketch.* Short answers that depend on recall are prompted by the following: *enumerate, give, list.*

In questions that call for extended discussion, it is again the verb that determines the approach to take in answering. For example, note the instructions implicit in the following:

analyze divide into components; explain features; describe structures, methods, or operations.

classify divide into groups according to shared characteristics. (See pp. 6–7 for more detail.)

compare identify differences as well as similarities. (See p. 7 for more detail.)

define tell what something is, or how it works.

describe present features, characteristics, details, perhaps including a sketch, graph, or diagram. (See p. 6 for more detail.)

discuss examine or analyze in an orderly way. This instruction allows for considerable freedom of approach, as long as you take into account contrary evidence or ideas.

evaluate analyze strengths and weaknesses, providing an overall assessment of worth.

explain show how or why something happens.

identify describe, illustrate, explain, or present examples.

outline identify steps or stages, without development.

show demonstrate or prove, mathematically, scientifically, or otherwise logically.

trace review chronologically, listing causes, effects, or stages or steps in a process.

These and other verbs tell you how to handle your answer. Pay attention to them right from the beginning of the test.

Make notes

As a preliminary strategy, jot down key ideas, details, and formulas on rough paper or the unlined pages of your answer book. These notes will keep you from forgetting something as you write. Use them to organize yourself once you start to answer in earnest.

Be direct

Get to your points quickly, adding examples and details as necessary. It's best to use a direct approach, backing up each general statement with specifics. Don't add unnecessary qualifications or elaborations (especially on objective exams), as they suggest a lack of confidence or knowledge. Remember that your exam is one of many to be marked by someone who has to work quickly, so the clearer your answers are, the better they will be received. For each answer, give details that prove you really know your material. General statements show you can assimilate information, but you get marks only for specifics—as long as they are accurate as well.

Write legibly

Poor handwriting makes markers cranky. When the person correcting your exam has to struggle to read your answers, you may get poorer marks than you deserve. If for some special reason (such as a physical handicap) your writing is hard to read, you may be able to make special arrangements to use a computer. If your writing is just not very legible, it's probably better to print. When writing an essay exam, it's a good idea to write on every second or even third line of the booklet. Doing so not only makes your answers easier to read but also leaves you space to make revisions and additions if there is time later on.

Keep to your time plan

Keep to your plan, and don't skip any questions. It's usually possible to score part marks for a question you can't fully answer, so put something down for every question if you can. If you find yourself running out of time, summarize what you have written and move on. If you have time, you can always go back to complete the answer once you've answered the more valuable questions to the best of your ability. If you ever change an answer, be sure to cross out the old one—neatly.

Reread your answers

No matter how tired or fed up you are, try to leave time to review your answers at the end of the exam. Check especially for readability. Revisions that make answers easier to read are always worth the effort.

WRITING AN OPEN-BOOK EXAM

Don't think that permission to take a cheat sheet or textbook into the exam room is a guarantee of success. Do not fall into the trap of relying too heavily on your reference material. It's easy to spend so much time rifling through pages and looking things up that there isn't time to produce thorough or accurate answers. The result may be worse than if you had been allowed no aids at all.

If you are allowed to bring in a cheat sheet, be careful to follow directions exactly. Normally, you will be given a definition of what you're allowed to bring—for example, a standard-sized sheet of paper with handwriting on one side only, not a photocopy. It makes sense to follow such instructions to the letter; otherwise, you might find yourself "sheetless" when it matters most.

In the exam itself, use your aids only to check numbers and look up specific, hard-to-remember details. For instance, if your subject is biotechnology, you can look up genetic formulas. For a statistics test, you can apply t-tests and chi-squared tests to given data. For an exam in thermodynamics, you can refer to criteria for equilibria and definitions for entropy. You can check classic references and find exact definitions of key concepts—as long as you know where to find them quickly. In other words, use the aids to make your answers precise and well illustrated. Don't expect to use them to reduce the time you spend studying and preparing.

WRITING A TAKE-HOME EXAM

If you are given a take-home exam, you have time to plan your answers, consult your texts and other sources, even work out answers with your classmates. The catch is that you probably still have less time than you would for an ordinary assignment. Use your time to produce a professional response to the exam question(s). After all, a 24- or 48-hour time limit is no different from a typical business situation, where a client demands instant results. Keep in mind that you were given this exam to test your overall command of the course material. Your reader is likely to be less concerned with specialized research than with evidence that you have understood and assimilated the principles presented in class.

Of course, one reason an instructor may have for assigning a take-home test is to present you with a complicated problem that is impossible to answer in two or three hours. In this case you're being tested on your efficiency in assessing a problem and developing a solution over time. Take as much time as necessary to analyze the demands of the test question so that you can offer a considered response, one that stands up to scrutiny.

The guidelines for a take-home exam are similar to those for a regular exam. The only difference is that you don't need to keep such a close eye on the clock:

- Unless told not to, use your word processor to provide the professional appearance that the time allows.
- Organize your answer so that the reader can easily follow it. Use headings if they are helpful.

- Use specifics (detailed diagrams, algorithms, equations, graphs) to back up your points.
- Where possible, show the range of your knowledge of course content by referring to a variety of examples rather than the same old ones.
- Focus on showing that you can analyze and evaluate material—that you can do more than simply repeat information.

WRITING A MULTIPLE-CHOICE TEST

Multiple-choice tests are particularly common in courses with large numbers of students, for they make marking manageable. The main difficulty with these tests is that the questions are designed to confuse the student who is not certain of the correct answers. If you tend to second-guess yourself or if you are the sort of person who sees two sides to every question, you may find such tests particularly difficult at first. Fortunately, practice almost always improves performance.

Preparation for multiple-choice tests is the same as for other kinds of exams that emphasize your ability to recall information. Although there is no sure recipe for doing well—other than a thorough knowledge of the course material—the following suggestions may help.

Look at the marking system

If marks are based solely on the number of right answers, pick an answer for every question, even if you aren't sure it's the right one. For a question with four possible answers, you have a 25-per-cent chance of being right—even if you picked the answers at random.

On the other hand, if there is a penalty for wrong answers—if marks are deducted for errors—make sure you guess only when you are fairly sure you are right, or when you are able to rule out most of the possibilities. Making wild guesses will do you more harm than good.

Do the easy questions first

Go through the test at least twice. On the first round, deal only with those questions that you can answer without difficulty, and don't waste time on troublesome questions. Since the questions are usually of equal value, start by getting all the marks you can on the ones you find easy. Save the more difficult questions to tackle on the next round. This approach has two advantages: first, you won't be forced, because you have run out of time, to leave out any questions that you could easily have answered correctly; second, when you come back to a harder question on the second round, you may find that you have figured out the answer in the meantime.

Make your guesses educated ones

If you have to guess, at least increase your chances of getting the answer right. Forget about intuition, hunches, and lucky numbers. More importantly, forget about so-called patterns of correct answers—the idea that if there have been two "A" answers in a row, the next one can't possibly be "A" as well. Many test-setters either don't worry about patterns at all or else deliberately elude pattern-hunters by giving the right answer the same letter or number several times in a row.

Remember that constructing good multiple-choice tests is a special skill that not all instructors have mastered. In many cases the questions they pose, though sound enough as questions, do not produce enough realistic alternatives for answers. In such cases, the test-setter may resort to some less realistic options—which you can spot if you keep your eyes open. James F. Shepherd [1] has suggested a number of tips that will increase your chances of making the right guess:

- Start by weeding out all the answers you know are wrong, rather than looking for the right one.
- Avoid any terms you don't recognize. Some students are taken in by anything that looks like sophisticated terminology and may assume that such answers must be correct. In fact, these answers are usually wrong (the unfamiliar term may well be a red herring, especially if it is close in sound to the correct one).
- Avoid extremes. Most often the right answer lies in between. For example, suppose that the answer choices are the numbers 800,000; 350,000; 275,000; and 15: the highest and lowest numbers are likely to be wrong.
- Avoid absolutes, especially on questions dealing with people. Few aspects of human life are as certain as is implied by such words as *everyone*, *all*, or *no one*; *always*, *invariably*, or *never*. Statements containing these words are usually false.
- Ignore jokes or humorous statements.
- Choose the best available answer, even if it is not indisputably true. Choose the long answer over the short (it's more likely to contain the detail needed to make it correct) and the particular statement over the general (generalizations are usually too sweeping to be true).
- Choose "all of the above" over individual answers. Test-setters know that students with a patchy knowledge of the course material will often fasten on the one fact they know. Only those with a thorough knowledge will recognize that all the answers listed are correct.

ONE FINAL TIP

If you have time at the end of the exam, go back and reread the questions. One or two wrong answers caused by misreading can make a significant difference to your score. However, don't start second-guessing yourself and changing a lot of answers at the last minute. Studies have shown that when students make eleventh-hour changes, they are often wrong. Stick with your original decisions unless you know for certain that you have made a mistake.

NOTE

[1]   James F. Shepherd, *College Study Skills*, 6th ed. Boston: Houghton Mifflin, 1997 and *RSVP: The College Reading, Study, and Vocabulary Program*, 5th ed. Boston: Houghton Mifflin, 1995.

cHApter 11

WRITING A RÉSUMÉ AND LETTER OF APPLICATION

Whether you are looking for a co-op placement, an apprenticeship program, a summer job, admission to graduate school, or permanent employment, you will have to write a résumé and letter of application. You may even need to write an application letter for admission to some courses, especially those with work–study options. The person who reads your application will not have time to waste, so you need to be brief yet precise, personal yet professional. Check with the career-services advisors at your college or university for models that are appropriate for students like you.

PREPARING A STANDARD RÉSUMÉ

Think of a résumé as more than just a summary of facts. It is essentially a marketing tool, designed to show how your talents and experience fit an employer's or organization's needs. You are expected to supply some basic information, but how you organize it and which details you emphasize are up to you. One good strategy is to put your most important or relevant qualifications first, so that they are noticed immediately. For most students, this means starting off with educational qualifications, but for others it may mean beginning with work experience. Within each section of the résumé, use reverse chronological order to feature the most recent item at the beginning.

Whatever arrangement you choose, your goal is to keep the résumé as concise as possible while including all the specific information that will help you "sell" yourself. A reader will lose interest in—and likely reject—a résumé that seems disorganized or looks as though it is padded. On the other hand, experience or skills that seem inconsequential may still represent an important attribute, such as a sense of responsibility or a willingness to work hard. For example, a job as a short-order cook is worth mentioning if you point out that it paid for your post-secondary education.

Here is a list of common résumé information, along with some suggestions on how to present it:

- **Name.** Your name is usually placed in capital letters and centred at the top of the page.
- **Contact information.** This includes your mailing address, phone and fax numbers, and e-mail address. If you have a temporary student address, remember to indicate where you can be reached after the term is over.
- **Career objective** (optional). It may be helpful to let the employer know your career goal, or at least your current aim for employment, for example: "a junior drafting position with opportunity for advancement." It's silly, however, to include such a statement if you are applying for a temporary position that is not in your field—a sales job, for example.
- **Education.** Include all of your degrees and related diplomas or certificates, along with the institutions that granted them and the date. If it will help your case, and if you are short of other qualifications, you may also list courses you have taken that are relevant to the job. List computer knowledge as one of your special skills (see below).
- **Academic awards or honours.** If you have several, list them in a separate section along with the years in which they were awarded. Include them with your education details if you have only one or two, especially if they are no longer recent.
- **Work experience.** Give the name and location of your most recent employers, along with your job title and the dates of employment. Instead of outlining your duties (which an employee may or may not carry out well), list your achievements on the job, using point form and action verbs. Here are two examples:

  - Designed, administered, and reported on a public awareness survey.
  - Supervised a three-member field crew.

If you have worked as a research or teaching assistant, be sure to state the type of work you did and the name of your supervisor. Include such details, either in the chronological listing of previous employment or in a separate category, as follows:

  - May–August 2001. Research assistant for Professor Marika Szabo, independently completing ten experiments and reporting the results in a paper entitled "The Liquid Limit of Leda Clay," Carleton University, Ottawa.

- **Special skills.** This category offers an opportunity to list expertise that may give you an advantage in a competitive market, such as experience with unusual computer programs or knowledge of a second language. If they are currently in effect, list such credentials as certificates in lifesaving or the handling of hazardous materials.

- **Other interests** (optional). Depending on the amount of information you have already included, and on the job you are applying for, you may choose to omit this section. Still, naming a few achievements or interests, such as athletics or music or travel, confirms that you are well rounded or especially disciplined. You should, however, avoid listing general activities that show passive or minimal involvement. For example, while reading is a commendable activity, putting it under hobbies says nothing about your versatility as an employee. Include only those interests that set you apart from the average applicant.

- **References** (optional). As a courtesy, always confirm a person's willingness to give you a good recommendation before you name him or her as a reference on your résumé. (You should be prepared to supply the names of at least three referees from a variety of contexts, such as school, work, and extracurricular activities.) Increasingly, employers are waiting to ask for references until they are serious about the prospective employee. Accordingly, if you are not required to give names, conclude your résumé with the following statement, centred: "References available upon request." As soon as you are asked to supply the names of referees (and it's possible for this to happen as soon as you apply), give the full name, complete title, address, phone number, and, if possible, e-mail address of each one.

STANDARD RÉSUMÉ

RAJ CHOUDHURY

Present Address (until 1 April 2005):
123 College Rd
Halifax NS B3H 2R2
Phone: 902-323-4567
Fax: 902-323-4568
E-mail: rchdhry@dal.ca

Permanent Address:
45 Main St
Ottawa ON K1K 1K1
Phone: 613-456-0000
Fax: 613-456-0001
E-mail: choudhury@intranet.ca

Career Objective: An entry-level position in software development, where my background in commercial applications would be an asset.

Education:
- M.Eng. in Electrical and Computer Engineering, Dalhousie University, expected in May 2005 (Thesis: "Machine Architecture and Linear Memory")
- B.Eng. in Electrical and Computer Engineering, University of Victoria, 2004

Honours and Awards:
- Dean's List, 2002–3, 2003–4, University of Victoria
- NSERC Industrial Undergraduate Research Award, 2004

Work Experience:
Summer 2004 – Software Engineer for Texas Instruments, Toronto
- Performed software validation and provided quality assurance.
- Designed a multi-headed debugging driver with Visual Studio C++.

Summer 2003 – Systems Engineer for Ford Motor Company in Windsor, Ontario
- Migrated paper forms to online format.
- Provided tech support for a variety of computer systems.
- Trained a college co-op student to take over plant website maintenance.

Summers 2001–2 – Research Assistant for Path Technologies, Gibson B.C.
- Performed daily and weekly lab tests and prepared reports of results.

Specialized Skills and Experience:
- Extensive computer skills. Operating Systems: MS-DOS, Windows XP, Solaris, Linnux. Languages: C/C++, SQL, HTML, DHTML/CSS, and JavaScript. Applications: Xemacs, Matlab, AutoCad, Cygwin.
- Strong background in tech support. Took courses in integrated circuits and high-speed PCB design and used these skills in my position with Texas Instruments.
- Certified in Standard First Aid & 2-Person CPR, WHMIS, and PADI Open Water Scuba diving.

Interests and Achievements:
- Member of University of Victoria varsity basketball team, 2001–3
- University of Victoria Engineering Society Director, 2001–4

References: Available upon request.

PREPARING A SCANNABLE RÉSUMÉ

More and more employers are depending on electronic media to short-list applicants for positions with their organizations. To revise your résumé so that it can be scanned for inclusion in a database or for electronic posting, take note of the following modifications to the standard printed format:

- **Presentation.** Minimize formatting features so that your résumé will be easy to scan. Use only two font sizes (the larger one for headings and the smaller one for contents), and put everything flush against the left margin. Use punctuation only when necessary to keep items separate, and keep lines as short as you can (no more than seventy characters and spaces).
- **Key words.** After listing your name and contact information, include a short list of words for which your résumé can be scanned. Supply nouns that refer to your qualifications and expertise as well as to the job you are seeking. (Refer to similar job descriptions to help you make the best choices.)
- **Filename.** Save your résumé in a file named with your last name followed by your first name (Raj Choudhury's file would thus be called choudhuryraj.txt or choudhuryraj.doc).

Whenever you send your résumé electronically, either as part of a message or as an attachment, include the same cover letter that you would if you sent everything by post. In fact, even when e-mailing or faxing an application, always mail or deliver an original (signed) copy of the letter and résumé—unless you have been explicitly instructed not to.

SCANNABLE RÉSUMÉ

The following example gives the first few lines of the standard résumé that appears on pages 99–100 revised to suit an electronic (scannable) format:

choudhuryraj.txt

RAJ CHOUDHURY
45 Main St
Ottawa ON K1K 1K1
Ph 613-456-0000
Fax 613-456-0001
choudhury@intranet.ca

KEY WORDS:
electrical and computer engineering, software engineering, debugging,
website maintenance, tech support, systems, research

POSITION DESIRED:
Software developer

EDUCATION:
Dalhousie University, 2004–5, M. Eng. in Electrical and Computer Engineering
(Thesis: "Machine Architecture and Linear Memory")

PREPARING A FUNCTIONAL RÉSUMÉ

A résumé with traditional categories is not the only kind that works. If you want
to emphasize your abilities and your versatility in addition to the jobs you've
had, prepare a *functional résumé*. A functional résumé has categories for experience in different areas of expertise (for example, research, field work, adminis-
tration, sales). Others may focus on personal attributes such as initiative,
teamwork, analytic ability, or communication skills. Of course, you tailor your
selection to match the requirements of the position you are applying for.

FUNCTIONAL RÉSUMÉ

CAROLINE PAGE
16 Harbour St
Toronto ON M4M 1V6
416-491-3020
cnpage@sympatico.ca

Objective: Work as an environmental consultant in wastewater management.

Profile: A highly organized environmental engineer (B.A.Sc, University of
Waterloo, 2004) with a positive attitude and consistent ability to meet
deadlines in challenging, high-pressure surroundings.

Environmental Engineering:
- Developed MATLAB code for modelling atrazine transport in an aquifer.
- Assisted in site characterization and site selection for active and passive
  water treatment systems.
- Conducted an audit of a paper mill freshwater system.

Field Work:
- Conducted water and sediment sampling at a mine site.
- Planted a constructed wetland for treatment of wood-waste landfill
  leachate.

Laboratory and Analysis:

- Identified, prepared, and analyzed specialized bacterial cultures for wastewater treatment.
- Conducted thermogravimetric analysis (TGA) and direct-current plasma (DCP) analysis of samples.
- Carried out experiments using a variety of biotechnology lab techniques (aseptic technique, culture growth, enumeration, gram staining, etc.).

Communication Skills:

- Fluent in French, both written and spoken
- Part-time teaching and research assistant at the University of Waterloo, January 2002 to present
- Instructor/Counsellor for Engineering Science Quest (a summer camp for pre-teen amateur scientists), Summer 2001

Software Tools:

- Skilled in HYSYS.Plant, including extensibility, and Aspen
- Proficient in MSOffice and Visual C++; working knowledge of MATLAB and Visual Basic

Other Achievements & Activities:

- Six-time recipient of the UW Engineering Upper Year Scholarship for academic excellence
- Member of the Dean's Honours List from 2000 to 2004
- Enjoy playing guitar and Celtic whistle
- Avid cyclist and runner
- Interested in environmental remediation and international development

References available upon request.

CHOOSING THE BEST CONTENT

The content of a résumé should be professional, so don't draw attention to weaknesses you may have, such as lack of experience in a particular area. (Never list a category and then write "None"—you don't want to suggest that you lack something!) Remember to tailor your list of special skills to suggest a fit with each job you apply for, so that the reader can see at a glance that you meet the job requirements. Finally, never claim more for yourself than is true. Including false information in a résumé is grounds for dismissal if it is discovered.

Keep in mind that you are not required to state anything about your age, place of birth, race, religion, or gender. (Use initials, rather than your given name, if you don't wish to reveal your gender until your interview.) To be sure that your application will be considered, of course, you must provide all the information requested when you are completing an application form that has set questions.

WRITING A LETTER OF APPLICATION

You should never use the exact same letter for all applications. Instead, craft each one to match the job and company in question and to catch the attention of the reader. Both the résumé and the letter of application are intended to open the door to the next stage in the job hunt—the interview. The key is to link your skills to the position, not just to state information. What matters is *not* what you want, but *what the employer needs*.

One challenge in writing a letter of application is to tell your reader about yourself and your qualifications without seeming too self-focused. Two tips can help:

1. Limit the number of sentences beginning with *I*. Instead, try burying *I* in the middle of some sentences, where it will be less noticeable, for example, "For two months last summer, I worked as a . . ."
2. Avoid, as much as possible, making unsupported, subjective claims. Instead of saying "I am a highly skilled manager," offer specifics like, "Last summer I managed a $50,000 field study with a crew of seven assistants." Rather than claim "I have excellent research skills," you might say, "Based on my volunteer work with first-year students, Professor Anson Park hired me as a lab assistant for his summer course in civil engineering."

Here is an example (to be imitated, *not* copied) of an application letter that relates the applicant's background to the current needs of a company:

1 April 2005
Steven Nazar, Personnel Director
Outlands Developments
110 Duplessis Blvd
Ottawa, ON N5N 1T7

Dear Mr. Nazar:

Your advertisement in the *Ottawa Citizen* for a Junior Environmental Officer caught my attention, since my qualifications match those you are seeking. As a student graduating with a B.Eng. in Environmental Engineering from the University of Regina, I would like to apply for the position.

Beyond my specialist academic program, I have had relevant environmental field experience. As my résumé indicates, I have spent two summers working with Professor Susan LeClerc in her studies of wetland pollution south of James Bay, helping both in the laboratory and in the wetlands. I also enjoy and am used to the kind of outdoor work you require. In my first summer as a university student, I worked as a tree planter in harsh conditions in northern British Columbia. If there is work available in eastern Canada, I am able to speak French well enough to converse with your French-speaking clients in Ontario and Quebec.

I would appreciate the chance to discuss with you how I could contribute to Outlands Developments. Please call or e-mail me to arrange an interview at your convenience. I look forward to hearing from you.

Sincerely,

Dale Gagnon

Dale Gagnon

FINAL WORDS OF ADVICE

When you apply for a job, your application will be one of many. Of course, it must pass a screening process before you will be invited to an interview. For this reason, it is essential that you submit a package that looks as professional as you will when you present yourself in person. Your application package will be judged not just by what you say but also by how you say it. That's why you must take the time to double-check for grammar and spelling errors and to make sure that your documents are well formatted. With applications, as with job interviews, first impressions count more than anything else.

chApter 12

WRITING FOR READABILITY

Engineering demands both objectivity and professionalism from writers. Your professional success depends on your ability to persuade your reader that your ideas are valid. Whether you are reporting a straightforward procedure or making recommendations that you want the reader to accept, your writing must always be easy to read and to understand. There is nothing unprofessional about writing that's simple and to the point.

Sentence length and style influence a reader's response to writing. These must never be obtrusive. In other words, the language you use to convey your ideas must never take attention away from those ideas. Studies of user-friendly language indicate the obvious: short words and short sentences are generally easier on readers, even sophisticated academic readers. People who have a lot of reading to do like it to be easy.

Because of its technical content, scientific writing is characterized by a specialized vocabulary and academic tone that automatically make it sound complicated. Novice writers often feel that they must adopt a similarly elaborate style in order to sound intelligent. This is not the case. To convince your reader that you are in control of your subject, your sentences must be precise and economical, not dense or convoluted. The most effective and readable style is still one that is clear and concise, confident and consistent. The watchwords are clarity and precision. Your goal is to make it as easy as possible for the reader to understand exactly what you mean—and to respond appropriately.

BE CLEAR

Use plain English
Plain words rather than flowery ones almost always make your sentences more readable. Many of our most common words—the ones that sound most natural and direct—are short. By contrast, most of the words that English has derived from other languages (like French and Latin and Greek) are longer and more complicated. Given the number of synonyms and choices, you should be wary of words loaded down with prefixes (*pre-, post-, anti-, pro-, sub-, maxi-,* etc.) and suffixes (*-ate, -ize, -tion,* etc.). Too much dependence on polysyllabic words

makes your writing hard to read. If you can substitute a short word for a longer one, do so:

Flowery	Plain
accomplish	do
ascertain	verify
cognizant	aware
commence	begin, start
conclusion	end
concur	agree
determinant	cause
efficacious	effective
endeavour	try
eventuate	occur
fabricate	build, create
finalize	finish, complete
firstly	first
initiate	begin
maximization	increase
modification	change
numerous	many
obviate	prevent
oration	speech
prioritize	rank
proceed	go
rectify	correct
remuneration	pay
requisite	needed, necessary
sanitize	clean
subsequently	later
systematize	order, arrange
terminate	end
transpire	happen, take place
utilize, utilization	use

Suggesting that you write in plain English does not mean that you should never pick an unfamiliar, long, or foreign word, especially if it is the only one that expresses a complicated concept concisely (for example, there is no simpler way to refer to *bioremediation* or *complementarity*). But do not needlessly clutter your sentence with longer words or phrases when shorter alternatives exist. Note how big words and long phrases can cloud rather than clarify meaning, as in the following example:

orig. The addition of the acid and the subsequent agitation of the solution resulted in the formation of crystals. (18 words)

rev. Crystals formed when the acid was added and the solution shaken. (11 words)

If you find yourself selecting words or phrases only because they look impressive, you may find your writing criticized for sounding awkward instead.

Choose clear wording

A dictionary is a wise investment. A good one will help you understand unfamiliar words or archaic and technical senses of common words. It will also help you use words properly by offering example sentences that show how certain words are typically used. A dictionary will help you with questions of spelling and usage as well. If you aren't sure if a particular word is too informal for your writing, or if you have concerns that a certain word might be offensive, a good dictionary will give you this information.

You should be aware that Canadian usage and spelling may follow either British or American practice, but usually combine aspects of both. There are a number of Canadian dictionaries available today that will help you to be consistent in your approach. It's also a good idea to make sure that the language option in your word-processing program is set to *English* (*Canada*). However, when you are a professional engineer writing for American clients, you will want to use American spelling.

A thesaurus lists words that are closely related in meaning. It can help when you want to avoid repeating yourself, or when you are fumbling for a word that's on the tip of your tongue. Your word processor also has a thesaurus feature that allows you to look up synonyms and antonyms easily. Be careful, though: make sure you distinguish between *denotative* and *connotative* meanings. A word's denotation is its primary or "dictionary" meaning. Its connotations are any associations that it may suggest; they may not be as exact as the denotations, but they are part of the impression the word conveys. If you examine a list of synonyms in a thesaurus, you will see that even words with similar meanings can have dramatically different connotations. For example, alongside the word *indifferent* your thesaurus may give the following: *neutral, noncommittal, careless, lackadaisical, fair,* and *unsympathetic.* Imagine the different impressions you would create if you chose one or the other of those words to complete this sentence: "Questioned about the experiment's chance of success, he was

_____ in his response." To write clearly, you must remember that a reader may react to the suggestive meaning of a word as much as to its "dictionary" meaning.

Avoid jargon

All fields have their own terminology, or *occupational dialect*. It may be unfamiliar to outsiders, but it helps specialists explain things to each other. As an engineering student, you are generally writing for experts, so there's no need to define standard technical terms or explain a methodology that's familiar to anyone with scientific training. In fact, by using the vocabulary of your discipline appropriately and correctly, you confirm that you are a serious student and a credible writer. The trouble is that people sometimes use special, technical language as jargon, thinking it will make them seem more professional. Too often the result is not clarity but confusion, especially if the words aren't used correctly. The guideline is easy: use specialized terminology only when it's called for to explain something more precisely and efficiently. If plain language will do just as well, use it, especially if your reader is not an expert. In particular, avoid using scientific-sounding words in contexts that are not scientific:

orig.   Consultation with managerial personnel furnished input for determining the viable parameters of the project.

rev.   The manager helped define the scope of the project.

Be precise

As a scientist, you already know how to be exact. Carry this habit into your writing. Always be as precise as you can. Avoid all-purpose adjectives like *major*, *significant*, and *relevant*, abstract general nouns like *situation* and *factor*, and vague verbs such as *involve*, *entail*, and *exist*, when you can be more specific:

orig.   Ensuring immediate access to emergency water supplies is a major element in effective disaster management.

rev.   In a disaster, rescuers must first ensure access to emergency water supplies.

Avoid generalizing with such qualifiers as *fairly, rather, somewhat*, and *quite*. Indeed, saying that something is *very* important carries less weight than saying simply that it is important. For example, compare these sentences:

This is an important decision.

This is a really important decision.

The shorter sentence has more impact. When you think that a word needs qualifying—and sometimes it will—first see if there's a more precise way of phrasing it. For example, the word *critical* conveys a greater degree of urgency than *important* and is more precise than something like *really important*; using *critical* will give a recommendation more weight:

> This is a <u>critical</u> decision.

If you are making qualitative judgments, you must be sure to back them up with specifics. In particular, watch how you use the word *relatively*. Its potential for misinterpretation is great unless you are actually considering two or more items. What does *relatively complex* mean anyway? Two other such weasel words are *basically* and *virtually*. Finally, watch how you use the qualifier *approximately*. Do not introduce an exact measure with this word:

✗ The receiver height was set at approximately 4.53 m.

✓ The receiver height was set at 4.53 m.

Be careful to avoid the mistake of qualifying absolutes. To say that something is *very unique* makes as little sense as describing something as *rather rectangular*. The following are other redundant descriptions to avoid:

in <u>close</u> proximity	revert <u>back</u> to
many <u>different</u> types	their <u>future</u> plans
<u>sudden</u> crisis	his <u>personal</u> opinion
this <u>particular</u> context	<u>successful</u> achievements
each <u>individual</u> participant	<u>true</u> facts

Avoid ambiguity

One good reason for having someone else read your final draft is to check for ambiguity—words or phrases with unintentional double meanings. For example, if you say "the *background* of the site was discussed," are you referring to the physical location or the context? Watch for words with multiple meanings, like *sound* and *solid*. Be particularly careful of the potentially confused meanings of *as* and *since*. You may find it safer to use unambiguous synonyms instead:

> *orig.* Sediments will be trapped <u>as</u> runoff is detained in the storm water management basins.

rev.   Sediments will be trapped <u>when</u> runoff is detained in the storm water management basins.

rev.   Sediments will be trapped <u>because</u> runoff is detained in the storm water management basins.

Pronouns can cause trouble too, especially if your reader can't tell what word the pronoun is referring to:

orig.   The seed requires water to germinate, and <u>it</u> must be warm.

Is it the seed or the water that must be warm? If there is any chance of ambiguity, restructure the sentence.

rev.   The seeds require water to germinate, and <u>they</u> must be warm.

rev.   The seeds require warm water to germinate.

One of the most commonly misinterpreted pronouns is the demonstrative *this*. In the example below, it's just not possible to tell whether it's the warning, the possibility, or the destruction that upsets taxpayers:

orig.   Experts warn that acid rain is destroying Canadian maple forests. <u>This</u> upsets most taxpayers.

rev.   <u>The possibility</u> that acid rain is destroying Canadian maple forests upsets most taxpayers.

Make sure there is just one word that the pronoun clearly refers to.

BE CONCISE

At one time or another, you will probably be tempted to pad your writing. Whatever the reason—because you need to write two or three thousand words and have only enough to say for one thousand, or just because you think length is strength and hope to get a better mark for the extra words—padding is a mistake. Readers suspect, quite legitimately, that you are only pretending to have something important to say.

Strong writing is always concise. It leaves out anything that does not serve some communicative or stylistic purpose, in order to say as much as possible in as few words as possible. Concise writing will help you do better on both your assignments and your exams, for you will never look as though you are blathering in desperation at having nothing to say. Start editing for economy by counting the words in your sentences and reducing that number whenever possible. The following guidelines will help.

Use adverbs and adjectives sparingly

Avoid the scattergun approach to adverbs and adjectives. Don't use combinations of modifiers unless you are sure they clarify your meaning. One well-chosen word is always better than a series of synonyms:

> *orig.*   As well as being <u>costly</u> and <u>financially extravagant</u>, the venture is <u>reckless</u> and <u>foolhardy</u>. (14 words)

> *rev.*   The venture is both <u>costly</u> and <u>foolhardy</u>. (7 words)

Avoid noun clusters

One recent trend for reducing sentence length is to use nouns as modifiers (as in the phrase <u>noun</u> *cluster*). In pairs, this practice is certainly useful: <u>kidney</u> *disease*, <u>hydrogen</u> *bomb*, <u>word</u> *processor*, <u>reaction</u> *time*, *S.I.* units are all well-established noun pairs. But avoid making up your own combinations, like *resonator junction isolator*, where it is difficult for the reader to understand if you are talking about *junction isolators for resonators* or *isolators for resonator junctions*. Frequent use of extended series can produce monstrous pile-ups. Breaking up noun clusters may not result in fewer words, but it will make your writing easier to read:

> *orig.*   computer services management group

> *rev.*   group of computer services managers

> *or*   group managing computer services

> *orig.*   volunteer pollution investigation committee

> *rev.*   volunteer committee to investigate pollution (*not* group investigating volunteer pollution!)

Avoid chains of relative clauses

Sentences full of clauses beginning with *which*, *that*, or *who* are usually wordier than necessary. Try reducing some of those clauses to phrases or single words:

> *orig.*   The solutions <u>that were discussed last night</u> have practical applications, <u>which will be easily grasped</u> by people <u>who have no technical training</u>. (22 words)

rev.   The practical applications of the solutions discussed last night are easily grasped by non-technical people. (15 words)

Reduce clauses to phrases or words

Independent clauses can often be reduced by subordination. Here are a few examples to imitate:

orig.   The report was written in a clear and concise manner, and it was immediately approved therefore. (16 words)

rev.   Written in a clear and concise manner, the report was immediately approved. (12 words)

rev.   Clear and concise, the report was immediately approved. (8 words)

orig.   The plan was of a radical nature and was a source of embarrassment to management. (15 words)

rev.   The radical plan embarrassed management. (5 words)

Watch for ineffective or accidental repetition

Although your word processor will point out where you've inadvertently typed the same word twice, you'll need your eyes to catch most redundancies. This is another good reason to proofread carefully:

orig.   The terrain slopes to the south with slopes of up to 6.0 per cent.

rev.   The terrain slopes to the south at angles of up to 6.0 per cent.

Sometimes the repetition comes in a different part of speech. It still calls for a revision:

orig.   The architects will issue a certificate of compliance showing that construction complies with building codes. (15 words)

rev.   The architects will certify that construction complies with building codes. (10 words)

Eliminate hackneyed expressions and circumlocutions

Because they are so commonplace and overused, hackneyed phrases can quickly come to mind when you're writing. While they flow easily from the pen, your reader may find them tired, stale, and unoriginal. Unnecessary words are deadwood. To keep your writing vital, chop ruthlessly:

Wordy	*Revised*
at the same time as	while
due to the fact that	because
at the end of the day	finally, all in all
at this point in time	now
consensus of opinion	consensus
despite the fact that	although
in the near future	soon
when all is said and done	[omit]
in the eventuality that	if
in all likelihood	likely
it could be said that	possibly, maybe
in all probability	probably
last but not least	finally

Avoid "it is" and "there is" beginnings

Many readers object to sentences that start with *It is* or *There are* because such writing often seems inflated. But it may not always be possible to avoid beginning sentences this way. For one thing, such constructions help you avoid a personal focus:

orig.   We have reason to be optimistic.

rev.   There is reason for optimism.

If your sentence includes a clause beginning with *that*, however, you may want to do some editing:

orig.   There are several problems that need to be resolved. (9 words)

rev.   Several problems need to be resolved. (6 words)

Be on the lookout for sentences that can be tightened up considerably by rewriting:

orig.   It is the purpose of the project to pursue new software development. (12 words)

rev.   The project will develop new software. (6 words)

orig.   It is certain that inflation will increase. (7 words)

rev.   Inflation will certainly increase. (4 words)

Use vigorous verbs

Verbs like *have*, *do*, and *make* often introduce wordy phrases that you can reduce by choosing an appropriate strong verb instead:

Wordy	Strong
have a tendency to	tend to
do an analysis of	analyze
do research on	study, investigate
make a discovery	discover
make an effort to	try

BE CONVINCING

Developing a confident, readable style means learning some standard techniques and practising them until they become habit.

Choose active over passive verbs

Active sentences are usually livelier and shorter than passive ones:

active: She presented the findings. (4 words)

passive: The findings were presented by her. (6 words)

Moreover, passive constructions tend to produce awkward, convoluted sentences. Writers of bureaucratic documents are among the worst offenders:

orig.   It <u>had been decided</u> that the utilization of small rivers in the province for purposes of hydroelectric power generation <u>should be studied</u> by the department and that a report to the deputy minister <u>should be made</u> by the director as soon as possible. (43 words)

The passive verbs in this mouthful take emphasis away from the issue and leave the sentence looking as though it had something to conceal. If a passive construction buries the "doer" of an action in a phrase beginning with "by," you can always rewrite to save words and emphasize the subject:

rev.   Once the department investigates using small rivers to generate hydroelectric power in the province, the director will report to the deputy minister without delay. (24 words)

In order to focus on results rather than on the people producing those results, scientific writing often relies on passive constructions—quite appropriately. In fact, four situations actually call for the passive rather than the active wording:

1. When you want to emphasize the results of actions rather than the person performing the action or achieving the results. This is generally the situation in lab reports:

   As a result, the concentration of radon <u>was reduced</u> by 40 per cent.

2. When the subject is the passive recipient of some action:

   The university <u>was founded</u> in 1959.

3. When you want to avoid an awkward shift from one subject to another in a sentence or paragraph:

   The sensor monitors light and <u>is checked</u> once a day.

4. When you want to avoid assigning responsibility or blame:

   Several errors <u>were made</u> in the calculations.

When passive verbs produce wordy or convoluted constructions, however, be sure to rewrite the sentence:

orig. If the fan <u>is located</u> in a remote space, noise <u>will be minimized</u> and the fan will thus be able <u>to be operated</u> throughout the night. (26 words)

rev. Minimizing noise by locating the fan away from the bedrooms will permit its operation throughout the night. (17 words)

If there are concise alternatives to passives, use them:

orig. Software reengineering <u>is concerned with</u> the redesign or reconstruction of a software system. (13 words)

rev. Software reengineering <u>involves</u> the redesign or reconstruction of a software system. (11 words)

Use strong subjects

In sentences that feature people and actions, it makes sense not to bury these in complicated phrases. When you have a choice, make the subject of your sentences concrete, not abstract:

orig. At the beginning of the term, <u>instructions</u> for handling hazardous materials were given to each student.

rev.   At the beginning of the term, <u>students</u> were given instructions for handling hazardous materials.

In most cases this principle calls for you to use an *active* instead of a *passive* verb:

orig.   When the function key <u>is pressed</u> by the operator, the RX screen <u>is activated</u>. [passive]

rev.   The operator <u>presses</u> the function key <u>to activate</u> the RX screen. [active]

If you are writing instructions, it is essential to address them to the person who will be following them. You accomplish this by using the *imperative*—a simple verb with *you* as the understood subject. Note the difference below:

orig.   To record the results, a three-step process <u>must be followed</u>.

rev.   <u>Follow</u> a three-step process to record the results.

Avoid hesitancy

It's normal for students to worry that they lack the knowledge to give a subject the development that it deserves. Avoid apologizing for your inexperience, however. State your information plainly without qualifications. Use words like *seem* and *appear* only in situations of genuine doubt, not because you are afraid you have not done enough research:

orig.   The tank <u>appears</u> to be located so as to be <u>fairly</u> accessible for periodic cleanout.

rev.   The tank's location makes it accessible for periodic cleanout by a professional contractor.

BE CONSISTENT

The demand for readability also calls for consistency. There should never be surprises for your reader. If you are constantly changing point of view or attitude or tone, your reader won't believe that you are in control of your ideas. After all, it's hard to trust someone who keeps changing the rules. Watch for and avoid situations where the wording seems to shift.

Keep a consistently appropriate tone

In Chapter 1, you learned about choosing a tone that matches the context of your writing. If you think of this in terms of clothing, it means selecting something to wear that makes you look good (not sloppy), yet doesn't make you feel uncomfortably overdressed. The corresponding tone and register lie generally between standard and formal. What's even more important, whether you are writing a cover letter or a dissertation, is that you not mix levels from sentence to sentence, or even within a sentence. Avril Lavigne may be able to wear a tie with a T-shirt, but on most people the combination would be too distracting to be effective. Consider this example from a cover letter for a job application:

orig.   As a project team member, I <u>interface</u> with the project leader, project members, and <u>pretty rarely</u> with the <u>end</u> consumer. (20 words)

Apart from the problem of parallel structure (see p. 143), this sentence contains standard English, jargon, and slang—all within the same sentence. The solution is to rework the sentence to make the language consistent:

rev.   On projects, I work with the project leader and team members, rarely with the consumer. (15 words)

Another typical inconsistency is a shift in tone from impersonal to personal; this often coincides with a shift from formal to informal:

orig.   The report discusses which recommendations should (in our opinion) get priority attention. A general plan of attack for making it past this phase will be included. (26 words)

rev.   The report discusses the recommendations that deserve primary attention. It includes a master plan and schedule. (16 words)

Generally the solution is to keep to the middle ground—not too formal, not too casual.

Shifting from one pronoun to another will also affect the consistency and formality of your writing. Where "you" is often too personal and too casual (except in personal communications and instructions), "one" is unnaturally formal. In your writing, then, avoid generalizing with either of these choices, and be especially careful not to combine the two approaches in the same document:

orig.   <u>Your</u> personal computer may have web connectivity, but Internet access doesn't mean <u>one</u> automatically has access to e-mail.

rev.   Most personal computers have web connectivity, but Internet access does not automatically mean access to e-mail.

Keep a consistent point of view

Where writers might once have referred to themselves, awkwardly, in the third person (as "the investigators" or "the authors"), scientific writing now generally permits "we" and a first-person point of view, especially when it makes sentences more readable. The level of formality is essentially your choice, but keep in mind that it is inappropriate to shift from an impersonal to a personal point of view in your writing:

orig. We note the deformation of the surface, and it is recommended that cryogenic treatment be attempted. (16 words)

rev. We note the deformation of the surface and recommend cryogenic treatment. (11 words)

Notice that the revised sentence not only offers a consistent point of view, but also features an active rather than a passive verb and is shorter, thus stronger.

BE OBJECTIVE

Your writing must be as free as possible of biases and subjective opinions. Your reader will be more likely to accept your findings if you follow these suggestions:

- Avoid unsubstantiated judgments. Be sure that any suggestions you make or conclusions you reach follow from the information you have provided. Never imply anything that you cannot prove. If your findings aren't foolproof, show where the uncertainty lies.
- Avoid subjective language. Words such as *terrible* or *wonderful* detract from the objective tone you want. Rather than saying "quarterly figures show an incredible increase," give the exact percentage of the increase and let the facts speak for themselves.

The overall tone to aim for depends on the circumstances—and particularly on the intended reader. If you are writing a short, informal report to someone you see often, familiar terms such as *I* or *you* do work well. On the other hand, many formal reports try to avoid the subjective impression created by personal pronouns. The result, unfortunately, is often a cumbersome load of passive constructions (see pp. 115–16). If you are writing on behalf of a group or an organization, you can use the pronoun *we*, which is less intrusive than awkward passive constructions. If you are writing as an individual, however, you don't have that option. In such a case, try to recast the sentence to keep an active verb while avoiding *I*:

✗ The purchasing system has been found to increase the duplication of forms.

✗ I found that the purchasing system increases the duplication of forms.

✓ The purchasing system increases the duplication of forms.

If you can't make this sort of revision, you are better to write the occasional *I* than to use convoluted passive constructions that strangle your meaning or substitutes like *the writer* or *the researcher* that make your writing seem old-fashioned.

USING BIAS-FREE LANGUAGE

As concern with political correctness increases, it becomes more and more important to avoid any suggestion of bias in the language we use—both spoken and written. Just as you consider your reader carefully when deciding on the appropriate tone to use, you will also have to be careful to use language that is as objective and neutral as possible.

The potential for bias is far-reaching, involving gender, race, culture, age, disability, occupation, religion, and socio-economic status. Although society hasn't come up with ideal solutions in every case, developing an awareness of sensitive issues will help you to avoid using biased language.

Gender

At one time, it was common to use *he* as a generic singular pronoun. Indeed you will still encounter this kind of usage in books published before 1975:

> If an employee discovers a way to cut costs, <u>he</u> will receive a bonus.

But as sensitivity to bias in language has increased, writers and speakers have become careful not to use *he* as a generic pronoun. Informally, we've solved the problem by using *they* instead, but this solution is acceptable only in speaking—never in any kind of formal writing. Rather than use an awkward combination of singular and plural, try these options for avoiding the problem:

- Pluralize the word and the pronouns that refer to it:

  > If <u>employees</u> discover a way to cut costs, <u>they</u> will receive a bonus.

- Use the passive voice:

  > A bonus <u>will be given</u> to an employee who discovers a way to cut costs.

- Restructure the sentence:

  > <u>An employee</u> who discovers a way to cut costs <u>will</u> receive a bonus.

- Use *he or she*, which is cumbersome and annoying, only as a last resort.

Avoid the abbreviated forms *he/she* and *s/he* except in the most casual writing.

Another trouble spot involves gender-specific nouns, such as *foreman*, *stewardess*, *draftsman*, and *waitress*. The solution in these cases is to prefer gender-free words, for example *supervisor*, *flight attendant*, *draftsperson*, and *server*.

Race and culture

The names used to describe someone's racial or cultural identity often carry with them negative connotations, for example the term *Negro*. The search for neutral language has produced alternatives such as *black* and *person of colour*, but these have not been universally accepted as bias-free. There are similar problems with the term *Indian*, with alternatives such as *Aboriginal*, *Native*, *Indigenous*, and *First Nations* each having its share of critics. The best solution is often to find out what the racial or cultural group in question prefers. Even if there isn't an easy answer, being aware of a potential problem is already a start. In scientific and technical writing, you are not likely to be dealing with the same issues of race, religion, or culture as you would in a sociology course. Still, it's important to remember that any reader may be highly sensitized to bias in language. It makes good sense to seek and use the most objective language you can.

There are areas beyond gender and ethnicity where the effort to develop and use neutral language has made an impact. For instance, we refer not to *old people* but to *seniors*, and to someone as having *special needs* rather than being *handicapped*. Whatever the situation, be sensitive to the power of the words you use and take the time to search for language that is bias-free.

MAKE IMPORTANT IDEAS STAND OUT

Experienced writers know how to manipulate sentences in order to emphasize certain points. The following are some of their techniques.

Use concrete details

Concrete details are easier to understand—and to remember—than abstract theories. If you are writing about abstract concepts for readers who are not experts in your field, be sure to provide specific examples and illustrations:

orig. The following are scientists who are dealing with problems associated with stochastic process: physicists, meteorologists, economists, and so on.

rev. The physicist measuring frequencies in the lab, the meteorologist forecasting rain, the economist verifying price fluctuations—all of these scientists are tackling problems related to stochastic process.

See how a few specific details can bring the facts to life? Adding concrete details and examples is another way to improve the readability of your writing.

Place key words in strategic positions

The positions of emphasis in a sentence are the beginning and, above all, the end. If you want to make a point convincingly, don't bury it in the middle of the sentence—feature it later:

> orig. The strongest part of the committee's report is its recommendations, not its findings.

> rev. The strongest part of the committee's report is not its findings but its recommendations.

Subordinate minor ideas

It is easy to connect incidents with a string of *ands*, as if everything were of equal importance:

> We performed the experiment, and we analyzed the results, and we made firm recommendations.

But you'll find it just as natural to *subordinate*—that is, to make one part of a sentence less important grammatically in order to emphasize another point:

> Once we performed the experiment and analyzed the results, we made firm recommendations.

Major ideas stand out more and connections become clearer when minor ideas are subordinated:

> orig. Fumes from insulation materials can build up along with carbon dioxide, mould, bacteria, and dust, and the result may be "sick building syndrome."

> rev. When fumes from insulation materials build up along with carbon dioxide, mould, bacteria, and dust, the result may be "sick building syndrome."

Make your most important idea the subject of the main clause. If you put this main clause at the end (see "periodic sentence" in the Glossary), it will carry more weight:

> orig. "Sick building syndrome" may result when fumes from insulation materials build up.

> rev. When fumes from insulation materials build up, "sick building syndrome" may result.

Vary sentence structure

As with anything else, variety adds life to writing. One way of adding variety, as you have seen, is to change the sentence order. Most sentences follow a standard pattern of **subject + verb + object (+ modifiers)**:

> The class president circulated a petition last week.
>   subject   verb   object   modifier

Placing a modifier at the beginning rather than in its natural place at the end of the sentence calls attention to it:

orig.   Unsolicited commercial e-mail, known as *spam*, is little more than a minor irritant for most Internet users.

rev.   For most Internet users, unsolicited commercial e-mail, known as *spam*, is little more than a minor irritant.

A full inversion of a sentence creates the greatest emphasis because it is so unusual. Save it for those times when you want to make a very strong point:

orig.   Astronomers did not learn of the existence of galaxies until the 1920s.

rev.   Not until the 1920s did astronomers learn of the existence of galaxies.

Use comparison and contrast

Just as a jeweller will highlight a diamond by displaying it against dark velvet, so too can you highlight an idea by placing it against a contrasting background:

orig.   A communications engineer conceives the overall design of a communications system.

rev.   Unlike the electronics engineer, whose job it is to design equipment, the communications engineer conceives the system itself.

Using parallel phrasing increases the effect of the contrast:

> Dioxin is not a name for one chemical but a general term for a group of chemicals—all of them toxic.

Parallel comparatives help you emphasize the increase or decrease of something in proportion to something else. The result is both economical and readable:

orig.   The water contained in an aquifer increases proportionally to the number of pores in the aquifer, and its circulation speed increases as the pore size increases. (26 words) *rev.*   The more pores in an aquifer, the more water it contains; the bigger the pores, the faster the water circulates. (20 words)

Use correlative constructions

Correlatives such as *both . . . and* or *not only . . . but (also)* can be used to emphasize combinations as well, as long as you keep both sides balanced and parallel (see pp. 142–3). Note the options for increased and reduced sentence length:

orig.   The model achieves the highest standards of energy efficiency, <u>and</u> it is cost effective <u>as well</u>. (16 words)

rev.   <u>Not only</u> does the model meet the highest standards of energy efficiency, <u>but</u> it is cost effective <u>as well</u>. (19 words)

rev.   The model is <u>both</u> energy efficient <u>and</u> cost effective. (9 words)

Vary sentence length

A short sentence can add impact to an important point, especially when it comes after a series of longer sentences. This technique can be particularly useful for conclusions. Don't overdo it, though. A string of long sentences may be monotonous, but a string of short ones can make your writing sound amateurish.

Still, scientific writing is likely to have more long sentences than short ones. Since short sentences are easier on readers, try breaking up clusters of lengthy ones. Check any sentence of over 20 words or so to see if it will benefit from being split. Use the readability indicator on your word processor to help you keep the average length of your sentences between 15 and 18 words. Never hesitate to tighten up a loose sentence either.

Use your ears

Your ears are probably your best guides. Make good use of them. Before producing a final copy of any piece of writing, read your draft out loud in a clear voice. The difference between cumbersome and fluent passages will be unmistakable.

SOME FINAL ADVICE: WRITE BEFORE YOU REVISE

No one would expect you to sit down and put all of this advice into practice as soon as you start to write. You would feel so constrained that it would be hard to get anything down on paper at all. It's better if you begin concentrating on these guidelines during the final stages of the writing process, when you are looking critically at what you have already written. Some experienced writers can combine the creative and critical functions, but most find it easier to write a rough draft before starting the detailed task of revising and editing.

As you examine that rough draft, consider ways of reducing the overall length as well as varying the average sentence length. In general, the shorter the sentences, the easier the text is to read. Note how the second of the two following paragraphs uses a lot fewer words than the first.

orig. The benefits of the project will include an understanding of the groundwater resources of the areas, their location, magnitude, and recharge characteristics. This understanding will be refined in the immediate well field area to produce a definition of the capture zones that will provide the basis for delineating well head protection areas around each well or well field. Groundwater protection measures in these areas will therefore be recommended or required by policies and programs currently being developed.

There are 77 words in the three sentences that make up this passage. The average sentence is 25.6 words long, and 50 per cent of the verbs are in the passive voice. This text is not easy to read.

rev. The project will identify the groundwater resources of the area, as well as their location, magnitude, and recharge characteristics. These data will help define the capture zones in the immediate well field area and delineate protection areas around each well head or field. Future policies and programs will recommend or require groundwater protection measures in these areas.

The number of words has been reduced to 56 from 77, leaving an average sentence length of 18.6 words with only 20 per cent passive verbs. The revision is much easier to read than the original.

The best advice is to take advantage of your situation as a student to try things out, to discover what your readers like or dislike, and to practise editing to reduce the total number of words you have written. By working at the readability of your writing, you will be well prepared for a career where your writing skills go hand in hand with your success.

NOTE

[1] Discussion of focus based on Robert Cluett and Lee Ahlborn, *Effective English Prose*. New York: L.W. Singer, 1965, p. 51.

chapter 13

COMMON ERRORS IN GRAMMAR AND USAGE

This chapter is a survey of those areas where students most often make mistakes. It will help you to keep a lookout for weaknesses as you are editing your work. Once you get into the habit of checking your work, it won't be long before you are correcting potential problems as you write.

The grammatical terms used here are the most basic and familiar ones; if you need to review some of them, see Chapter 14 or the glossary. For a thorough treatment of grammar and usage, consult a complete text such as *The Canadian Writer's Handbook* (Toronto: Oxford University Press, 2005).

If English is not your first language, there is a section at the end of this chapter that focuses on the most typical errors of non-native speakers. As you work to increase your proficiency, keep track of the mistakes you typically make and concentrate on eliminating them as you edit. It is also a good idea to have your writing reviewed by a colleague who speaks English as a first language. This person can point out idiomatic and other errors that you may have missed.

PROBLEMS WITH SENTENCE UNITY

SENTENCE FRAGMENTS

To be complete, a sentence must have both a subject and a predicate in an independent clause. If it doesn't, it's a fragment. There are times in informal writing when it is acceptable to use a sentence fragment in order to give emphasis to a point, as in

✓ Will the municipality reduce property taxes? Not likely.

Here the sentence fragment *Not likely* is deliberate. The writer intended it to be understood as a short version of *It is not likely that the municipality will reduce property taxes.* Unintentional sentence fragments, on the other hand, usually seem incomplete rather than shortened:

✗ One application is the algorithm for a chess program. Based on an actual game situation.

The last "sentence" is incomplete because it has neither a subject nor a verb. (Remember that a participle such as *based* is a verbal, or "part-verb," not a verb.) The fragment can be made into a complete sentence by adding a subject and a verb:

✓ It is based on an actual game situation.

More economically, you could join the fragment to the preceding sentence:

✓ One application is the algorithm for a chess program based on an actual game situation.

Be particularly careful not to separate dependent clauses from the previous sentence. Watch for such subordinators as *whereas*, *while*, and *because*.

✗ Some companies are exemplary corporate citizens. Whereas others are interested only in making profits.

One good test for a complete sentence is to make sure that it fits naturally into the following space: "It is true that _____." If the result sounds wrong—as it would with the sentence fragment beginning *whereas* above—it makes sense to revise it:

✓ Some companies are exemplary corporate citizens, whereas others are interested only in making profits.

RUN-ON SENTENCES

Many people consider a run-on sentence one that continues beyond the point where it should have stopped:

✗ Mosquitoes and blackflies are annoying, but they don't stop tourists from coming to spend their holidays in Canada, and such is the case in Ontario's northland.

This example reveals a problem of over-coordination. The sentence could be improved by removing the word *and* and replacing the comma after *Canada* with a semicolon or period.

The grammatical problem called a run-on sentence occurs when two independent clauses are jammed together without any punctuation at all. (An independent clause is a clause that is a complete sentence.) Two independent clauses should not run together, as they seem to do in the following example:

✗ Flat-screen technology is so new its cost is prohibitive.

✓ Flat screen technology is so new that its cost is prohibitive.

Here the problem is corrected by adding the word *that*, which effectively turns the second independent clause (*its cost is prohibitive*) into a dependent, or subordinate, clause. The problem cannot be corrected by simply adding a comma, as the writer of the next example has done:

✗   In physics there is matter and antimatter, everything must be balanced.

This error is known as a comma splice. There are three ways of correcting it:

1. by putting a period after *antimatter* and starting a new sentence:

   ✓   . . . and antimatter. Everything . . .

2. by replacing the comma with a semicolon:

   ✓   . . . and antimatter; everything . . .

3. by making one of the independent clauses subordinate to the other, so that it can't stand by itself:

   ✓   In physics, because there is matter and antimatter, everything must be balanced.

The comma splice is occasionally forgivable when clauses are very short and arranged in tight sequence:

orig.   The rainbow has seven bands, Saturn has seven rings, the concept has seven features.

However, it's still better to revise such a sentence:

✓   The rainbow has seven bands, Saturn has seven rings, <u>and</u> the concept has seven features.

Contrary to what many people think, words such as *however*, *therefore*, and *thus* cannot be used with a comma to join independent clauses:

✗   The coefficient used for the calculation is still correct, therefore no new modelling has been done.

Correct this mistake by beginning a new sentence after *correct* or by replacing the comma with a semicolon:

✓   The coefficient used for the calculation is still correct; therefore, no new modelling has been done.

The only words that can be used without a semicolon to join independent clauses are the coordinating conjunctions—*and, or, nor, but, for, yet,* and *so*—

and subordinating conjunctions such as *if, because, since, while, when, where, after, before,* and *until*:

✓ The coefficient used for the calculation is still correct, so no new modelling has been done.

FAULTY PREDICATION

When the subject of a sentence is not grammatically connected to what follows (the predicate), the result is called *faulty predication*:

✗ The <u>reason</u> they chose this design is <u>because</u> it is well suited to indoor environments.

The problem with this sentence is that *because* means essentially the same thing as *the reason (that)*. The subject needs a noun clause to complete it:

✓ The reason they chose this design is that it is well suited to indoor environments.

Another solution is to rephrase the sentence:

✓ They chose the design because it is well suited to indoor environments.

Faulty predication also occurs with *is when* and *is where* constructions:

✗ The best time for the tests <u>is when</u> the subjects are well rested.

Again, you can correct this error in one of two ways:

1. Follow the *is* with a noun phrase to complete the sentence:

   ✓ The best time for the tests <u>is the morning, when</u> the subjects are well rested.

2. Change the verb:

   ✓ Run the tests when the subjects are well rested.

PROBLEMS WITH SUBJECT–VERB AGREEMENT

IDENTIFYING THE SUBJECT

Formal writing always requires the verb to agree in number with its subject. In other words, singular subjects call for singular verbs; plural subjects call for plural verbs. Sometimes, however, when the subject does not come at the beginning of the sentence, or when it is separated from the verb by other information, you may inadvertently use a verb form that does not agree, as in the example that follows:

    ✗   Our design work, including earthwork calculations and cost estimates, are based on these figures.

The subject here is *work*, not *calculations and estimates*; therefore, the verb should be singular:

    ✓   Our design work, including earthwork calculations and cost estimates, is based on these figures.

EITHER, NEITHER, EACH

The indefinite pronouns *either*, *neither*, and *each* always take singular verbs:

    ✗   Neither of the models are flawless.

    ✓   Neither of the models is flawless.

    ✓   Each of them has flaws.

COMPOUND SUBJECTS

When you use *or*, *either . . . or*, or *neither . . . nor* to create a compound subject, the verb is expected to agree with the last item in the subject:

    ✓   Neither the TA nor her students were able to solve the equation.

    ✓   Either the students or the TA was misinformed.

You may find that it sounds awkward to use a singular verb when a singular item follows a plural item:

    orig.   Neither the transistors nor the circuit was modified.

In such instances, it's worth rephrasing the sentence:

    rev.   Neither the circuit nor the transistors were modified.

Unlike the word *and*, which creates a compound subject and therefore takes a plural verb, the phrases *as well as* and *in addition to* do not create compound subjects. The verb remains singular:

    ✓   Noise, interference, and channel distortion corrupt information transmissions.

✓ Noise, as well as interference and channel distortion, corrupts information transmissions.

When the main verb is a form of *be* (*is, are, was,* or *were*), you often have a choice of sentence order. Note the subject–verb agreements below:

✓ My area of research is biomechanics and motor control.

✓ Biomechanics and motor control are what I research.

Remember that you can always revise your sentences when you are writing.

Subject–verb agreement is often ignored in spoken English (which is much less formal than writing, remember). Orally, sentences beginning with *there,* for example, tend to be followed by the singular verb, even when the subject is a plural. Avoid such casual structures when you are writing:

✗ There is a number of problems to be resolved.

✓ There are a number of problems to be resolved.

✓ A number of problems need to be resolved.

Subject–verb agreement errors often result from a misunderstanding of the true subject in phrases containing *of.* In the example above, *a number of* is grammatically equivalent to *many,* so it is right to use a plural verb. But many similar constructions are singular, not plural, because the true subject comes after the definite or indefinite article (*the* or *a*), not *of.* When you use the following, be sure to use a singular verb:

a series of _____
the set of _____
a range of _____
a variety of _____ } is available.
the group of _____
a multitude of _____

COLLECTIVE NOUNS

A collective noun is a singular noun that comprises a number of members; examples include words such as *family, class, group,* and *team.* If the noun refers to the members as one unit, it takes a singular verb:

✓ The class is studying communication systems.

If, in the context of the sentence, the noun refers to the members as individuals, the verb becomes plural:

✓ The <u>class</u> <u>are</u> submitting their projects on Friday.

It's advisable to rewrite such a sentence to avoid the awkward sound of the singular and plural together:

✗ The <u>class</u> <u>is</u> submitting their projects on Friday.

✓ <u>Members</u> of the class <u>are</u> submitting <u>their</u> projects on Friday.

QUANTITIES

A number of nouns and pronouns are used to measure quantities that can be either enumerated or portioned out (see pp. 144–6 for a discussion of countable and uncountable nouns). You must be especially careful to distinguish between singulars and plurals so that your choice of verb will be appropriate:

✓ <u>Most</u> of the <u>noise</u> <u>was</u> eliminated.

✓ <u>Most</u> of the <u>noises</u> <u>were</u> accounted for.

With the words that follow, the rule is to use a plural verb if you are measuring a number of individual items (*microchips, electrodes, test tubes*) and a singular verb if you are measuring a portion of something that cannot be counted (*equipment, software, water*):

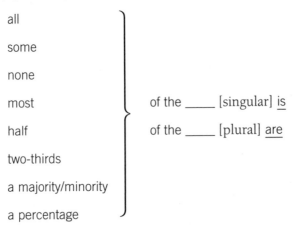

all

some

most

half

two-thirds

a majority/minority

a percentage

of the _____ [singular] <u>is</u>

of the _____ [plural] <u>are</u>

The following sentences show the difference:

✓ <u>None</u> of the <u>experiment</u> <u>was</u> videotaped.

✓ <u>None</u> of the <u>experiments</u> <u>were</u> videotaped.

UNUSUAL PLURALS

A number of nouns cause real trouble for writers because they do not follow the traditional pattern of forming plurals by adding an s.

Singular	*Plural*
datum	data
criterion	criteria
phenomenon	phenomena
stratum	strata

Watch for these words in your writing, and be sure to use them correctly:

- ✗ The criteria was met.
- ✓ One criterion was met.
- ✓ One of the criteria was met.
- ✓ All the criteria were met.

In addition to these, there are a number of words that form plurals by adding s only in certain instances and have alternative plural forms in other contexts. Consult a dictionary before using words like *medium* and *antenna* in the plural.

Finally, be aware that in scientific writing, *data* is always plural. In non-scientific contexts, however, you will hear *data* used acceptably as a singular synonym for *information*.

TITLES

The name of a business or organization is always treated as a singular noun, even if it contains plural words. The same is true of book titles. Use a singular verb with these:

- ✓ Essentials of Optics is an excellent textbook.
- ✓ Goodman & Goodman is handling the legal dispute.

TENSE PROBLEMS

When you are speaking, your tenses usually come automatically, but it's easy to run into difficulty when writing. A few general rules can help you avoid problems.

THE PAST PERFECT

If you have a reference point in the past and you want to mention something that happened *prior to* that time, use the *past perfect* (*had* followed by the past participle). The time sequence will *not* be clear if you use the simple past for both:

✗   The second study <u>revealed</u> that the earlier results <u>were</u> misinterpreted.

✓   The second study <u>revealed</u> that the earlier results <u>had been</u> misinterpreted.

Similarly, when you are reporting what someone said in the past—that is, when you are using *past indirect discourse*—use the past perfect form to distinguish what's happening at the time from what happened prior to that time:

✗   The CEO said that the project <u>was approved</u>.

✓   The CEO said that the project <u>had been approved</u>.

IF–THEN CONDITIONS

When you are describing regularly occurring consequences, use the present tense in both the condition (*if*) clause and the consequence (*then*) clause:

✓   If the temperature <u>drops</u> below −6°, the liquid <u>freezes</u>.

When you are predicting a future consequence, use the present tense in the *if* clause and the future in the *then* clause:

✓   If the temperature <u>drops</u> below −6°, the liquid <u>will freeze</u>.

When the situation is hypothetical, it is conventional—especially in formal writing—to use the *subjunctive* form in the condition clause and *would* + the base verb in the consequence clause:

✓   If the solution <u>precipitated</u>, the experiment <u>would fail</u>.

Note that the *subjunctive* form is exactly the same as the past tense. The subjunctive form of the verb *be* is always *were*. Another way of expressing the subjunctive is to use *were to* + the base verb:

✓   If the solution <u>were to precipitate</u>, the experiment <u>would fail</u>.

When you are describing a hypothetical instance in the past, use the *past subjunctive* (it has the same form as the past perfect) in the *if* clause and *would have* + the past participle for the consequence. It is an error to use *would have* in both clauses:

✗ If the solution would have precipitated, the experiment would have failed.

✓ If the solution had precipitated, the experiment would have failed.

WRITING ABOUT SCIENCE

When you are describing a situation with a historical context, use the past tense:

✓ In 1993, Claude Berron introduced a new class of channel encoders, which he named turbocodes.

To discuss applications that are timeless (those that are sometimes called "scientific truths") use the present tense:

✓ Turbocodes achieve high rates with low interference.

To establish a relationship between past and present in writing, use the present perfect form (*have* + the past participle):

✓ To date, many tests have been performed.

Do not hesitate to combine past and present tenses in the same paragraph as long as the contexts are appropriate. Never shift without a good reason:

✓ Tests were performed on 14 November, and results have been analyzed. The company now recommends further study.

Be sure to maintain the present tense for all reports of current or timeless actions, processes, or states.

PRONOUN PROBLEMS

PRONOUN REFERENCE

The noun that a pronoun refers to is called a *referent* or *antecedent*. There must always be a clear antecedent for every pronoun. If the referent doesn't appear in the same sentence as the pronoun, it must appear in the preceding sentence:

✗ Groundwater specialists have developed a variety of strategies to decontaminate it.

Even though *groundwater* appears in the sentence, it is being used as an adjective, not a noun. Therefore, it cannot serve as referent or antecedent for the pronoun *it*. You must either replace *it* or rephrase your sentence:

✓ Specialists have developed a variety of strategies to decontaminate groundwater.

When a sentence contains more than one noun, make sure there is no ambiguity about the antecedent:

> ✗ The public wants increased <u>environmental responsibility</u> along with <u>lower taxation</u>, but the government does not favour it.

What does the pronoun *it* refer to: *responsibility*, *taxes*, or even *the public*?

> ✓ The public wants increased <u>environmental responsibility</u> along with <u>lower taxes</u>, but the government does not advocate <u>spending increases</u>.

Another problem with pronouns relates to the same singular-plural agreement issues that occur with subjects and verbs (see pp. 129–33). Singular pronouns have singular nouns as antecedents; plural pronouns refer to plural nouns:

> ✗ A spokesperson for GVA <u>Transit</u> said that <u>their</u> ridership had doubled in the past year.

> ✓ A spokesperson for GVA <u>Transit</u> said that ridership had doubled in the past year.

In speaking, it is common to use *they* and *their* to refer to a singular noun—particularly when the noun is a person of unknown gender—but this practice does not yet extend to formal writing. Rewrite the sentence to avoid the problem, either by pluralizing everything or by rewriting the sentence to avoid the pronouns:

> ✗ <u>Every</u> co-op <u>student</u> should submit <u>their</u> work report by the beginning of <u>their</u> next school term.

> ✓ <u>Every</u> co-op <u>student</u> should submit <u>a</u> work report by <u>the</u> beginning of the next school term.

> ✓ <u>All</u> co-op <u>students</u> should submit <u>their</u> work <u>reports</u> by the beginning of <u>their</u> next school term.

USING "IT," "WHICH," AND "THIS"

Using *it*, *which*, and *this* without a clear referent can lead to confusion:

> ✗ Although the directors wanted to meet in January, <u>it</u> [<u>this</u>] didn't take place until May.

> ✓ Although the directors wanted to meet in January, <u>the conference</u> didn't take place until March.

When you use *which*, make sure that it refers to its noun antecedent and not to a general idea:

✗ The directors wanted to meet in January, <u>which</u> didn't happen until March.

✓ The directors planned a winter meeting, which didn't happen until March.

If you don't want your sentences to confuse readers, make sure that your pronoun clearly refers to a specific noun or pronoun.

USING "ONE"

People sometimes use the pronoun *one* to avoid *I* in formal writing. Although common in Britain, such a reference may seem too formal for a North American audience, even a bit pompous:

orig. If <u>one</u> were to apply for the grant, <u>one</u> would find <u>oneself</u> engulfed in so many bureaucratic forms that <u>one's</u> patience would be stretched thin.

While there is nothing grammatically incorrect in this example, it sounds a little stiff or pretentious. The best alternative is to recast the sentence with a plural subject:

rev. <u>Researchers</u> applying for the grant could find <u>themselves</u> engulfed in so many bureaucratic forms that <u>their</u> patience would be stretched thin.

If you avoid using *one*, you will automatically avoid making the error of mixing the third-person *one* with the second-person *you*:

✗ When <u>one</u> uses a bank machine, <u>you</u> are using a CNC system.

✓ A <u>person</u> using a bank machine is using a CNC system.

USING "ME" AND OTHER OBJECTIVE PRONOUNS

Remembering that it is wrong to say "My supervisor and me were invited," many people use the subjective form (*I*) of the pronoun when the objective form *me* is correct:

✗ The committee invited Dorcas and <u>I</u> to present our findings.

✓ The committee invited Dorcas and <u>me</u> to present our findings.

The verb *invited* requires an object; *me* is the objective case. A good way to tell which form is correct is to ask yourself how the sentence would sound with only the pronoun. You will know by ear that the subjective form—"The committee invited *I*"—is not appropriate.

Knowing that *I* should be avoided in the previous example, some people prefer to substitute *myself*, but this usage is equally inappropriate and ungrammatical. *Myself, yourself, ourselves*, and so on, are reflexive pronouns to be used *only* when their referent has already appeared, usually as the subject, in the sentence:

✓ <u>She</u> wrote <u>herself</u> a note to remind <u>herself</u> to return the book.

Avoid using reflexive pronouns as substitutes for objective forms:

✗ The final exam schedule causes problems for <u>myself</u>.

✓ The final exam schedule causes problems for <u>me</u>.

Problems also arise with prepositions, which should be followed by a noun or pronoun in the objective case:

✗ <u>Between</u> you and <u>I</u>, this result doesn't make sense.

✓ <u>Between</u> you and <u>me</u>, this result doesn't make sense.

There are times, however, when the correct case can sound stiff or awkward:

orig. The reporter wanted to know <u>to whom</u> the award had been given.

Rather than keep to a correct but awkward form, feel free to reword the sentence:

rev. The reporter wanted to know <u>who</u> had received the award.

EXCEPTIONS FOR PRONOUNS FOLLOWING PREPOSITIONS

The rule that a pronoun following a preposition takes the objective case has exceptions. When the preposition is followed by a clause, the pronoun should take the case required by its position in the clause:

✗ The students were curious <u>about whom would be elected</u>.

Although the pronoun follows the preposition *about*, it is also the subject of the verb *would be elected* and therefore requires the subjective case:

✓ The students were curious <u>about who would be elected</u>.

Similarly, when a gerund (an *-ing* word that acts partly as a noun and partly as a verb) is the subject of a clause or phrase, the word that modifies it takes the possessive form:

✗ Our drafting instructor objected to <u>us</u> asking for an extension.

✓ Our drafting instructor objected to <u>our</u> asking for an extension.

✓ The drafting instructor objected to the <u>students'</u> asking for an extension.

PROBLEMS WITH MODIFIERS

Adjectives modify nouns; adverbs modify verbs, adjectives, and other adverbs. Never use an adjective to modify a verb:

✗ He played <u>good</u>. (adjective with verb)

✓ He played <u>well</u>. (adverb modifying verb)

✓ He played <u>very well</u>. (adverb modifying adverb)

✓ He played <u>really well</u>. (informal)

✓ He had a <u>fine</u> style. (adjective modifying noun)

✓ He had a <u>very fine</u> style. (adverb modifying adjective)

The examples above feature one-word adjectives and adverbs. Many combinations can act in similar ways—as adjectival and adverbial modifiers. The following represent some of the most common ones:

She is a student <u>in residence</u>. (adjectival phrase)

The students live <u>in residence</u>. (adverbial phrase)

Here is a place <u>to begin</u>. (adjectival phrase)

<u>To begin</u>, open the book. (adverbial phrase)

The TA <u>preparing the slides</u> is new. (adjectival phrase)

The TA discovered an error <u>while preparing the slides</u>. (adverbial phrase)

Everyone understood the material <u>prepared by the TA</u>. (adjectival phrase)

Being familiar with these types of modifiers will help you to avoid the problems described below.

MISPLACED MODIFIERS

Modifiers need to be put as close as possible to the words they refer to. If there is some distance between a modifier and the word it modifies, a reader may misinterpret the sentence.

✗ Students can find valuable information about eating nutritiously <u>on the Internet</u>.

✓ <u>On the Internet</u>, students can find information about eating nutritiously.

Be particularly attentive to words like *hardly*, *nearly*, *even*, *only*, and *almost*, which can modify many of the words in a sentence. Put them directly before the words they are meant to modify—just so that there is no room for misinterpretation:

✓ <u>Only</u> this study surveys the transformations.

✓ This study <u>only</u> surveys the transformations.

✓ This study surveys <u>only</u> the transformations.

✓ This study surveys the <u>only</u> transformations.

SQUINTING MODIFIERS

Remember that clarity largely depends on word order: to avoid confusion, the connections between the different parts of a sentence must be clear. Modifiers should therefore be as close as possible to the words they modify. A *squinting modifier* is one that, because of its position, seems to be working in two directions at the same time:

✗ Computers that malfunction <u>often</u> need to be replaced.

Does *often* refer to the rate of malfunction or the rate of replacement? Changing the order of the sentence or rephrasing it will make the meaning clearer:

✓ Computers need replacing if they malfunction <u>often</u>.

✓ <u>Often</u>, computers that malfunction need to be replaced.

Other ambiguous modifiers can be corrected in the same way:

✗ Dr. Hutt gave a lecture on artificial intelligence, <u>which</u> has several extended applications.

✓ Dr. Hutt's <u>lecture</u> on artificial intelligence <u>has</u> several extended applications.

✓   Dr. Hutt lectured on <u>artificial intelligence</u>, <u>which</u> has several extended applications.

SPLIT INFINITIVES

Many readers object to the positioning of modifiers between the two parts of an infinitive (*to* and the base verb). Indeed, it's often more elegant to move the modifier to another position, either earlier or later, in the phrase. This revision is recommended whenever it is easy to make:

orig.   To <u>graphically</u> represent time requires four coordinates.

rev.   To represent time <u>graphically</u> requires four coordinates.

DANGLING MODIFIERS

Modifiers that have no grammatical connection with anything else in the sentence are said to be *dangling*. Sentences that begin with modifiers need special care. If it isn't clear who or what is doing the action expressed by the modifier, the dangling construction needs to be repaired:

✗   <u>Developing</u> a third model, <u>success</u> was eventually achieved.

Who is doing the developing? Here are two more examples:

✗   Before <u>setting out</u> to model the system, <u>it</u> is important to define the intended benefits.

✗   To <u>understand</u> the concept, <u>knowledge</u> of market risk is essential.

Who is doing the setting out or the understanding? Clarify the meaning by making sure the subject in the modifier is explicit:

✓   <u>Developing</u> a third model, the <u>designers</u> finally achieved success.

✓   Before setting out to model the system, the <u>project team</u> must define the intended benefits.

✓   To <u>understand</u> the concept, <u>students</u> need a knowledge of market risk.

One type of dangling modifier occurs when the subject is hidden by a passive verb:

✗   To <u>maximize</u> the validity, a target user <u>group</u> has to <u>be designated</u>.

✓   To <u>maximize</u> the validity, <u>testers</u> <u>must designate</u> a target user group.

In another situation, changing an active verb in the modifier to a passive verb will solve the problem:

✗ After modifying the filter, it performed extremely well.

✓ After the filter was modified, it performed extremely well.

In conclusion, it makes sense to watch for problem modifiers when you are editing, for they occur far too frequently in scientific and other kinds of writing.

PROBLEMS WITH PAIRS AND PARALLELS

COMPARISONS

Make sure that your comparisons are complete. The second element in a comparison should be equivalent to the first, whether the equivalence is stated or merely implied:

✗ Today's students have a greater understanding of calculus than their parents.

This sentence suggests that the two things being compared are *calculus* and *parents*. Adding a second verb (*do*) that matches the first one (*have*) shows that the two things being compared are parents' understanding and students' understanding:

✓ Today's students have a greater understanding of calculus than their parents do.

A similar problem arises in the following comparisons:

✗ A design engineer's responsibilities are similar to an architect.

✗ The area of the landfill site is twice as large as the proposed development.

In both cases, the writer is neglecting one of the primary principles of comparison—that the left side and right side must be equal and comparable:

✓ A design engineer's responsibilities are similar to an architect's.

✓ The area of the landfill site is twice as large as that of the proposed development.

PARALLEL PHRASING

A series of items in a sentence should be phrased in parallel wording. Make sure that all the parts of a parallel construction (A, B, and C) are in fact equal:

✗ He liked the pay, being able to vary his hours, and also appreciated the many benefits.

✓ He liked the pay, the flexible hours, and the many benefits.

Once you have decided to use the same pattern in the first two elements, the third must have it as well. For clarity as well as elegance, keep similar ideas in similar form:

✗ The products are extremely strong, dimensionally stable, and they do not contain formaldehyde.

✓ The products are extremely strong, dimensionally stable, and free of formaldehyde.

The rule also applies to lists, where parallel elements are indicated with bullets:

✓ Communication systems use coding for three major reasons:
  • to reduce the volume of information
  • to protect it against intruders
  • to personalize it

CORRELATIVES (COORDINATE CONSTRUCTIONS)

Constructions such as *both . . . and*, *not only . . . but also*, and *neither . . . nor* demand special care. The coordinating term must not come too early or else one of the parts that come after will not connect with the common element. For the implied comparison to work, the two parts that come after the coordinating term must be grammatically equivalent:

✗ Mechanical systems should be not only simple and reliable but require little maintenance.

✓ Mechanical systems should not only be simple and reliable but require little maintenance.

PROBLEMS FOR SECOND-LANGUAGE WRITERS

If English is not your first language, you have probably spent more time in English grammar and writing classes than the average student. The following explanations point out some of the most persistent trouble spots to watch for as you edit your work. When in doubt about vocabulary or idioms, consult the latest editions of the *Oxford Advanced Learner's Dictionary* (2005) and the *Oxford ESL Dictionary* (2005).

NOUN RULES

Use the determiner that's right for the context

Most nouns can be introduced by a word called a *determiner*. (The articles *a*, *an*, and *the* are the most common determiners, but others, called *quantifiers*, have similar functions.) Because nouns can be singular or plural, countable or uncountable, general or specific, it is usually the determiner that tells what kind of noun will follow. Choosing the appropriate determiner for the context will prevent you from sending mixed messages to your reader about the kind of noun you are using.

English nouns can be categorized in terms of quantity either by number or by amount. Singular countable nouns (such as *lake* or *contaminant*) are easily confused with uncountable nouns (such as *water* or *pollution*) because they both take singular verbs and because neither of them has an added –s. Plural countable nouns (*lakes*, *contaminants*) are easier to spot, but many nouns play dual roles, acting as countable or uncountable according to the context. It's the choice of determiners that will make the difference.

1. Use the determiners *a*, *an*, *one*, *another*, *each*, *every*, *either*, and *neither* only with singular countable nouns. If you remember the rule that every singular countable noun *must* have a determiner of some sort or other, you will avoid making errors like the one below:

   ✗ ITS encourages commuters to take bus rather than drive car.

   ✓ ITS encourages commuters to take a bus rather than drive a car.

2. Animals and people are always countable. It is a mistake not to use a determiner when they are used in the singular.

   ✗ The computer is often compared to the brain of human being.

   ✓ The computer is often compared to the brain of a human being.

3. Do not use singular countable determiners with uncountable nouns:

   ✗ Every slang or jargon must be avoided in formal writing.

   ✓ All slang or jargon must be avoided in formal writing.

4. Uncountable nouns don't need a determiner when they are used in a general sense. If you use a singular word without a determiner, you automatically tell the reader that it's uncountable. Be sure that's what you intend.

   ✓ Many people are afraid of change.

   ✗ There's been <u>change</u> in plans.

   ✓ There's been <u>a change</u> in plans

5. The following determiners can all be used before plural (countable) nouns: *other, all, some, more, most, plenty of, a lot of*:

other courses	all students
some books	more requirements
most colleges and universities	a lot of exams

   But these determiners are also used to introduce uncountable nouns:

other coursework	all hardware
some research	more evidence
most equipment	a lot of studying

   Be careful not to confuse your singulars and plurals:

   ✗ <u>Some lab</u> need <u>more spaces</u> for machinery.

   ✓ <u>Some labs</u> needs <u>more space</u> for machinery.

6. Watch out especially for nouns that can be either countable (one ____) or uncountable (a lot of ____) according to the context. For example, the word "experience" as a countable noun refers to a single eventful occurrence: "Meeting the astronaut was quite *an experience*." When referring to someone's background, however, use uncountable determiners: "He doesn't have *much experience*." Always use determiners that clarify your meaning:

   ✗ Dr. Frank had <u>a</u> trouble solving the equation.

   ✓ Dr. Frank had <u>some</u> trouble solving the equation.

   Words like *attention, difficulty, damage, effort, exercise, interest, life, power, promise, proof, respect,* and *time* are only a few of those that create similar difficulties for second-language writers.

7. All numbers higher than *one* are used only with countable plurals (*two eyes, three wheels, four legs,* and so on), as are the following quantifiers: *these, those,*

many, several, few, fewer, both, and *a couple of.* Be sure that the noun that follows them is indeed a plural. Sometimes, you will have to use a countable word or phrase like "a piece of" together with an uncountable noun:

✗ Imperial measures are still used in <u>many equipment</u>.

✓ Imperial measures are still used in <u>many pieces of equipment</u>.

8. The following quantifiers introduce uncountable nouns only: *much, little, less,* and *an amount of.* You will make a mistake if you use one of them in front of a plural:

✗ Channel coding produces <u>less types</u> of errors than expected.

✓ Channel coding produces <u>fewer types</u> of errors than expected.

9. The definite article *the,* the possessive pronouns (*my, your, his, her, its, our, their, whose*), the interrogatives *what* and *which,* and the determiners *no* and *any* can be used before any noun at all. But when you use *the,* you must already have a specific context for your noun. It is a mistake to use it when you mean *any*:

✗ <u>The groundwater</u> is an important source of water for agriculture.

✓ <u>Groundwater</u> is an important source of water for agriculture

10. Before using a proper name, be sure you know whether it takes the determiner *the.* Nouns that are capitalized won't normally be introduced by *the* unless they also contain a phrase with *of* in it: it's *Vancouver,* but <u>*the*</u> *City of Vancouver; Waterloo College,* but <u>*the*</u> *University of Waterloo; Scotiabank,* but <u>*the*</u> *Bank of Montreal.* When the proper noun is included as a modifier, however (as in *the* <u>*English*</u> *language* or *the* <u>*Calgary*</u> *Flames*), you must use *the* for the sake of specificity:

✗ They went to a conference in United States.

✓ They went to a conference in <u>the</u> United States.

VERB RULES
Watch agreement with singulars and plurals
Countable nouns can be singular or plural, where uncountable nouns have only a singular form. In addition to regular rules for subject–verb agreement, you must pay careful attention to the following situations.

1. With present-tense verbs and a *singular* subject, be sure to add –*s* to the verb:

   ✗ An RGP lens offer high oxygen transmissibility.

   ✓ An RGP lens <u>offers</u> high oxygen transmissibility.

   When one of the following singular pronouns is the subject of the sentence, the verb must be singular as well: *one, each, either, neither, another, much, little, less.*

   ✗ Of the two sets of figures, <u>neither are</u> easy to manipulate.

   ✓ Of the two sets of figures, <u>neither is</u> easy to manipulate.

2. When referring to countable items in a set, you may use the prepositional phrase *of the* before the item to measure quantities. Remember that the word following *of the* will always be plural: "one of the *books*," "both of the *tests*," "some of the *results*." Remember also that the verb agrees with the word before *of*: "*one* of the books *is*," "*both* of the tests *are*," "*some* of the results *were*." Such constructions are worth checking twice to avoid errors:

   ✗ <u>One</u> of the most complicated <u>application</u> of AI <u>are</u> computer games.

   ✓ <u>One</u> of the most complicated <u>applications</u> of AI <u>is</u> computer games.

   With uncountable sets (masses), the word following *of the* is always singular and the verb is singular as well: "*much* of the *test is* invalid"; "*some* of the *equipment was* missing."

   With pronouns that can be either uncountable or plural (*all, any, more, most, some, none*), subject–verb agreement depends on whether the pronoun's referent is singular or plural: "*all* of the *material is* ready"; "*all* of the *materials are* ready." See below for other situations.

3. In classifications, expressions like *type of, sort of,* and *kind of* are quite restrictive in terms of what follows: agreement will depend on whether the main noun is countable or uncountable. With countable nouns, agreement rules require everything to be all singular or all plural: "What *sort* of *label is* required?" "What *kinds* of *labels are* needed?"

   With uncountable nouns, the expression can be singular or plural, but the noun itself will always remain singular:

   ✗ The program could handle various types of <u>informations</u>.

   ✓ The program could handle various types of <u>information</u>.

4. Rules for subject–verb agreement do not apply to modal auxiliaries (*can, could, shall, should, will, would, may, might, must*), which do not have separate singular and plural forms. If you aren't sure whether a subject is singular or plural, you will be safe if you can use a modal:

✓ The criteria will need validating.

Be sure, however, that you use the root form of the verb following a modal auxiliary:

✗ Later, the principal investigators <u>could discussed</u> the project.

✓ Later, the principal investigators <u>could discuss</u> the project.

VERB FORMS

Be is the verb most often used in English—both as a main verb and as an auxiliary. *Have* is the next most common one. It makes sense, then, to watch how you use these two verbs in your writing.

Use continuous verbs for action in progress

Be followed by the present participle forms the continuous verb form to emphasize action in progress at a point in time in the past ("she *was reading*"), present ("she *is reading*"), or future ("she *will be reading*"). Use the continuous to add the meaning of "being in the process of" to your context: "I am [in the process of] studying for my finals." Verbs that express states of being and sense perceptions instead of action do not take the continuous form, however. Among these are the verbs *appreciate, believe, contain, hear, intend, know, mean, need, own, possess, see, understand, want.*

When the verbs *be* and *have* are used in the continuous form, they have specific meanings: *be* means "behave" ("Joshua *is being* unusually cooperative today"), and "have" refers to temporary duration ("He *is having* dinner"; "she *is having* a party"). Always be careful to choose the appropriate form.

✗ We expect that everyone <u>is understanding</u> the course outline.

✓ We expect that everyone <u>understands</u> the course outline.

Use perfect forms to express completion

Have followed by the past participle produces the perfect form, which suggests completion of an activity prior to a point in time in the past, present, or future. Use the present perfect rather than the past tense to bring things up to date:

✗ We will be interviewing all next week because seventeen candidates <u>submitted</u> an impressive CV.

✓   We will be interviewing all next week because seventeen candidates have submitted an impressive CV.

Be careful with passive forms

Be followed by the past participle produces the *passive voice* (see pp. 115–16), which shows the subject of the sentence *receiving* the action of the verb rather than *doing* it. Be sure to keep such relationships distinct:

✗   An atom composes of a nucleus surrounded by orbiting electrons.

✓   An atom is composed of a nucleus surrounded by orbiting electrons.

Differentiate your participles

Because *be* can be used as an auxiliary with both the past and present participles, it is especially important to choose the appropriate participle form for the context. In other words, always be sure to distinguish between *doing* an action (verb + *ing*) and *receiving* an action (verb + *ed*):

✗   I am interesting in applying for a position with your company.

✓   I am interested in applying for a position with your company.

Use only gerunds in prepositional phrases

Prepositions like *in*, *of*, *on*, *for*, and so on may be followed by only one possible form of a verb: the verb ending in *–ing*, which is called a *gerund*. Be sure to use only this form in prepositional phrases:

✗   Designers enhance the SNR either by reduce the noise effects or increase the signal level.

✓   Designers enhance the SNR either by reducing the noise effects or increasing the signal level.

An apparent exception to this rule is the word *to*, which may be followed by a gerund or the base form of a verb, depending on the context. When *to* is being used as a preposition, it must be followed by a gerund; when it is being used as part of an infinitive, it must be followed by the base form of the verb. This double role explains the difference between "She used to do calculus" and "She is used to doing calculus." Be sure that you know which *to* is called for by the context:

✗   I am looking forward to meet you.

✓   I am looking forward to meeting you.

Include required verbs

Don't leave out the auxiliaries or the main verbs that convey the meaning in the sentence:

✗   He <u>working</u> for that oil company since February.

✓   He <u>has been</u> working for that oil company since February.

IDIOM RULES

Idiom is the term used for a construction we can't explain except to say that it "sounds right." Idioms aren't predictable, and they aren't logical. The following are typical situations where you want to be careful that things sound right.

Pay attention to word endings

As you add to your vocabulary, it's worth noting the suffixes that mark the various parts of speech (*-ment, -ness, -er, -ence* for nouns; *-ify, -ate, -en, -ize* for verbs; *-al, -ful, -ent, -like, -less* for adjectives; *-ly* for adverbs). Be sure to use the appropriate word for the context:

✗   Please send the following files at your <u>convenient</u>.

✓   Please send the following files at your <u>convenience</u>.

Be sure the suffix you have used is legitimate:

✗   This insulation is valuable for its <u>strongness</u> and <u>durableness</u>.

✓   This insulation is valuable for its <u>strength</u> and <u>durability</u>.

Include expected prepositions

1. Some prepositions (words like *of, for, in, on,* and so on) express conventional relationships. The following sentences represent typical examples:

✓   I am a student <u>in</u> the department of Mechanical Engineering <u>at</u> the University of Toronto <u>in</u> the GTA.

✓   I'll meet you <u>at</u> noon <u>on</u> Monday <u>at</u> the lab <u>on</u> King Street.

Although *at* specifies time or place here and *on* generalizes, the relationships cannot be applied to other situations haphazardly:

✗   This work will be presented <u>in</u> the graduate research conference <u>at</u> April 2-4, 2004.

✓ This work will be presented <u>at</u> the graduate research conference <u>on</u> April 2–4, 2004.

2. Verb or adjective constructions completed with prepositions don't usually allow for any choice. From *consist of* to *insist on* and *convenient to*, it is worth maintaining a list to refer to whenever you are writing.

Avoid unneeded prepositions

1. Do not include prepositions after verbs that do not require them:

✗ He lacked <u>of</u> motivation to find a job.

✓ He lacked motivation to find a job.

Lack is used as a noun followed by *of* in the expression *have a lack of*. But because it uses four words instead of one, you should prefer the single verb *lack* for the sake of sentence economy.

2. With time expressions introduced by *last*, *next*, *this*, or *every* (*last night*, *next Monday*, *this month*, or *every week*), it is redundant to use a preposition:

✗ The midterm is <u>on</u> next Monday.

✓ The midterm is <u>next Monday</u>.

3. A few key idioms are completed by either gerund phrases or prepositional phrases:

> to have trouble/difficulty/a problem <u>doing</u> something
> > *or*
> to have trouble/difficulty/a problem <u>with</u> a topic (*or* in a subject)

> to spend or waste time/money <u>doing</u> something
> > *or*
> to spend or waste time/money <u>on</u> it

> to keep busy <u>doing</u> something
> > *or*
> to keep busy <u>at</u> it.

It's redundant to use the gerund and the preposition together:

✗ The professor spent three hours <u>on explaining</u> the project.

✓ The professor spent three hours <u>explaining</u> the project.

Use the idiomatic verb form called for by the main verb

1. Some verbs must be followed by an infinitive; others, by a gerund. Some (*begin, cease, continue, dread, forget, hate, like, love, prefer, remember, start, stop, try*) are followed by either form, sometimes with a change in meaning. Be sure you use the right idiom:

   ✗ Chemical reactions result when atoms <u>try sharing</u> electrons with other atoms.

   ✓ Chemical reactions result when atoms <u>try to</u> share electrons with other atoms.

2. There are eight verbs (*have, make, let, help, see, watch, hear,* and *feel*) that are followed by an object and the root form: "They *made* you *learn* this." Memorize these idioms, and avoid mistakes with them in your writing:

   ✗ Because of her high average, her faculty <u>let</u> her <u>to take</u> six courses in the winter term.

   ✓ Because of her high average, her faculty <u>let</u> her <u>take</u> six courses in the winter term.

3. There are nine verbs (*ask, demand, insist, prefer, recommend, request, require, suggest, urge*) that may be followed by a *that*-clause containing a verb in the subjunctive (the uninflected root form of the verb): "She *suggested that* he *be* consulted." Only four of these verbs (*ask, prefer, require, urge*) allow the clause to be rephrased with an infinitive phrase: "They urged her *to accept* the job." Avoid using infinitive phrases with the other five verbs:

   ✗ She suggested <u>him to take</u> some time off before finding a job.

   ✓ She suggested <u>that he take</u> some time off before finding a job.

Watch word order

1. Word order in declarative sentences follows a basic pattern of subject followed by verb. The order is inverted in questions, whether they are information questions beginning with an interrogative (*What* is the density? *How long* does the reaction take?) or questions where the expected answer is "yes" or "no" (Is the frequency modulated? Did the program work?). When these questions are reported in sentences, however, the original word order is preserved. Be careful, then, to respect the difference between *direct* and *indirect* questions:

✗ Why the *e* number is so important to scientists? (*direct*)

✓ Why is the *e* number so important to scientists? (*direct*)

✓ The student asked why the *e* number is so important to scientists. (*indirect*)

2. The subject–verb word order is also reversed when a sentence begins with a restrictive modifier introduced by *only* or a negative like *not, never,* or *seldom.* Regular word order applies if such modifiers appear later in the sentence:

✓ Only once has the computer lost a match.

✓ Rarely does the computer lose a match.

✓ The computer rarely loses a match.

The same principles apply to sentences introduced by *not only* and *neither* and/or *nor*. It is a mistake not to invert the subject and verb after these correlative conjunctions if you use them to join complete sentences:

✗ Not only CNC performs operations that people used to do, but it does work that was previously impossible to do.

✓ Not only does CNC perform operations that people used to do, but it does work that was previously impossible to do.

Avoid ungrammatical repetition.
1. When you combine two sentences, use either coordination or subordination. It is redundant to use both:

✗ Although there are some limitations, but this method does identify clear trends.

✓ Although there are some limitations, this method does identify clear trends. (*subordination*)

✓ There are some limitations, but this method does identify clear trends. (*coordination*)

2. Avoid repetition in relative clauses. Once you've used a relative pronoun or adverb, be sure to delete the original referent:

✗ Seismologists are needed in countries where there have been major earthquakes there.

✓ Seismologists are needed in countries <u>where</u> there have been major earthquakes.

Distinguish between "it is" and "there is"

Despite sharing the main verb *be*, "it is" and "there is" (or "there are") constructions are idiomatically quite different. They cannot substitute for each other: *It is time to work* is different from *There is time to work*. One test of whether it is appropriate to use "there is" is to try substituting *exists* for *is* (or *exist* for *are* if you are trying to use "there are"). If you can't make the substitution, try another idiom:

✗ <u>It is</u> a number of applications for packet filtering.

✓ <u>There are</u> a number of applications for packet filtering.

✓ <u>There exist</u> a number of applications for packet filtering. *(test)*

Be careful to include *it* or *there* in front of *is*. Even though neither word conveys much meaning, it is essential idiomatically:

✗ <u>Is</u> theoretically possible to control traffic flow even in a large city.

✓ <u>It is</u> theoretically possible to control traffic flow even in a large city.

Avoid errors with comparisons.

1. One- and two-syllable adjectives and some adverbs express the comparative by adding *–er* and a phrase beginning with *than*: *harder than x, easier than y, sooner than z*. Longer words and nouns show the comparison with *more* instead: *more difficult than x, more research than y*. It is redundant to use both methods of comparison together:

   ✗ Coding makes communication <u>more</u> faster and cheaper.

   ✓ Coding makes communication <u>increasingly</u> faster and cheaper.

   If you can use *more* in a comparison, then you can express the opposite with *less*, as long as you are comparing modifiers. (If you are using nouns, then you'll have to use *fewer* if the noun is plural and countable [see pp. 145–6].) If your comparison uses *-er* rather than *more*, you can express the opposite with the phrase *not as . . . as* instead.

   ✗ Plastics are <u>less hard</u> than ceramics but have higher impact resistance.

   ✓ Plastics are <u>not as hard as</u> ceramics but have higher impact resistance.

2. Don't forget to complete phrases including *so, such, too,* and *enough* for expressions of degree. Follow *so* or *such,* with a *that*-clause: *The paper had so many errors that it was rejected.* With *too,* use an infinitive phrase: *It was too complicated to correct.* With *enough,* use either construction. In writing, it is an·error not to complete such expressions. Revise to avoid the problem:

    ✗   In nature, there are <u>so many</u> examples of symmetry.

    ✓   In nature, there are <u>many</u> examples of symmetry.

3. Use standard phrases to establish comparisons: *different from* (not *than*), *similar to,* and *the same as.* Be sure that you always include *the* when you use the word *same*:

    ✗   At equilibrium, forward and reverse reactions occur at <u>same</u> rates.

    ✓   At equilibrium, forward and reverse reactions occur at <u>the same</u> rates.

chapter 14

PUNCTUATION

Punctuation poses so many problems that it deserves a chapter of its own. If your punctuation is faulty, your readers will be confused and may have to backtrack; worse still, they may not be convinced that you are in control of your writing. Punctuation marks are the traffic signals of writing. Use them with precision to keep readers moving smoothly through your work.

(Items in this chapter are arranged alphabetically: *apostrophe, brackets, colon, comma, dash, ellipsis, exclamation mark, hyphen, italics, parentheses, period, quotation marks, semicolon,* and *solidus/slash.*)

APOSTROPHE [']

The apostrophe forms the possessive case for nouns and some indefinite pronouns.

1. **Add an apostrophe followed by "s" to**

   - all singular and plural nouns not ending in "s":

     > Schrödinger's cat; women's studies; Bill and Lynda's graph

   - singular proper nouns ending in "s":

     > Ross's proposition; Willis's autobiography

     (Note, however, that the final "s" should be omitted if the name has a number of syllables already and would sound awkward, as in *Socrates'* or *Copernicus'.*)

   - indefinite pronouns:

     > everyone's responsibility; anybody's guess

2. **Add an apostrophe to plural nouns ending in "s":**

   > our families' pets; the Board of Directors' decision

3. **Use an apostrophe before or after "s" to show time measurements:**

> a month's notice; two weeks' time

4. **Use an apostrophe to show contractions of words:**

> we'll see; you're welcome; the '90s

Caution! Don't confuse *it's* (the contraction of *it is* or *it has*) with *its* (the possessive of *it*), which has no apostrophe.

BRACKETS [ ]

Brackets are square enclosures, not to be confused with parentheses (which are round).

1. **Use brackets to set off an editorial remark within a quotation.** They show that the words enclosed are not those of the person quoted:

> Before her marriage soured Mileva Einstein Maric liked to joke that she and Albert were "one stone [ein Stein]."

When a direct quotation is unavoidable, use brackets to enclose *sic* after an error, such as a misspelling, to show that the mistake appeared in the original. (Most of the time you will paraphrase to avoid reporting errors):

> Banting's discovery of insulin can be traced to brief jottings in his lab book: "Diabetus [*sic*]. Ligate pancreatic ducts of dog."

2. **Use brackets to indicate references in scientific writing.** Include the number of the citation in brackets when you make the reference in the text of your work:

> Dr. Knuth named the approach "literate programming" [3].

Then use the same number in brackets in the *References* section at the end to provide full documentation of the source. See Chapter 15.

3. **Use brackets within parentheses to indicate an additional parenthetical insertion.** (This is the inverse of mathematical "fences.")

> Spammers (i.e. those who send spam [unsolicited commercial e-mail]) work hard to ensure that their message looks like any regular e-mail message a user might receive.

COLON [:]

A colon indicates that something will follow: an elaboration, a list, a quotation.

1. **Use a colon before a formal statement or series:**

    ✓   The following students will be presenters: Anna, Dieter, and Hugh.

    It is considered informal, and often incorrect, to use a colon if the words preceding it do not form a complete sentence:

    ✗   The filters are classified as: lowband, bandpass, and highpass.

    ✓   The filters are classified as lowband, bandpass, and highpass.

    On the other hand, a colon often precedes a vertical list, even when the introductory part is not a complete sentence:

    ✓   The filters are classified as:
        – lowband
        – bandpass
        – highpass

    Even so, it is still preferable—and more professional—to recast the introductory phrase as a complete sentence.

2. **Use a colon for formality before a direct quotation, especially when a complete sentence precedes the quotation:**

    The leaders of the anti-nuclear group repeated their message: "The world needs bread before bombs."

3. **Use a colon between numbers expressing time and ratios:**

    4:30 p.m.

    The ratio of calcium to potassium should be 7:1.

COMMA [,]

Commas are the trickiest of all punctuation marks; even experts differ on when to use them. Most agree, however, that too many commas are as bad as too few, since they make writing choppy and awkward to read. Certainly recent writers use fewer commas than earlier stylists did. Whenever you are in doubt, let clarity be your guide. The following are the most widely accepted conventions.

1. **Use a comma to separate two independent clauses joined by a coordinating conjunction (*and, but, for, or, nor, yet, so*).** By signalling that there are two clauses, the comma will prevent the reader from confusing the beginning of the second clause with the end of the first:

   ✗ Pine is softer than oak and cedar is harder than oak.

   ✓ Pine is softer than oak, and cedar is harder than oak.

   When the second clause has the same subject as the first, you have the option of omitting both the second subject *and* the comma:

   ✓ Rebuilding costs more at the outset, but it helps avoid expensive maintenance later.

   ✓ Rebuilding costs more at the outset but helps avoid expensive maintenance later.

   If you mistakenly punctuate two sentences as if they were one, the result will be a run-on sentence (see pp. 127–9). If you use a comma but forget the coordinating conjunction, the result will be a comma splice:

   ✗ The Weil reaction of the capacitor is small, its impact is negligible.

   ✓ The Weil reaction of the capacitor is small, so its impact is negligible.

   Remember that words such as *however*, *therefore*, and *thus* are conjunctive adverbs, not conjunctions. If you use one of them to join two independent clauses, the result will again be a comma splice:

   ✗ Enantiometers have the same molecular structures and physical properties, however they cannot be superimposed.

   ✓ Enantiometers have the same molecular structures and physical properties; however, they cannot be superimposed.

   Conjunctive adverbs are often confused with conjunctions. You can distinguish between the two if you remember that a conjunctive adverb's position in a sentence can be changed:

   ✓ Enantiometers have the same molecular structures and physical properties; they cannot, however, be superimposed.

   The position of a conjunction, on the other hand, is invariable; it must be placed between the two clauses:

✓ Enantiometers have the same molecular structures and physical properties, <u>but</u> they cannot be superimposed.

A good rule of thumb, then, is to use a comma when the linking word can't move.

2. **Use a comma between items in a series.** Place a coordinating conjunction before the last item:

✓ Coding is a procedure that makes communication faster, cheaper, more reliable, and more private.

✓ Software reengineering redesigns a system to improve its quality, understandability, and maintainability.

The comma before the conjunction is optional for single items in a series:

✓ Fractals are found in vegetables, leaves or snowflakes.

For phrases in a series, however, use the final comma to help prevent confusion:

✗ Linseed is a superior material because it is made from natural products (linseed oil, flax, jute and wood fibres).

In this case, a comma would prevent the reader from thinking that *linseed oil* is made from *jute fibres* as well as *wood fibres*:

✓ Linseed is a superior material because it is made from natural products (linseed oil, flax, jute, and wood fibres).

This is the reason many writers always add a comma before the conjunction as soon as there are three or more items in a series. One rule is certain— remember not to put a comma at the end of the series if the series begins the sentence:

✗ Heat distribution, electric charge diffusion, wave propagation, and even chemical reactions, have mostly a natural exponential form.

✓ Heat distribution, electric charge diffusion, wave propagation, and even chemical reactions have mostly a natural exponential form.

3. **Use a comma to separate adjectives preceding a noun when they modify the same element.**

✓ It is a pretty, clever device.

However, when the adjectives do not modify the same element, you should not use a comma:

✗ It is a familiar, domestic task.

Here *domestic* modifies *task*, but *familiar* modifies the whole phrase *domestic task*. A good way of checking whether you need a comma is to see if you can reverse the order of the adjectives. If you can (*pretty, clever device* or *clever, pretty device*), use a comma; if you can't (*domestic familiar task*), omit the comma:

✓ It is a familiar domestic task.

4. **Use commas to set off an interruption (i.e. "parenthetical element"):**

✓ The results, as expected, were inconclusive.

✓ It is important, however, that results be consistent.

Remember to put commas on both sides of the interruption:

✗ It is important however, that results be consistent.

✗ The build-up of these fumes, along with mould, bacteria, and dust can lead to "sick building" syndrome.

✓ The build-up of these fumes, along with mould, bacteria, and dust, can lead to "sick building" syndrome.

5. **Use commas to set off words or phrases that provide additional but non-essential information:**

✓ Our TA, Chandra Elliot, gives clear explanations.

✓ The video, a documentary on recycling, was popular among students.

In these examples, *Chandra Elliot* and *a documentary on recycling* are *appositives*: they give additional information about the nouns they refer to ("TA" and "video"), but the sentences would make sense without them. Here's another example:

✓ Polymers involve macromolecules, which have high molecular weights.

The phrase *which have high molecular weights* is a *non-restrictive modifier* because it doesn't limit the meaning of the word it modifies (*macromolecules*). Without that modifying clause, the sentence would still make sense. Since the information the clause provides is not necessary to the meaning of the sentence, you use a comma to set it off.

In contrast, a *restrictive modifier* is one that provides essential information. It must not be set apart from the element it modifies, and commas should not be used:

✓ Many people who are legally blind can read using a closed circuit TV.

Without the clause *who are legally blind*, the reader would not know which specific group of people can read this way.

To avoid confusion, be sure to distinguish carefully between essential and additional information. The difference can be important:

Students, who are unwilling to work, should not receive grants.

Students who are unwilling to work should not receive grants.

The first example makes an unacceptable generalization about students, which you will understand if you imagine parentheses in place of the commas.

The issue is never simple, as you can see above. In the example that follows, adding or omitting a comma changes the meaning just as significantly:

✓ There is really only one problem which calls for immediate action.

To avoid misinterpretation in such cases, it makes sense to follow the practice of using *which*, following the comma, only with non-restrictive (i.e. non-essential) modifiers; use *that* (without the comma) to introduce restrictive modifiers:

✓ There is really only one problem that calls for immediate action. (*restrictive*)

✓ There is really only one problem, which calls for immediate action. (*non-restrictive*)

6. **Use a comma after an introductory phrase, especially when omitting it would cause confusion:**

✗ After extensive planning tests were performed with real data.

✓ After extensive planning, tests were performed with real data.

✗ If the samples are random calculations need adjusting.

✓ If the samples are random, calculations need adjusting.

7. **Use a comma to separate elements in titles, dates, and addresses:**

> David Gunn, President

> February 2, 2004 (Commas are generally omitted if the day comes first: 2 February 2004)

> 117 Hudson Drive, Edmonton, Alberta

> They lived in Dartmouth, Nova Scotia.

8. **Use a comma before a quotation in a sentence:**

> Einstein said, "God is subtle, but he is not malicious."

For more formality, if the quotation is preceded by a complete sentence, use a colon (see p. 158).

9. **Do not use a comma between a subject and its verb:**

> ✗ The metals and other ions in the contaminated groundwater, increase the water's conductivity.

> ✓ The metals and other ions in the contaminated groundwater increase the water's conductivity.

10. **Do not use a comma between a verb and its object:**

> ✗ The second section explains, what solutions are possible.

> ✓ The second section explains what solutions are possible.

11. **Do not use a comma before "and" or "or" when linking two words, phrases, or dependent clauses:**

> ✗ In the simulation, two robots think independently, and cooperate to achieve a common goal.

> ✓ In the simulation, two robots think independently and cooperate to achieve a common goal.

12. **Do not use a comma in place of the colon to introduce a list:**

> ✗ Two AI tools were considered as possible components, natural language processors and neural networks.

> ✓ Two AI tools were considered as possible components: natural language processors and neural networks.

DASH [—]

A dash abruptly and dramatically draws attention to the words that follow. Never use dashes as casual substitutes for other punctuation. Overuse can detract from the calm, well-reasoned effect you want to create.

1. **Use a dash to stress a word or phrase:**

> Pressure is a physics concept crucial to medicine—especially in lung physiology.

> Their solution was well received—at first.

2. **Use a pair of dashes to set off an important interruption:**

> Hawking postulates that if the universe has no boundary—no beginning and no end—then it is self-contained.

Note the effect of parentheses in the same context. Dashes emphasize; parentheses add an aside:

> Hawking postulates that if the universe has no boundary (no beginning and no end) then it is self-contained.

Be careful to distinguish between hyphens and dashes. Two hyphens typed together with no spaces on their side represent a dash. This is the most space-efficient way of showing the feature, and word processors automatically convert this to a dash (called an *em dash* because of its length) as you continue typing. Another method is to use an *en dash*, one hyphen with single spaces left on either side.

ELLIPSIS [. . .]

1. **Use ellipsis points (three spaced dots) to show an omission from a quotation:**

> He reported that "to many farming families in the West, the drought in the Thirties [. . .] resembled a biblical plague, even to the locusts."

Use brackets around the ellipsis to indicate that you, not the original author, have left out the words.

If the omission comes just before the words quoted, an ellipsis is not used:

He reported that the drought "resembled a biblical plague, even to the locusts."

If the omission comes at the end of a quoted sentence, add the original period (without a space) right after the ellipses:

He reported that the drought "resembled a biblical plague [. . .]."

2. **Use an ellipsis to show that a series of numbers continues indefinitely**:

$$y = 1, 3, 5, 7, 9, \ldots$$

In mathematical copy, put commas or operational signs after each term and after the ellipsis points (without an intervening space) if followed by a final term:

$$x_1, x_2, \ldots, x_n$$

EXCLAMATION MARK [!]

An exclamation mark helps to show emotion or feeling, usually in informal writing like e-mails (Go figure!). Use it only in those rare cases, in non-scientific writing, when you want to give a point emotional emphasis:

Prof. Furness predicted that the dollar would rise against the yen. Some forecast!

HYPHEN [-]

1. **Use a hyphen if you are forced to divide a word at the end of a line.** Although it's generally best to start a new line if a word is too long, there are instances—for example, when you're formatting text in narrow columns—when hyphenation might be preferred. The hyphenation feature in word processors has taken the guesswork out of dividing words at the end of the line, but if you must use manual hyphenation, here are a few guidelines:

- Divide between syllables.
- Never divide a one-syllable word.
- Never leave one letter by itself.
- Divide double consonants except when they come before a suffix, in which case divide before the suffix:

ar-rangement

fall-ing

pass-able

When the second consonant has been added to form the suffix, keep it with the suffix:

refer-ral

begin-ning

- Do not divide a hyphenated compound word except at the hyphen:

✗   co-op-erative

2. **Use a hyphen to separate the parts of certain compound words:**

- compound nouns:

    kilowatt-hour; brother-in-law

- compound verbs:

    test-drive; mass-produce

- compound modifiers:

    matrix-based consideration; first-aid kits

Do not hyphenate a compound modifier that includes an adverb ending in -ly:

✗   a highly-developed prototype

✓   a highly developed prototype

Spell-checking features today will help you determine which compounds to hyphenate, but there is no clear consensus, even from one dictionary to another. As always, consistency in your writing style is most important.

3. **Use a hyphen with certain prefixes (*all-*, *self-*, *ex-*, *e-*) and with prefixes preceding a proper name**. Practices do vary, so consult a dictionary when in doubt.

    all-inclusive; self-imposed; ex-president; e-commerce

Use *former* rather than *ex-* in formal situations:

> Dr. Ling is the former chair of this department.

4. **Use a hyphen to emphasize contrasting prefixes**:

> The technician assessed both pre- and post-test findings.

5. **Use a hyphen to separate written-out compound fractions and compound numbers from one to ninety-nine:**

> seven-tenths full; two-thirds of a cup; twenty-two participants

6. **Use a hyphen to join a cardinal number and the unit of measurement when they precede what they modify:**

> a five-step process; 16-point type; a six-legged robot

7. **Use a hyphen to separate parts of inclusive numbers or dates**:

> the years 1890-1914; pages 3-10

ITALICS [*ITALICS*]

1. **Use italics for the titles of books, journals, magazines, plays, films, and lengthy musical pieces, as well as for the names of ships, trains, and spacecraft:**

> *The Discipline of Design* is one of my favourite textbooks.

Note: for articles, chapter titles, and unpublished dissertations (as well as short poems or musical pieces), use quotation marks. If the title itself contains the title of another work, be sure to set it off in appropriate fashion:

- When both titles are those of major works, use quotation marks for the internal one:

  > His latest book is *"Columbia"—What Went Wrong?*

- When the internal title is a major work but the main title is not, use italics:

  > For more detail, see her recent article, "Special Effects in *The Return of the King*."

- When neither title is a major work, use single quotation marks:

  > The article is entitled "Assonance in 'In Flanders' Fields.'"

2. **Use italics (or quotation marks) to identify a word or phrase that is itself the subject of discussion:**

> The term *op amp* is one of many blended words used in electrical engineering.

3. **Use italics for foreign words or expressions that have not been natural-ized in English, including Latin names for species and subspecies:**

> All owls belong to the sub-order *Striges*.

4. **Use italics for the text of equations as well as for defining theorems, rules, etc.:**

> $E = mc^2$

PARENTHESES [( )]

1. **Use parentheses to enclose an explanation, example, or qualification.** Parentheses show that the enclosed material is of incidental importance to the main idea. They make an interruption that is more subtle than one marked off by dashes but more pronounced than one set off by commas:

   ✓ The frequency domain brings out the dynamic (non-random) characteristics of a signal.

   ✓ Only clusters with a population of greater than 3,000 (30 per cent of the entire image) are processed.

Remember that punctuation should not precede parentheses but may follow them if required by the sense of the sentence:

   ✓ In cases that require special formatting (smoothed edges, shading, or shadowing), the characters must be modified.

If the parenthetical statement comes between two complete sentences, it should be punctuated as a sentence, with the period, question mark, or exclamation mark *inside* the parentheses:

   ✓ The process requires substantial execution time. (Turnaround can take as much as 24 hours.) Nevertheless, the savings outweigh the costs.

2. **Use parentheses to translate acronyms the first time you use them:**

   ✓ There are different types of FACTS (Flexible AC Transmission Systems) controllers.

   ✓ The concept explains how the central nervous system (CNS) operates.

3. **Use parentheses for in-text author or year references.** See Chapter 15 for details.

PERIOD [.]

1. **Use a period at the end of a sentence.** A period indicates a full stop, not just a pause.

2. **Use a period with abbreviations.** Canada's adoption of the metric system in 1970 contributed to a trend away from the use of periods in many abbreviations. It is still common, although not mandatory, to use periods in abbreviated titles (Mrs., Dr., Rev., etc.), academic degrees (M.Sc., Ph.D., etc.), expressions of time (6:30 p.m.), and place names (B.C., N.W.T., P.E.I., N.Y., D.C.). However, in official postal use, two-letter state and provincial abbreviations do not require periods (BC, NT, PE, NY, DC). In addition, most acronyms for organizations do not use periods (CIDA, CBC, UNESCO, WTO), nor do general acronyms (RPM, GST, EMF, STP).

3. **Use a period at the end of an indirect question.** Do not use a question mark:

   ✗ Users were asked if they found the manual useful?

   ✓ Users were asked if they found the manual useful.

   ✗ I wonder where she went?

   ✓ I wonder where she went.

4. **Use a period for questions that are really polite commands:**

   Would you please send him the report by Friday.

   May I congratulate you on your promotion.

QUOTATION MARKS [" "OR ' ']

American and British methods of punctuating quotations differ. American practice generally favours double quotation marks, while British practice generally favours single quotation marks. Sometimes the decision is based on space constraints (as happens with newspaper headlines, which use only single quotation marks). In Canada, either style is accepted as long as you are consistent. The guidelines outlined below are based on the American conventions, which are more common than the British ones in Canada.

1. **Use quotation marks to signify direct discourse (the actual words taken from a speaker or a text):**

   > In 1912, Einstein wrote the following to a friend: "Compared with this problem [formulating the general theory of relativity], the original theory is child's play."

2. **Use quotation marks to show that words themselves are the issue:**

   > The tennis term "love" comes from the French word for "egg."

   Alternatively, you may italicize the terms in question.

   Only in informal writing are quotation marks occasionally used to show with a slang word or inappropriate usage that the writer is aware of the difficulty. You mark text this way only if you would use your fingers to make imaginary quotation marks when you are face to face with someone.

   > Several of the "experts" did not seem to know anything about the topic.

   In general, it's better to let the context show your attitude or, better still, to choose another term.

3. **Use quotation marks to enclose the titles of chapters, poems, short stories, songs, presentations, films, and articles in books or journals.** (In contrast, titles of books, paintings, or music are italicized.)

   > The most provocative article in the July 2003 issue of *Transactions* is "Virtual Gaming" by Jerome Kim.

4. **Use single quotation marks to enclose quotations within quotations:**

   > He said, "Several of the 'experts' did not know anything about the topic."

   Note that British style reverses this pattern so that double quotation marks enclose quotations within quotations.

PLACEMENT OF PUNCTUATION WITH QUOTATION MARKS

The following guidelines for punctuating quotations are based on American rather than British conventions:

- A comma or period always goes inside the quotation marks:

  The method involves identifying the "core business," the "extended enterprise," and the "business ecosystem."

- A semicolon or colon always goes outside the quotation marks:

  Cybernetics relates to the recently developing "sciences of complexity": AI, neural networks, and complex adoptive systems.

- A question mark, dash, or exclamation mark goes inside quotation marks if it is part of the quotation but outside if it is not:

  One of the more important development questions is "How much investment money can be raised?"

  Did Prof. Hagen actually describe the Casuistic Theory of Value as "passing the buck"?

- If a reference is given parenthetically (in round brackets) at the end of a quotation, the quotation marks precede the parentheses, and the sentence punctuation follows them:

  Lipsey suggested that we should "abandon the Foreign Investment Review Agency" (Paisley 94).

Remember that questions, exclamation marks, and dashes are rare in scientific writing, but they have their place in informal communications.

SEMICOLON [;]

1. **Use a semicolon to join independent clauses (complete sentences) that are closely related:**

   Some samples contained sediment; others were clear.

A semicolon is especially useful when the second independent clause begins with a conjunctive adverb, such as *however, moreover, consequently, nevertheless, in addition,* or *therefore* (usually followed by a comma):

> Daylight is the most efficient source of building lighting; however, its
> full potential has yet to be demonstrated.

Some editors disagree, but it's usually acceptable to follow a semicolon with
a coordinating conjunction if one or both clauses are complicated by other
commas:

> On July 14, 2004, her assistant put the report in the mail; but the
> response was, unfortunately, negative.

2. **Use a semicolon to mark the divisions in a complicated series when
   individual items themselves need commas.** Using a comma to mark the
   subdivisions and a semicolon to mark the main divisions will help to prevent mix-ups:

> ✗   He invited Professor Ludvik, the vice-principal, Christine Li, and
>   Dr. Hector Jimenez.

Is the vice-principal a separate person?

> ✓   He invited Professor Ludvik, the vice-principal; Christine Li; and
>   Dr. Hector Jimenez.

Only in a case such as this do the elements separated by the semicolon not
need to be independent clauses.

SOLIDUS/SLASH [/]

1. **Use the solidus, or slash, to offer alternatives when either of a pair of
   words is to be selected:**

> Addresses should include name, street, city, province/state, country,
> and postal code.

While *he/she* and *s/he* are gaining in popularity as gender-neutral pronoun
pairs, be wary of using them in any formal writing. Unless space is an issue,
write these out in full: *he or she.*

2. **Use a solidus to separate parts of a web address, or URL:**

> http://www.oup.com/ca

If you are obliged to break a lengthy URL at the end of a line, do so only after a solidus:

The CSE's website, <http://www.councilscienceeditors.org.publications/corrections6th.cfm>, offers up-to-date guidelines.

cHApter 15

DOCUMENTATION

Much of the writing you do requires you to consult secondary sources for project ideas as well as to become and stay familiar with current research. Although scientific writing calls for few direct quotations, it is still essential to acknowledge your sources, not just if you quote directly from them but also when you refer to observations, conclusions, theories, or ideas presented in them. If you don't acknowledge these sources, you let your reader assume that the words, ideas, or concepts are yours. Such an omission is considered plagiarism, and penalties are severe (see Chapter 2).

The purpose of documentation is less to avoid charges of plagiarism than to show the body of knowledge that your work is building on. Academic writing is based on the premise that researchers are not working in a vacuum but are indebted both to scholars who came before them and to colleagues. By documenting your sources, you show that you recognize your indebtedness and are ready to make your own contribution to your field.

USING DIRECT QUOTATIONS

If you are not writing a technical paper, judicious use of direct quotations can add authority to your writing. However, never quote a passage just because it sounds impressive; be sure that it really adds to the discussion. Perhaps it expresses an idea with special force or cogency or gives substance to a debatable point. Quote directly only when you need to present the source's exact words. (If you allude to a source, rather than quote directly, follow the conventional methods of referencing presented later in this chapter.) The following are situations that justify word-for-word quotations from primary or secondary sources:

- **Literary content.** An analysis or evaluation of someone's writings (prose or poetry) calls for exact quotations.
- **Expert opinion.** A representative statement or a memorable comment from an acknowledged authority is worth citing, especially if it is the subject for discussion.

- **First-hand reports.** In media accounts and news releases, an accurate record from witnesses adds necessary specificity.

When you are convinced that only a direct quotation will serve your purposes, the following are guidelines you should follow:

1. Integrate the quotation so that it makes sense in the context of your discussion and fits grammatically into a sentence:

   ✗ Bill Gates could not foresee the future. "640 K ought to be enough for anybody" is now highly ironic.

   ✓ Bill Gates's 1981 prediction that "640K ought to be enough for anybody" is ironic in light of today's exponential leaps in computer engineering.

2. If the quotation is less than four lines long, include it as part of your text, enclosed in quotation marks. If the quotation is four lines or longer, set it as a block of free-standing text, double-spaced and indented from the left-hand margin (without quotation marks). If the quotation consists of more than one paragraph, indent the first line of the second (and all subsequent paragraphs) an additional three spaces.

   If you are quoting brief lines of poetry, they can be included as part of your text. Use a slash (/) to indicate the end of a line. For verse quotations longer than four lines, write the words line for line as originally written.

3. Be accurate whenever you are using quotation marks. Reproduce the exact wording, punctuation, and spelling of the original. (You can always acknowledge a typo or mistake in the original by inserting the word *sic* in square brackets after it—see p. 157). If you want to insert an explanatory comment of your own into a quotation, enclose it in square brackets:

   As Jones points out, "Biology now has a statistical machine [cladistics] to order the world."

4. If you want to omit something from the original, use ellipsis points. (See Chapter 14 for details.)

DOCUMENTING YOUR SOURCES

Your purpose for including a list of references at the end of your document is to make it as easy as possible for any reader to track your sources. That's why each reference will include as much of the following information as possible:

- Name of author or authors, in the order listed in the original work.
- Publication date.
- Title of article, posting, paper, or chapter in quotations marks.
- Title, underlined or italicized, of book, journal, periodical, or collection, including volume number if applicable.
- Name of editor or translator, identified by the abbreviations "ed." or "trans."
- Place of publication and publisher, for books only.
- Volume number, issue number, and page numbers, for journals and periodicals.
- Site sponsor/organization, URL, and date of last access, for websites.

List only those works that you have actually cited in the text of your writing.

There are many systems of documentation, and the one you use will depend on your subject as well as on the preference of your instructor, your department, or your employer. It makes sense from the beginning to find out whether there is a preferred documentation style and set of guidelines for its use. For easy reference, the most common systems are presented later in this chapter. Remember, though, that style guides are constantly undergoing revision, especially with the wealth of online information currently available. Always check the appropriate website or the latest edition of the relevant manual to be sure that you have the most up-to-date information available.

Be aware as well that technical societies may produce their own specifications, available on their websites. If you are preparing a paper for publication, you will be expected to follow the guidelines of the organization exactly, and there may be major or minor variations from the standards you have learned to follow in other contexts. It is a mark of professionalism to follow requirements exactly.

There is one absolute principle in documenting anything—the demand for consistency. Once you have committed to following a particular referencing style, you must continue to use it throughout whatever it is that you are writing.

If you are not told to follow a specific style manual or set of guidelines, you are still expected to acknowledge your sources. In scientific writing, the most common system of documentation is also the simplest and most economical. The following guidelines outline the system for IEEE publications [1], which is followed in this handbook. Keep to these conventions if no others have been specified for you.

IEEE STYLE

IN-TEXT CITATION SEQUENCING

Number your citations consecutively, putting the reference numbers in square brackets and punctuating afterwards if necessary. The first reference in your text will be [1], the next new reference will be [2], and so on. Once a source has been assigned a number, it is referred to by that number whenever it appears in the text:

> Labossière's groundbreaking study [1] was first challenged by Gormon [2] and later disputed by Huang [3]. Gormon's later work [4] confirmed the validity of Labossière's original hypothesis [1].

Putting reference numbers in square brackets both in the text and in the list of references is a preferred alternative to raised numerals that might be confused with superscript in scientific abbreviations or exponents. If you are referencing several sources at once, include all reference numbers in the same citation, giving each one its own square brackets. Refer to multiple references this way:

> Ultrasound images contain speckle noise [1]–[3] that makes tumours difficult to detect by eye alone.

If you make a later reference to a work you have already cited, use the number you assigned the work originally. Don't include the same work more than once, with different numbers, in your reference list.

REFERENCE LISTS

A convenient method for preparing a comprehensive list of sources at the end of your work merges traditional formats for endnotes and bibliographies. If you are using the in-text citation sequencing method, you will be listing references in numerical order, according to their order of appearance in your work. Put the bracketed number flush with the left margin, and use a hanging indent if your entry extends beyond the initial line. To conserve space, use initials rather than first names for authors. If you are referring to only a page or two rather than the entire work, list page numbers. Follow the punctuation conventions below:

> [1] I. Author, U. Writer, and T. Editor, "Chapter," in <u>Book</u>. Place: Publisher, Year.
>
> [2] I. Author and U. Writer, "Article," <u>Periodical</u>, Vol. 1, No. 1 (Year), pages.
>
> [3] I.M. Author, "Name," Website, Organization [online]. <URL> (date accessed).

You may notice that the examples in this handbook show titles underlined. Authors submitting work for publication use underlining as a clear indication to the publisher that certain words—including titles—should be set in italics. It's easy to put titles in italics while you type, of course, but the underlining makes the titles stand out. Most professors won't object if you use italics instead of underlining in your reference lists (in fact, CSE titles are not underlined at all); however, check with your instructor or department if you are in doubt.

The following examples provide models for scientific references. Remember to give as much information as necessary for your reader to locate each source.

Book with one author

The author's name follows the citation number and is not inverted. Capitalize important words in the title:

[1] J. Gruska, Quantum Computing. Toronto: McGraw-Hill, 1999.

Book with more than one author

If the book you are citing has two or more authors, list all the names, separated by "and" (and commas, in the case of three or more authors).

[2] N.R. Grist, D.O. Ho-Yen, E. Walker, and G.R. Williams, Diseases of Inflection: An Illustrated Textbook, 2nd ed. Oxford: Oxford University Press, 1992.

Book with a group or corporate author

[3] University of Chicago Press, The Chicago Manual of Style, 15th ed. Chicago: University of Chicago Press, 2003.

In the case of a revised or subsequent edition, include this information following the title, as shown above. (A revised edition would be shown as "rev. ed.")

Book with an editor, compiler, or translator

If the book has an editor or compiler and no author, give the editor's or compiler's name followed by "ed." or "comp.":

[4] R. Kling, ed., Computerization and Controversy. Toronto: Academic Press, 1996.

If the book has a translator, editor, or compiler as well as an author, put the author's name before the title and the other name after the title, introduced by the appropriate abbreviation.

[5] N. Copernicus, <u>On the Revolutions of the Heavenly Spheres</u>. Trans. A.M. Duncan. New York: Barnes & Noble, 1976.

Selection in an edited work

The title of the selection, placed in quotation marks and in lower case but for the first letter of the first word of the title and subtitle, follows the author's name and precedes the name of the edited work. Notice that the word "in" precedes the name of an edited book but is *not* used before the names of journals, periodicals, magazines, or newspapers containing a referenced article:

[6] R.H. Waterman, P.I. Peters, and J.R. Phillips, "The 7-S framework," in <u>The Strategy Process</u>, ed. J.B. Quinn, H. Mintzberg, and R.M. James. New Jersey: Prentice-Hall, 1988.

Article in a journal or periodical

[7] P. Maes, "Artificial life meets entertainment: Lifelike autonomous agents," <u>New Horizons of Commerical and Industrial AI</u>, Vol. 38, No. 11 (1995), pp. 108–114.

In cases where each issue is paginated separately, the issue number may follow the volume number, separated by a comma and "no." as shown above. Alternatively, it may be shown in brackets, without "no." and without a comma to separate it from the volume number. With the latter method, the issue number (in parentheses) is followed by a colon, the page number(s), and the date (in parentheses):

[7] . . . <u>and Industrial AI</u> 38 (11): 108–114 (1995).

Either method is acceptable, but you must use one consistently.

If the work has not yet appeared in print, include words to that effect in parentheses directly after the reference:

[8] M. Foumani, A. Khajepour, and M. Durali, "Optimization of engine mount characteristics using experimental numerical analysis," <u>Journal of Vibration and Control</u> (accepted for publication).

Article in a newspaper

If the section of the newspaper containing the article you are referencing is identified, give its name, number, or letter:

[9] B. Jang, "Investors, motorists find comfort in big oil," Business, <u>The Globe and Mail</u>, 23 October 2001, B16.

If the article is unsigned, begin the note with the title of the article.

Article in a magazine

When referencing a magazine article, you have the option of including the volume number. If you choose to include it, put the date of issue in parentheses, followed by a colon rather than a comma before the page reference.

> [10] Lynn Bowen, "Elusive treasure: Fortune seeking in the Athabasca tar sands," The Beaver, February/March 1999, 22–27.

> *or* [10] Lynn Bowen, "Elusive treasure: Fortune seeking in the Athabasca tar sands," The Beaver 79, No. 1 (February/March 1999): 22–27.

Either method is acceptable as long as you use it consistently.

Technical report

Even if a technical report has been printed in-house (i.e. by the organization itself), you list it as a publication. Include all necessary information for locating it:

> [11] International Data Corportation, "Worldwide Internet services and market trends forecast, 1998–2003," New York, Rep. 47–53, May 1999.

Paper presented at a conference

Cite this as you would a journal article:

> [12] H. Pi, "A neural approach to futures trading," presented at NNCM '96 in Singapore, 1996.

If the paper is subsequently published, use the conventional reference format for a publication:

> [13] D. Rayside and K. Kontogiannis, "Extracting Java library subsets for deployment on embedded systems," WRCE Proceedings, October 1998, pp. 315–319.

Dissertation

Refer to an unpublished dissertation this way:

> [14] L. Fu, "Realtime vehicle routing and scheduling in dynamic and schostic traffic networks," Ph.D. dissertation. Dept. of Systems Design, Univ. of Alberta, 1996.

Lecture notes

Give as much detail as necessary. For online course material, refer to online source referencing below.

> [15] C. MacGregor, User-centred design course notes. SD 348, Univ. of Waterloo, March 2003.

Patent

Include the country of origin, patent number, and day:

> [16] R.W. Schemendauer, Master/Slave hydraulic system for farming implements, Can. patent 2 015 835, Jul. 22, 1997.

Audio-visual sources

For unusual items, specify the type and availability:

> [17] CANDU reactor [overhead transparency], VD-648, Atomic Energy of Canada. Toronto: Stoddart, 1986. Available: 34 Lesmill Rd. Toronto M3B 2T6.

Online sources

The most up-to-date information is now available instantly on the Internet, and references must therefore include full details about the source, the site, and the sponsoring organization. Provide the full URL (not just the home-page address), and identify the date you last visited the site (to show when the information was current). List this information at the end of a standard reference after inserting "online" in square brackets like this: [Online]. Remember that your main aim, as always, is to make it possible for your reader to access the source of your information. Be especially careful to report the URL accurately. (The value of using angle brackets is that you keep the URL integral.)

> [18] P. Ford-Martin, "Understanding blood tests: Diabetes blood tests-fasting plasma glucose," Diabetes, About Inc. [Online]. <http://diabetes.about.com/library/weekly/aa122600a.htm> (current May 30, 2003).

Note that if you have to break a URL so that it fits properly on a line (as above), do so after a slash. Don't add extra spaces or use hyphens.

ALPHABETICAL REFERENCING

Some professors will ask you to list your references in alphabetical order at the end of your document rather than in their order of appearance in the text. Follow their recommendations by assigning a number to each reference only once everything has been alphabetized. (For entries, use the same format as that described above, for there is no expectation of reversed first names and surnames.) Thus your reference list will be in numerical and alphabetical order at the same time. To complete the process, go back to your document and make sure your references are keyed to the numbers listed at the end. When the reference list is alphabetized, numbers in the text will therefore not appear in sequence:

> Ultrasound images contain speckle noise [2],[5],[6] that makes tumours difficult to detect by eye alone.

STANDARD STYLE SHEETS

If you have professors, colleagues, or situations calling for a specific reference style, it is likely to be APA, CSE, CMS, or MLA. Below you will find examples of each of these formats as well as additional references for you to consult. Note the minor differences distinguishing each of these, and follow the conventions exactly.

APA STYLE

The American Psychological Association system of documentation is the one most commonly used in the social sciences, business, and nursing. The APA system uses in-text citations, which name authors and dates in parentheses after the information cited, rather than providing reference or note numbers. Complete bibliographical information is included in a list of references at the end. Some examples are listed below. For more detailed information, consult the *Publication Manual of the American Psychological Association* (5th ed.). The APA website also provides up-to-date information about documenting electronic sources: <http://www.apastyle.org/elecref.html>.

IN-TEXT CITATIONS
Source with one author
If the author's name is given in the text, cite only the year of publication in parentheses.

Helmsteadt (2002) made a significant contribution to the climate change debate.

Otherwise, give both the name and the year:

The latest analysis (Christensen, 2003) disproved government statements.

Source with more than one author

If the work you are citing has two authors, include both names every time you cite the reference in the text. The APA uses an ampersand (&) when the names are in parentheses but "and" in the text:

Earlier research showed that neonates did not distinguish between small frequency differences (Leventhal & Lipsitt, 1964). However, Morrongiello and Clifton (1984) found that neonates orient better to high- than to low-frequency sounds.

If there are three, four, or five authors, cite all the names when the reference first occurs and afterwards cite only the first author, followed by "et al.":

Pola, Wyatt, and Lustgarten (1992) studied eye movements. [. . ..]
Research found that subjects suppressed eye movements (Pola et al., 1992).

If the work you are citing has six or more authors, cite only the surname of the first author followed by "et al."

Source with a group or corporate author

Corporations, associations, and government agencies serving as authors are usually given in full each time they appear. Some group authors may be named in full the first time and abbreviated in subsequent citations if this provides the reader with enough information to easily locate the entry in the reference list:

A recent study examines the effectiveness of treating low-back pain in the first two weeks following injury (Institute for Work & Health [IWH], 2000). [. . ..] The same study also looks at the effectiveness of bed rest in speeding up recovery (IWH, 2000).

Work with no known or declared author

If the work you are referencing has no known or declared author, cite the first few words of the title, as well as the year:

In the pyroelectric sensor, the infrared light generates surface electric charge off a substrate ("Motion sensing lights," 2002). [The full title of the source is "Motion Sensing Lights and Burglar Systems Work, Study Shows."]

Specific parts of a source
If you are referring to a particular part of a source, you must indicate the page, chapter, figure, table, or equation. Always give page numbers for quotations:

(Felderhaus, 1991, p. 299)
(Christenssen & Schor, 1994, pp. 2601–2602)
(Stenson, 1998, chap. 2)
(Li & Knowles, 2004, fig. 2)

Note that the APA abbreviates page numbers with "p." for a single page and "pp." for several pages.

Online sources
In-text citations for electronic sources use the same formatting principles outlined above for print sources, with the following exceptions:

- If your source has no page numbers, use the paragraph number or section number, if one is available:

    (Edson, 2004, para. 10)

- If sections, pages, and paragraphs are not numbered, cite the heading and the number of the paragraph following it to direct the reader to the specific location you are referring to:

    (Black, 2003, Introduction, para. 6)

REFERENCES
Here are the conventions for recording entries in an APA *References* section:

- Entries begin with the author's surname, followed by his or her initials (full given names are not used).
- In entries for works with more than one author, all authors' names are reversed, with the name of the last author preceded by an ampersand (&) rather than "and."
- The date of publication appears immediately after the names of the author(s).

- Entries for different works by the same author are listed chronologically. Two or more works by the same author with the same publication year are arranged alphabetically by title.
- For titles of books and articles, only proper nouns and the first word of the title and of the subtitle (if there is one) are capitalized. The same is not true of journal titles.
- Titles of articles or selections in books are *not* enclosed in quotation marks.

Book with one author

Klein, N. (2000). No logo: Taking aim at the brand bullies. Toronto: Vintage Canada.

Book with more than one author

Doty, D.I., & Pincus, M. (2001). Publicity and public relations (2nd ed.). New York: Barron's.

For books with more than six authors, list only the first six followed by "et al" and a period.

Book with a group or corporate author

American Medical Association. (1994). Guides to the evaluation of permanent impairment (4th ed.). Chicago: American Medical Association.

Book with no known or declared author

The Canadian encyclopedia: Year 2000 edition. (1999). Toronto: McClelland & Stewart.

Book with a volume number

Musling, J.M., & Bornstein, R.F. (Eds.). (1998). Empirical studies of psychoanalytic theories: Vol. 7. Empirical perspectives on the psychoanalytic unconscious. Washington, DC: American Psychological Association.

Book with an editor

Yerema, R.W. (Ed.). (2001). The career directory. Toronto: Mediacorp.

Selection in an edited book

> Schluter, D. (1998). Ecological speciation in post-glacial fishes. In P.R. Grant (Ed.), Evolution on islands (pp. 145–162). Oxford: Oxford University Press.

Note that the page numbers of the selection are given, preceded by "pp."

Article in a journal

> Caladine, C.R. (1978). Buckminster Fuller's "tensegrity" structures and Clerk Maxwell's rules for the construction of stiff frames. International Journal of Solids Structures, 14, 161–172.

Note that the page numbers of the article are given but are not preceded by "pp.," as they would be in entries for newspaper articles and selections in books.

When a journal has continuous pagination, the issue number should not be included. If each issue begins on page 1, give the issue number in parentheses before the page numbers and immediately following the volume number, with no punctuation separating them and a comma following the parentheses. The volume number is underlined; the issue number and its parentheses are not:

> Furuya, H., & Hansaor, A. (1993). Double-layer tensegrity grids as deployable structures. International journal of space structures, 8 (1), 135–143.

Article in a newspaper

> Keenan, G. (2004, January 6). Ford boss hopeful for Oakville future. The Globe and Mail, pp. B1, B21.

Note that when a newspaper or magazine article continues on a non-consecutive page, the first page is given, followed by a comma and the page(s) it continues on.

If the newspaper article is unsigned (that is, if it has no listed author), begin the entry with the title:

> Westcoast profit jumps in second quarter. (2001, July 27). The Globe and Mail, p. B9.

Article in a magazine

> Karnovsky, M.J. (1965). A formaldehyde-glutaraldehyde fixative of high osmolity for use in electron microscopy. Journal of Cell Biology, 27, 137–144.

Note that if the magazine has a volume number, it should be included after the magazine title, underlined. For monthly or bi-monthly magazines, give the month(s) in full; for weekly magazines, give the month (in full) and day.

Website

When citing original content from an online source, you should include the author of the content, the date of publication or last update, the title of the work, the retrieval date, and the complete URL:

> Health Canada. (2003, January 15). Best practices in mental health reform: Discussion paper. Retrieved May 22, 2004, from http://www.hc-sc.gc.ca/hppb/mentalhealth/pubs/sic_paper/e_disc8.html

Article in an online journal

If you are referencing an article in an online publication that is identical to the print edition, use the same format as for a print version of the article. Add "Electronic version" in square brackets after the article title to indicate that the version you read was online:

> Townsend, R.L. Jr., Werner, J-J., & Nguyen, M-H. (1995, July/August). Using technology to bring ATM to the desktop. [Electronic version]. AT&T technical journal, 25–34.

If the article has been altered, updated, or written specifically for an online publication, you must indicate the date you retrieved it and the URL:

> Fredrickson, B.L. (2000, March 7). Cultivating positive emotions to optimize health and well-being. Prevention & Treatment, 3, Article 0001a. Retrieved November 20, 2000, from http://journals.apa.org/prevention/volume3/pre003001a.html

Remember to break a URL that goes to another line after a slash or before a period. Do not insert (or allow your word-processing program to insert) a hyphen at the break.

CSE STYLE

The Council of Science Editors (formerly the Council of Biology Editors) recommends both an author–date system, like APA, and also a numerical-sequence system using raised numerals to direct the reader to a list of references at the end of the paper, like IEEE. This system is commonly used in the life sciences. The following guidelines are based on the principles laid out in the sixth edition of *Scientific Style and Format: The CBE Manual for Authors, Editors, and Publishers* (1994):

- Superscript numbers in the text correspond to numbered references in a *References* or *Cited References* section at the end of the document.
- If several sources are being referenced at once, all relevant reference numbers should be given in the same citation, separated with commas and no spaces. With a sequence of three or more citation numbers (e.g., 7, 8, 9), use only the first and last number in the sequence, separated with a hyphen:

  Several studies[1,5,12–15] have shown . . ..

- When citing material that you have not read yourself but have seen cited by others, give the citation number for the original, followed (in parentheses) by "cited in" and the citation number for the source in which you found the material:

  According to Wilcox and Wolf[18(cited in 19)], ...

- In the *References* or *Cited References* section, references are listed in order of their appearance in the text. For each entry, follow these conventions exactly:

  1. The note number followed by a period and two spaces.
  2. The author's last name followed by initials without punctuation and then a period.
  3. The title of the article or selection, followed by the title of the journal or book, with *no* underlining or italics or quotation marks. Only the first word of the title and proper nouns are capitalized.
  4. The place of publication followed by a colon.
  5. The name of the publisher followed by a semicolon.
  6. The date of publication.
  7. The range or total number of pages.

REFERENCES
Book with one author

> 1. Tomasello M. Constructing a language: a usage-based theory of language acquisition. Cambridge (MA): Harvard Univ Pr; 2003. 388 p.

Note that the last element of the entry ("388 p.") indicates the total number of pages in the book.

Book with two or more authors
If the book you are referencing has more than one author, give the names of all authors up to a maximum of ten, after which additional authors are replaced by "and others." Names should be inverted and separated by commas. Note that "and" is not used:

> 2. Peterson LM, Russell AF. Active and passive movement testing. New York: McGraw-Hill; 2002. 418 p.

Book by a group or corporate author

> 3. National Advisory Committee on Immunization. Canadian immunization guide. Ottawa: Canadian Medical Assoc; 2002. 278 p.

Book with an editor

> 4. Case-Smith J, editor. Pediatric occupational therapy and early intervention. 2nd ed. Boston: Butterworth-Heinemann; 1998. 324 p.

Selection in an edited book

> 5. Rogers AG. Understanding changes in girls' relationships and in ego development: three studies in adolescent girls. In: Westenberg A, Blasi A, Cohen LD, editors. Personality development: theoretical, empirical, and clinical investigations of Loevinger's conception of ego development. New Jersey: Erlbaum; 1998. p 145–62.

Article in a journal

> 6. Baranski JV, Petrusoc WM. Testing architectures of the decision–confidence relation. Can J Exp Psych 2001;55:196–206.

Note that the CSE abbreviates names of journals and magazines.

Article in a magazine

> 7. Hollingham R. In the realm your senses. New Scientist 2004 Jan 31:40–3.

Article in a newspaper

> 8. MacDonald G. CBC on trial. Globe and Mail 2001 Jul 28; Sect R:12, 16.

> 9. [Anonymous]. Woman again registers her cows as voters. Toronto Star 2004 Feb 22; Sect F:2 (col 6).

Note that when a newspaper article continues on a non-consecutive page (as in the first example), the first page is given, followed by a comma, a space, and the page(s) it continues on. For an article without an identified author, use "[Anonymous]."

Article in an online journal

> 10. Pechenik JA, Wendt DE, Jarrett JN. Metamorphosis is not a new beginning. BioSci Online [Internet]. 1998 [cited 1998 Nov 17]; 48:90110. Available from: http://www.aibs.org/latitude/latpublications.html

Website

> 11. Preventing skin cancer [Internet]. Health Canada; 2001 Nov [updated 2004 Feb; cited 2004 Feb 22]. Available from: http://www.hc-sc.gc.ca/english/iyh/diseases/cancer.html

Pending the publication of the seventh edition of *Scientific Style and Format*, you can find out more about the CSE's recommendations for citing electronic sources by visiting their website: <http://www.councilscienceeditors.org/publications/citing_internet.cmf>.

CMS STYLE

The Chicago Manual of Style (CMS) outlines two methods of documentation: the *author–date* system, preferred in the natural and social sciences, follows the same principles as APA style with only minor stylistic differences; the *documentary-note* method uses superscript numerals to direct the reader to footnotes at the bottom of the page or endnotes listed separately at the end of the document. In scientific writing, footnotes or endnotes are used not to cite references but to expand upon the content of the paper—on the *very rare* occasions where such elaboration is impossible in the text. Some journals, for example, will use a footnote to provide biographical details of the author(s).

Despite the convenience of footnoting software, use notes *only* if you have been specifically directed to do so. The following are some examples of notes using the Chicago method. For additional examples, consult *The Chicago Manual of Style: The Essential Guide for Writers, Editors, and Publishers* (15th ed.) or the University of Chicago Press website: <http://www.press.uchicago.edu/Misc/Chicago/cmosfaq/cmosfaq.html>.

NOTES

Footnotes appear at the bottom of the page or column that contains the reference. Endnotes are placed on a "Notes" page after any appendices and before a bibliography. The notes are single-spaced and can be typed with either a first-line indent (as in the examples below) or a hanging indent. Although the note numbers in the text are superscript, the note numbers that precede the notes themselves are not. If you have been asked to cite your references with notes, prepare your notes according to the following conventions.

Book with one author

The name of the author follows the note number and is not inverted. It is followed by a comma and the title of the book, with all important words capitalized. The publication details follow the title in parentheses:

> 1. Michael B. Decter, Four Strong Winds: Understanding the Growing Challenges to Health Care (Toronto: Stoddart, 2002).

Book with more than one author

If the book you are referencing has two or three authors, all of the authors' names are given, separated by "and" and (in the case of three authors) commas:

> 2. Ira Marc Price and Linda Comac, Coping with Macular Degeneration (New York: Penguin Putnam, 2000).

> 3. J. Frederick Little, Leo A. Groarke, and Christopher W. Tindale, Good Reasoning Matters! A Constructive Approach to Critical Thinking (Toronto: McClelland & Stewart, 1989).

If the book you are referencing has more than three authors, you can use the name of only the first author, followed by either "et al" or "and others" and a period, without intervening punctuation:

4. Janice Laflamme et al., <u>Notions of Independence: Eighteenth-Century Views on Freedom</u> (Vancouver: Ruff Books, 2000).

Book with a group or corporate author

5. University of Chicago Press, <u>The Chicago Manual of Style</u>, 15th ed. (Chicago: University of Chicago Press, 2003).

In the case of a revised or subsequent edition, include this information following the title, as shown above. A revised edition would be "rev. ed."

Book with an editor, compiler, or translator

If the book you are referencing has an editor or compiler and no author, give the editor's or compiler's name first, followed by "ed." or "comp.":

6. S.E. Gontarski, ed., <u>The Grove Press Reader 1951–2001</u> (New York: Grove, 2001).

If the book you are referencing has a translator, editor, or compiler as well as an author, the author's name should come before the title with the translator's, editor's, or compiler's name following the title, introduced by the appropriate abbreviation:

7. Denyse Baillargeon, <u>Making Do: Women, Family and Home in Montreal During the Great Depression</u>, trans. Yvonne Klein (Waterloo: Wilfrid Laurier University Press, 1999).

Selection in an edited book

The title of the selection, set in quotation marks, follows the author's name and precedes the name of the edited work. Note that a title within a title is enclosed in quotation marks:

8. J.D. Salinger, "Slight Rebellion Off Madison," in <u>Wonderful Town: New York Stories from "The New Yorker,"</u> ed. David Remnick, 87–90 (New York: Modern Library, 2000).

Article in a journal

If an issue number is given, it follows the volume number, separated by a comma and "no." In a reference to the article as a whole, the entire page range should be included. A reference to a particular section should give relevant page numbers only:

9. Taras Kuzio, "Nationalism in Ukraine: Towards a New Framework," Politics 20, no. 2 (2000): 77–86.

Article in a newspaper

Since a newspaper may have several editions in a given day, and items may be moved or eliminated in various editions, page numbers should be omitted. If the section of the newspaper containing the article you are referencing is identified, give its name, number, or letter:

10. Brent Jang, "Investors, Motorists Find Comfort in Big Oil," Business, Globe and Mail, 23 October 2001, sec. B.

If the article is unsigned, begin the note with the title of the article.

Article in a magazine

Even if a magazine is numbered by volume and issue, it is usually cited by date only:

11. Adrienne Clarkson, "An Immigrant's Progress," Maclean's, 1 July 2001, 26–27.

Online sources

Whether referencing electronic journals (as in the following example), magazines, or newspapers, follow the format of their print counterparts, with the addition of a URL and, especially if the information is time-sensitive, the date of access:

12. Giuliano Bonoli, "Social Policy through Labour Markets: Understanding National Differences in the Provision of Economic Security to Wage Earners," Comparative Political Studies 36, no. 9 (2003): 1007–1030, http://80-www.ingenta.com.ezproxy.library.dal.ca/isis/shopping/cart/ShoppingCart/ingenta;jsessionid=v4rfa91eobla.crescent (accessed January 15, 2004).

To cite a website, include as much of the following as can be determined: author of the content, title of the page, title or owner of the site, URL, date of access (if the document is particularly time-sensitive).

Shortened citations

If you are referring repeatedly to the same source, you can use the abbreviation "Ibid." and the page number for subsequent references, provided that there is no intervening reference to a different source. In cases where a reference to a different source intervenes, you can use a shortened citation, which should include enough information to lead the reader to the appropriate entry in the bibliography, and normally consists of the last name of the author and a shortened version of the title:

13. Teresa MacNeil, "Assessing the Gap between Community Development Practice and Regional Development Policy," in <u>Community Organizing: Canadian Experiences</u>, ed. Brian Wharf and Michael Clague (Toronto: Oxford University Press, 1997), 152.

14. Ibid., 155.

15. Robert Page, <u>Northern Development: The Canadian Dilemma</u> (Toronto: McClelland & Stewart, 1986), 17.

16. MacNeil, "Assessing the Gap," 158.

If all works cited in a document are included in a bibliography, even the first citation of a particular work can be very concise.

BIBLIOGRAPHY

The bibliography is a list of all the sources you have used in your paper, including works you may have consulted but not referred to directly. It is placed on a separate page at the end, arranged alphabetically by the authors' last names, single-spaced, with hanging indents. If you are asked to keep primary and secondary source materials separate, or list online sources separately from paper sources, use subheadings. Do not number your entries.

Book with one author

Gruska, J. <u>Quantum Computing</u>. Toronto: McGraw-Hill, 1999.

Book with more than one author

If the book you are referencing has two authors, invert the name of the first author only and separate the names with a comma and "and":

Price, Ira Marc, and Linda Comac. <u>Coping with Macular Degeneration</u>. New York: Penguin Putnam, 2000.

When referencing a book with three or more authors, semicolons may be used to separate the authors' names:

Grist, Norman R.; Darrel O. Ho-Yen; Eric Walker; and Glyn R. Williams. <u>Diseases of Infection: An Illustrated Textbook</u>. 2nd ed. Oxford: Oxford University Press, 1992.

If the book you are citing has four or more authors, you may also follow the first author's name (inverted) with a comma and "et al." or "and others":

> Grist, Norman R., et al. <u>Diseases of Infection: An Illustrated Textbook</u>. 2nd ed. Oxford: Oxford University Press, 1992.

Book with a group or corporate author

> Human Resources Development Canada. <u>Changing Patterns in Women's Employment</u>. Ottawa: Queen's Printer, 1998.

Book with an editor or translator

If the book has an editor and no author, give the editor's name first, followed by the abbreviation "ed.":

> Gontarski, S.E., ed. <u>The Grove Press Reader 1951–2001</u>. New York: Grove, 2001.

If the book has an editor or translator as well as an author, give the author's name first and give the translator's or editor's name after the title, introduced by "Edited by" or "Translated by":

> Copernicus, Nicolas. <u>On the Revolutions of the Heavenly Spheres</u>. Translated by A.M. Duncan. New York: Barnes & Noble, 1976.

Selection in an edited book

> Salinger, J.D. "Slight Rebellion Off Madison." In <u>Wonderful Town: New York Stories from "The New Yorker,"</u> edited by David Remnick, 87–90. New York: Modern Library, 2000.

Article in a journal

Since a bibliographic entry is a reference to the article as a whole, the entire page range should be given:

> Kuzio, Taras. "Nationalism in Ukraine: Towards a New Framework." <u>Politics</u> 20, no. 2 (2000): 77–86.

Article in a newspaper

> Picard, André. "Despite health benefits, men don't eat vegetables." <u>Globe and Mail</u>, 26 July 2001, A7.

If you are referencing an unsigned article, the entry should begin with the title of the article.

Online sources

> Benoli, Giuliano. "Social Policy through Labour Markets: Understanding National Differences in the Provision of Economic Security to Wage Earners." Comparative Political Studies 36, no. 9 (2003) 1007–1030. http://80-www.ingenta.com.ezproxy.library.dal.ca/isis/shopping/cart/ ShoppingCart/ingenta;jsessionid=v4rfa91ebola.crescent (accessed January 15, 2004).

The preceding example lists an electronic journal, but the same guidelines apply to electronic magazines and newspapers: follow the format of the print counterparts, with the addition of the URL and, especially if the information is time-sensitive, the date of access. To list a website, include as much of the following as can be determined: the author of the content; the title of the page; the title or owner of the site; the URL; and the access date.

MLA STYLE

If you are taking elective courses in the humanities, the Modern Language Association is the accepted authority for documenting your sources. MLA style uses in-text citations, which give the author's last name and the page number in parentheses after the information cited. Complete bibliographical information is then given in an alphabetical list, titled *Works Cited*, on a separate page at the end of the paper.

The following examples illustrate the most common types of references as they would appear in citations and in the *Works Cited* list. If you don't see what you're looking for, consult the *MLA Handbook for Writers of Research Papers* (6th ed.). Some guidelines, mostly for documenting electronic sources, are also available on the FAQ page of the MLA website: <www.mla.org>.

IN-TEXT CITATIONS
Book or article with one author

Put in parentheses (round brackets) only the information needed to identify a source clearly—usually the author's (or editor's) last name and the page number of the text referred to:

> Einstein later described his original theory of relativity as "child's play" (Lawden 46).

Place the parenthetical reference at the end of the sentence or clause it documents. Note that there is no punctuation between the author's name and the page number.

If the author's name is already given in the text, put in parentheses only the place of the reference:

> Harris sees the logic in Hegel's argument (72–4).

If you are citing an entire work, try to include the author's (or editor's) name in the text rather than in parentheses:

> In Elements of Relativity Theory, D.F. Lawden considers both historical and scientific contexts of Einstein's work.

Source with more than one author

If the work has two or three authors, include all of the names in the citation:

> The same argument was applied to the universities (Matthews and Steele 50–62).

If the work has four or more authors, use only the first author's last name and "et al."; use the same form in the *Works Cited* section:

> The result, some claim, is "cultural suicide" (Jones et al. 42).

Book or article with a group or corporate author

If you are citing a document prepared by a corporate author or government agency, give the name of the organization or agency or a shortened form. It is often clearer if you include this information in your sentence rather than in your citation:

> Until a correction appeared on the website, Canada Post Corporation showed the abbreviation for both Nunavut and Northwest Territories as "NT" (14).

Two or more works by the same author

If you need to refer to more than one work written by the same author, use a shortened version of the appropriate title with each citation:

> It's useful to think of business communication as presenting a problem for which there may be no single solution (Northey, Impact 25).

If the author's name appears in the text, include only the title and page number(s) in parentheses. If the author's name and the title appear in the text, indicate only the page number(s) in parentheses:

In Impact: A Guide to Business Communication, Northey suggests that it's useful to think of business communication as a problem for which there may be no single solution (25).

Electronic sources

In-text citations for electronic sources use the same formatting principles outlined above for print sources. However, since many electronic sources do not have page numbers, you may have to cite a paragraph or section number instead. Note that you use a comma after the name here:

("Stocks", sec. 2)
(Douglas, pars. 12–15)

If your source has no page, section, or paragraph numbers, include only the name of the author or a shortened version of the work's title (if there is no listed author) in your parenthetical references. Do not use page numbers of a printout of the source, as the pagination may vary in different printouts.

WORKS CITED

Your list of works cited should contain only those works you have actually referred to in the text. (Do not include works that you consulted but did not cite directly.) The following are some formatting guidelines, followed by examples of common entries in a *Works Cited* list. If the kind of source you are using isn't shown in any of the examples here, consult the *MLA Handbook* or the MLA website.

- Begin your *Works Cited* section on a separate page but continue the page numbering.
- Double-space the entire list, both between and within entries and between the title and the first entry. Do not number entries, but list them alphabetically by the author's or editor's surname. If no author is given, alphabetize according to the first significant word in the title.
- Format with hanging indents: begin each bibliographic entry at the margin and indent any subsequent line five spaces.
- Separate the main divisions by periods.

Book with one author

Robinson, Jeffrey. Prescription Games: Money, Ego, and Power Inside the Global Pharmaceutical Industry. Toronto: McClelland & Stewart, 2001.

Two or more works by the same author

Entries for two or more works by the same author are arranged alphabetically by the first significant word in the title. List the author's name in the first entry only; in subsequent entries, use three em-dashes (or five en-dashes) followed by a period:

> Robb, R.A. <u>Three-dimensional Biomedical Imaging: Principles and Practice</u>. New York: VCH Publishers, 1994.
>
> ———. "VR Assisted Surgery Planning: Using Patient Specific Anatomic Models." <u>IEEE Engineering in Medicine and Biology</u> Mar./Apr. 1996: 60–69.

Book with an editor

> Kerr, Philip, ed. <u>The Penguin Book of Lies</u>. London: Viking Penguin, 1990.

If the book has a compiler rather than an editor, use the abbreviation "comp." rather than "ed."

If you are listing a book with more than one editor, follow the guidelines given above for a book with more than one author, listing the editors' names followed by "eds." (or "comps." where appropriate).

Selection in an edited book

> Pascal, Blaise. "A Contentious Dispensation from Keeping One's Word." <u>The Penguin Book of Lies</u>. Ed. Philip Kerr. London: Viking Penguin, 1990. 89–108.

Make sure to give inclusive page numbers for the entire piece, not just for the material you used.

Article in a journal

When listing a journal article, give the title of the article, the journal title, the volume number, the year of publication, and the inclusive page numbers. Omit introductory articles ("A," "An," or "The") in the journal title:

> Einstein, Albert, B. Podolsky, and N. Rosen. "Can Quantum-Mechanical Description of Reality be Considered Complete?" <u>Physical Review</u> 47 (1935): 777–780.

If the issue in which the article appears is paginated separately—that is, if all of the issues in a volume are not paginated together continuously, as in the example above—then you must also include the issue number, following the volume number and separated from it by a period. Abbreviate all months except for May, June, and July:

> Chambliss, M.L., and J. Conley. "Answering Clinical Questions." Journal of Family Practice 43.2 (Aug. 1996): 97–103.

Article in a magazine or newspaper

The guidelines are the same except that with newspapers the page number also includes a letter identifying the section in which the article is found. For both, you must include the date shown on the issue:

> Snyder, Peter Etril. "Buffalo Revered As Food." Record [Kitchener] 31 May 2003: J11.

Not all newspaper references are this straightforward. Bear in mind the following guidelines:

- As with journals, omit introductory articles in the title.
- If the city of publication is not included in the name of a locally published newspaper, add this in square brackets after the title: *Herald* [Halifax]. You do not need to add the city of publication for nationally published newspapers.
- When an article has no listed author, begin the entry with the article title.
- If the newspaper section is identified by a number rather than a letter, use "sec." followed by the section number and page number, and separate this information from the date with a comma rather than a colon:

  > "Study Links Long Life to Gardening." Peterborough Times-Tribune 22 Oct. 2000, sec. 3: 2.

- In the case of a particular edition used—such as an early or late edition or one published in a particular location—this information follows the date and a comma and is itself followed by the colon and page number.
- When an article is continued on a page that is not the next consecutive page, the page number is followed by a plus sign (+) and a period.

Article in an online journal

When referencing an article retrieved from an online journal, MLA specifies that you list everything as you would for a published journal. If the article does not have page numbers, give the numerical range or total number of paragraphs or sections in the article, if these are numbered. Give the date you retrieved the article followed, in angle brackets, by the URL:

> Waynant, R.W., and V.M. Chenault. "Overview of Non-Invasive Fluid Glucose Measurement Using Optical Techniques to Maintain Glucose Control in Diabetes Mellitus." LEOS Newsletter 2.2 (1998): 16 secs. 28 Mar. 2003 <http://www.ieee.org/organizations/pubs/newsletters/leos/ apr98/overview.htm>.

As always, if you have to break a URL so that it fits on a line, do so after a slash. Do not insert (or allow your word-processing program to insert) a hyphen at the break.

Website

References to original content from online sources should contain the following information: the author of the content; the title of the page; the title of the site; the date of publication; the name of the organization that maintains the site (if different from the title of the site); the date of access; the URL in angle brackets. Note that if no author is given, the entry should begin with the title of the page:

> "Best Practices in Mental Health Reform: Discussion Paper." Health Canada Online. 15 Jan. 2003. Health Canada. 7 Feb. 2004 <http://www.hc-sc.gc.ca/hppb/mentalhealth/pubs/disc_paper/ e_disc8.html>.

> Physionet. 4 Feb., 2003. MIT. 1 May, 2003. <http://www.physionet.org>.

NOTE

[1] "Preparation of Papers for IEEE Transactions and Journals (April 2002)," [Online template] IEEE <www.ieee.org> (Current 12 February 2004).

chapter 16

CATCHLIST OF MISUSED WORDS AND PHRASES

This chapter offers a catchlist of words and phrases that are often misused. A periodic read-through will refresh your memory and help you avoid needless mistakes.

a, an. When you want to generalize about a single item, these are alternatives to the word *one*. Use **a** before a consonant sound and **an** before a vowel sound (*a, e, i, o, u*) or silent *h*:

> This product has a history of recalls.

> It will take an hour to repair.

accept, except. Accept is a verb meaning *to receive affirmatively*; **except**, when used as a verb, means *to exclude*:

> She accepted the scholarship.

> He was excepted from the language requirements.

acoustics. This word is singular as it refers to the science, but plural with respect to the acoustic properties of a building:

> Acoustics looks at how a building's acoustics are planned.

advice, advise. Advice is a noun, **advise** a verb:

> He was advised to ignore the advice of others.

affect, effect. Affect is a verb meaning *to influence*. **Effect** can be either a noun meaning *result* or a verb meaning *to bring something about*, usually with reference to change:

> The eye drops affect his vision.

> The effect of higher government spending is higher inflation.

> One job of the production engineer is to effect improvements.

all ready, already. To be **all ready** is simply to be ready for something; **already** means *beforehand* or *earlier*:

> The students were all ready for the test.

> Three days later, the test had already been marked.

all right. Write as two separate words: *all right*. (The single word *alright* is not an accepted spelling.) **All right** can mean *safe and sound, in good condition, okay*; *correct*; or *satisfactory*:

> Is everyone all right?

> The student's answers were all right.

(This second example is ambiguous: does it mean that the answers were all correct or simply satisfactory? In such cases, it is better to use a clearer word.)

all together, altogether. **All together** means in a group; **altogether** is an adverb meaning *entirely*:

> He was altogether insistent on keeping the papers all together.

allusion, illusion. An **allusion** is an indirect reference; an **illusion** is a false perception:

> His joke about relatives was an allusion to Einstein.

> What looks like water on the road is often an optical illusion.

a lot. Write as two separate words: *a lot*.

alternate, alternative. **Alternate** means *every other* or *every second* thing in a series; **alternative** refers to a *choice* between options:

> The two sections of the class attended labs on alternate weeks.

> The students could do a research paper as an alternative to writing the exam.

among, between. Use **among** for three or more persons or objects, **between** for two:

> Between you and me, there's trouble among the committee members.

amount, number. Note the difference between what's countable and not countable when choosing between these two words. **Amount** indicates quantity when units are not discrete and not absolute (i.e. uncountable); **number** indicates quantity when units are discrete and absolute (i.e. countable):

> A large <u>amount</u> of electricity was consumed.

> A large <u>number</u> of students were registered.

See also **less, fewer**.

analysis. The plural is **analyses**.

ante-, anti-. Distinguish the spellings here. **Ante-** means *before*, as in <u>ante</u>cedent or <u>ante</u>date. **Anti-** means *opposite* or *against*, as in <u>anti</u>dote or <u>anti</u>matter.

anyone, any one. Write the two words to give numerical emphasis; otherwise, **anyone** is written as one word:

> <u>Any one</u> of the proposals is reasonable.

> <u>Anyone</u> can write a reasonable proposal.

anyways. Non-standard informal English. Use **anyway** instead.

as, because. As a synonym of *because*, **as** is ambiguous because it may be confused with *while* or *when*:

> ✗   <u>As</u> he was working, he ate at his desk.

> ✓   <u>Because</u> he was working, he ate at his desk.

> ✗   She arrived <u>as</u> he was leaving.

> ✓   She arrived <u>when</u> he was leaving.

aspect, respect. Distinguish carefully between these two nouns when **aspect** means *angle* and **respect** means *point*:

> This <u>aspect</u> of the problem needs expansion in two <u>respects</u>.

as to. A common feature of bureaucratese. Replace it with a single-word preposition such as *about* or *on*:

> ✗   They were concerned <u>as to</u> the range of disagreement.

> ✓   They were concerned <u>about</u> the range of disagreement.

bad, badly. **Bad** is an adjective meaning *not good*:

> The weather turned bad.

> He felt bad about turning in his assignment late.

Badly is an adverb meaning *not well*. When used with the verbs **want** or **need**, it means *very much*:

> The results were recorded badly.

> The results badly needed corroboration.

basis, bases. **Basis** is singular; **bases** is plural.

beside, besides. **Beside** is a preposition meaning *next to*:

> She worked beside her assistant.

Besides has two uses: as a preposition it means *in addition to*; as a conjunctive adverb it means *moreover*:

> Besides her assistant, there was no one in the lab.

> She left because she was tired. Besides, there was no more work to do.

between. See **among**.

bring, take. Use **bring** for action coming closer to the speaker (*here*) and **take** for action going away (*there*):

> Bring me your résumé the next time you come.

> Take your résumé when you go to your interview.

cite, sight, site. To **cite** something is to *quote* or *mention* it as an example or authority; **sight** can be used in many ways, all of which relate to the ability to see; **site** refers to a specific *location*, the place where something is located, as in *website*.

classic, classical. Use **classic** to mean *memorable* or *standard of excellence*. **Classical** is normally the choice in scientific writing (as well as music):

> Gaussian distribution predicts the classic bell curve.

> Classical physics does not account for black holes.

climactic, climatic. Climactic describes a *climax*; **climatic** refers to *climate*.

complement, compliment. As verbs, **complement** means *to complete or enhance*, while **compliment** means *to praise*. Make this distinction clear, especially when you use adjective endings (**-ary**):

> The two experiments produced complementary results.
>
> The professor's comments on the report were complimentary.
>
> New subscribers were promised complimentary alarm clocks.

compose, comprise. Both words mean *to constitute or make up*, but **compose** is preferred. **Comprise** is correctly used to mean *include, consist of*, or *be composed of*. Using **comprise** in the passive ("is comprised of")—as you might be tempted to do in the second example below—is frowned on in formal writing, not the least because it uses three words where one will do:

> Four students compose the group representing the faculty.
>
> All systems comprise rules that govern them.

continual, continuous. Continual means *repeated over a period of time*; **continuous** means *constant* or *without interruption*:

> The strikes caused continual delays in building the road.
>
> Five days of continuous rain delayed the project further.

could of. This construction is nonstandard, as are **might of, should of**, and **would of**. Replace *of* with *have*:

> ✗ He could of done it.
>
> ✓ He could have done it.
>
> ✓ They might have been there.

council, counsel. Council is a noun meaning *an advisory or deliberative assembly*. **Counsel** as a noun means *advice* or *lawyer*; as a verb it means *to give advice*.

> The college council meets on Tuesday.
>
> A camp counsellor may need to counsel parents as well as children.

criterion, criteria. A **criterion** is *a standard for judging something*. **Criteria** is the plural of *criterion* and thus requires a plural verb:

These are the criteria for evaluating the new product.

data. The plural of **datum**. **Data** refers to the set of information, usually in numerical form, that is used for analysis as the basis for a study. Informally, **data** is often used as a singular noun, but in formal contexts, especially scientific contexts, treat it as a plural:

These data were gathered in an unsystematic fashion. Therefore they are inconclusive.

different from, different than. Although **different than** is common in informal contexts, use **different from** in writing:

The results were different from what had been predicted.

deduce, deduct. To **deduce** something is *to work it out by reasoning*; to **deduct** means *to subtract or take away* from something. The noun form of both words is **deduction**.

defence, defense. Both spellings are correct: **defence** is standard in Britain and is somewhat more common in Canada; **defense** is standard in the United States.

defuse, diffuse. Although they sound similar, these words have quite different meanings. It is a bomb that you **defuse** and information that you **diffuse** (or send out).

delusion, illusion. A **delusion** is a belief or perception that is distorted; an **illusion** is a false perception of reality:

He had delusions of grandeur.

The pool he thought he saw was an illusion.

dependent, dependant. **Dependent** is an adjective meaning *contingent on* or *subject to*; **dependant** is a noun.

Suriya's graduation is dependent upon her passing algebra.

Chedley is a dependant of his father.

device, devise. The word ending in **-ice** is the noun; the word ending in **-ise** is the verb.

diminish, minimize. To **diminish** means *to make or become smaller*; to **minimize** means *to reduce* something to the smallest possible amount or size.

discreet, discrete. **Discreet** means *tactful* or *prudent*; **discrete** means *separate and distinct*, generally the meaning applicable in scientific writing:

> The interviewer was <u>discreet</u> in asking about previous jobs.

> <u>Discrete</u> samples were collected.

disinterested, uninterested. **Disinterested** implies impartiality or neutrality; **uninterested** implies a lack of interest:

> As a <u>disinterested</u> observer, he was in a good position to judge the issue fairly.

> <u>Uninterested</u> in the proceedings, he yawned repeatedly.

dominant, dominate. **Dominant** is an adjective meaning *exerting control over* or *ranking above* something. **Dominate** is a verb meaning *to rule*:

> The <u>dominant</u> values are reported in Fig. 1.

> Safety should <u>dominate</u> all construction decisions.

due to. Although increasingly used to mean *because of*, **due** is an adjective and therefore needs to modify something:

> ✗ <u>Due to</u> his impatience, we lost the contract. [<u>Due</u> is dangling.]

> ✓ The loss was <u>due to</u> his impatience.

economic, economical. Use **economic** in reference to *the economy* and **economical** in reference to *savings*.

e.g., i.e. E.g. means *for example*; **i.e.** means *that is*. It is incorrect to use them interchangeably.

eminent, imminent. Eminent means *prominent* or *distinguished*; **imminent** refers to time and means *soon*.

entomology, etymology. **Entomology** is the study of insects; **etymology** is the study of the derivation and history of words.

especially, specially. **Especially** means *particularly* where **specially** means *for a special purpose*:

> The device was specially designed for wheelchair users.
>
> Cost price is an especially important consideration in manufacturing.

etc. Avoid **etc.** (*et cetera*) in formal writing. End a list with two or three examples introduced by *such as*:

> ✗ The project leaders discussed risk, interest rates, etc.
>
> ✓ The project leaders discussed such variables as risk and interest rates.

exceptional, exceptionable. **Exceptional** means *unusual* or *outstanding*, whereas **exceptionable** means *open to objection* and is generally used in negative contexts:

> His accomplishments are exceptional.
>
> There is nothing exceptionable in his behaviour.

farther, further. Where **farther** generally refers to distance, **further** suggests extent:

> The aquifer lies farther south than expected.
>
> She explained the proposal further.

firstly. Use **first** or **first of all** to avoid annoying readers who consider **firstly** old-fashioned or pretentious.

focus. The plural of the noun may be either **focuses** (also spelled *focusses*) or **foci**.

foreword, forward. A **foreword** (or *preface*) refers to front matter in a book or dissertation; **forward** describes a direction:

> In his foreword, the author praised his team for continually moving the project forward.

good, well. **Good** is an adjective that modifies a noun; **well** is an adverb that modifies a verb. In medical contexts, however, **well** also means *healthy*.

> He is a good rugby player.
>
> The experiment went well.
>
> The patient reported feeling well.

hardy, hearty. To distinguish these sound-alike words, reserve the sense of *durable* for **hardy** and *energetic* for **hearty**:

> Corn is a hardy crop.
>
> Corn chowder makes a hearty meal.

he/she, his/her. In formal writing, never resort to these abbreviations. If it is impossible to avoid generalizing in the singular, write out **he or she**, or the equivalent pronoun forms, in full.

> ✗   A co-op student should make sure his/her résumé is always up to date.
>
> ✓   A co-op student should make sure his or her résumé is always up to date.
>
> ✓   Co-op students should make sure their résumés are always up to date.

hopefully. In formal writing, use **hopefully** as an adverb meaning *full of hope*:

> She scanned the horizon hopefully, looking for signs of the missing boat.

Its informal use as a substitute for *it is to be hoped that* is frowned upon in formal writing.

> ✗   Hopefully the results will be published.
>
> ✓   The investigators hope to publish the results.

i.e. This is not the same as **e.g.** See **e.g.**

illusion. See **delusion.**

incite, insight. **Incite** is a verb meaning *to stir up*; **insight** is a noun meaning (often sudden) *understanding*.

infer, imply. To **infer** means *to deduce or conclude by reasoning*. It is often confused with **imply**, which means *to suggest or insinuate*. Note the give-and-take in these words (we **infer** X from Y, where Y **implies** X to us):

> We infer from the data that there will be cost overruns.

> The data imply that there will be cost overruns.

inflammable, flammable, non-flammable. Despite its **in-** prefix, **inflammable** is not the opposite of **flammable**: both words describe things that are *easily set on fire*. The opposite of **flammable** is **non-flammable**. To prevent any possibility of confusion, it's a good idea to stop using **inflammable** altogether.

inset, insert. Something that is **inset** is literally "set in," as a picture within a picture. Don't confuse this word with **insert**, a noun referring to something added separately:

> The histogram appears as an inset on the map of Cape Breton.

> A weekly regional paper comes as an insert in the Saturday *Record*.

intense, intensive. While both words refer to heavy concentrations, **intense** is a more subjective word, reflecting one's response to or impression of something; **intensive** is used as a more objective description:

> He found the course very intense and had difficulty keeping up with the workload.

> It was an intensive course designed to cover a lot of material in a short period of time.

irregardless. **Irregardless** may be found in dictionaries, but it is considered nonstandard English. It is also redundant. Use **regardless** instead.

its, it's. **Its** is a possessive pronoun; **it's** is a contraction of *it is* or *it has*. It is an error to put an apostrophe anywhere in *its* to show possession:

> ✗   Every problem has its' solution.

> ✗   Every problem has it's solution.

> ✓   Every problem has its solution.

> ✓   It's time to leave.

lead, led. **Lead** (the metal) sounds like **led** (the past form of the verb **to lead**). Be careful to distinguish the spellings.

✗ The investigation <u>lead</u> to a public inquiry.

✓ The investigation <u>led</u> to a public inquiry.

✓ The investigation <u>will lead</u> to a public inquiry.

less, fewer. **Less** is used not with plurals but with singular and uncountable units (as in "less information"). **Fewer** is the word to use with plurals (as in "fewer details"). However, **less** is also regularly used as a pronoun measuring statistics, distances, sums of money, or units of time, which are often thought of as amounts:

Abstracts should be kept to 150 words or <u>less</u>.

lie, lay. To **lie** means either *to assume a horizontal position* or *to tell a lie*; to **lay** means *to put [something] down*. The changes of tense often cause confusion:

Present	Past	Past participle
lie	lay	lain
lie	lied	lied
lay	laid	laid

like, as. **Like** is a preposition, but it is often used casually—and inappropriately—as a conjunction. To join two independent clauses, use the conjunction **as, as if,** or **as though** instead:

✗ The transformer looked <u>like</u> it was overloaded.

✓ The transformer looked <u>as though</u> it was overloaded.

✓ The residue looked <u>like</u> sand.

loose, lose. **Loose,** as an adjective, means the opposite of tight; **lose,** as a verb, means misplace or be defeated. Watch the spelling.

✗ The battery was <u>loosing</u> its charge.

✓ The battery was <u>losing</u> its charge.

media, medium. Use **media** as the plural of the singular word **medium**:

The <u>media</u> have reported the ban on urea formaldehyde as an insulation <u>medium</u>.

might of. See **could of**.

minimize. See **diminish**.

mitigate, militate. To **mitigate** means *to reduce the severity of* something; to **militate against** something means *to oppose* it.

myself, me. **Myself** is an intensifier of (not a substitute for) *I* or *me*. If you use it, make sure to use *I* or *me* in your sentence first:

   ✗   Please contact John or <u>myself</u> if you have questions.

   ✓   Please contact John or <u>me</u>.

   ✗   Jane and <u>myself</u> are presenting our findings.

   ✓   Jane and <u>I</u> are presenting our findings

   ✓   I completed the research <u>myself</u>.

off of. Drop the redundant **of**:

   ✗   The fence kept children <u>off of</u> the premises.

   ✓   The fence kept children <u>off</u> the premises.

orient, orientate. As a verb, **orient** means *to position something properly, to determine its bearings*. Although **orientate** is now commonly used with the same meaning, the shorter word is preferred, especially when positioning something according to compass points.

partake, take part. **Partake** means *to share*, while **take part** means *to participate*. Both are followed by the preposition *in*, but they are *not* synonyms:

   ✗   The candidate said that she liked to <u>partake</u> in sports.

   ✓   The candidate said that she liked to <u>take part</u> in sports.

passed, past. **Passed** is the past form of the verb **pass**. **Past** refers either to time or to one place farther than another:

     <u>Past</u> the bridge, they <u>passed</u> a sportscar.

people, persons. Legal contexts (for example, elevator licences) use **persons** as the plural of **person** in case of liability. For all other purposes, use **people**:

    ✗   The media reported two <u>persons</u> missing after the ferry sank.

    ✓   Twenty <u>people</u> registered for the first-aid class.

per cent, percentage. **Per cent** (from the Latin *per cent*) is used for numbers written as words (*four per cent*); with digits, use the symbol instead (*4.0%*). **Percentage** means proportion or amount and is used in generalizing about measurements:

    What <u>percentage</u> of students graduate with honours?

    Twenty-five <u>per cent</u> of students graduate with averages over 80%.

phenomenon. **Phenomenon** is a singular noun; the plural is **phenomena**. Not to be used as a synonym for *occurrence*, **phenomenon** refers to an exceptional circumstance.

practice, practise. **Practice** can be a noun or a modifier; **practise** is always a verb. (Note, however, that the standard American spelling of the verb is **practice**.)

    In a <u>practice</u> game, players <u>practise</u> their skills.

precede, proceed. To **precede** is *to go before* (earlier) *or in front of* others; to **proceed** is *to go on* or *to go ahead*:

    The dean's welcome will <u>precede</u> the awarding of certificates.

    The presentation will <u>proceed</u> without interruption.

prescribe, proscribe. These words are sometimes confused, although they have quite different meanings. **Prescribe** means *to advise the use of* or *to impose authoritatively*. **Proscribe** means *to reject, denounce, or ban*:

    The professor <u>prescribed</u> the conditions under which the equipment could be used.

> The student government proscribed the publication of unsigned editorials in the newspaper.

preventive, preventative. Although both are used to describe measures of prevention, the shorter word, **preventive**, is preferred.

principle, principal. **Principle** is a noun meaning *a general truth or law*; **principal** can be used as either a noun or an adjective, meaning *chief*.

quote, quotation. In formal writing, use **quote** as a verb, not as a synonym for **quotation**, which is a noun.

> The media quoted the mayor, who had asked city planners to present quotations [not *quotes*] on the project.

rational, rationale. **Rational** is an adjective meaning *logical* or *able to reason*. **Rationale** is a noun meaning *explanation*:

> That was not a rational decision.

> The president's memo explained the rationale for the decision.

real, really. **Real**, an adjective, means *true* or *genuine*; **really**, an adverb, means *actually*, *truly*, *very*, or *extremely*:

> The nugget was of real gold.

> The gold nugget was really valuable.

remanent, remnant. **Remanent** is an adjective for describing residual magnetization (or "remanence"). **Remnant** is a noun naming something left over or remaining.

sceptic, septic. British and Canadian spelling prefers **sceptic** for a person who doubts or disbelieves (the American spelling is *skeptic*). Be careful not to confuse it with the lookalike **septic**, which is used with ulcers and sewers.

seasonable, seasonal. **Seasonable** means *usual or suitable for the season*; **seasonal** means *of, depending on, or varying with the season*:

> Meteorologists predict the return of seasonable temperatures later in the week.

> In the summer, employment figures are adjusted to account for seasonal employment increases.

should of. See **could of.**

simple, simplistic. Both words refer to something that is *easy* or *basic*. **Simplistic**, however, has the negative connotation of *oversimplification*, so it should not be used simply as a synonym.

> The solution was simple.

> His simplistic answer annoyed the examiners.

stimulant, stimulus. A **stimulant** temporarily increases some vital process in an organ or organism, where a **stimulus** incites the organism to act in the first place.

than, then. **Than** is a conjunction linking unequal comparisons; **then** is an adverb of time or sequence:

> A is shorter than B.

> Shorten A, then B.

that, which. **That** can introduce a restrictive clause, and **which** can introduce a clause that is either restrictive or nonrestrictive (see p. 162).

> They studied cybernetics, which is a modern academic domain that touches all traditional disciplines.

Modern grammar checkers point to an error when there is no comma before **which**, so it is safe to make the distinction:

> He followed the format that the company recommends.

> He followed IEEE format, which the company recommends.

their, there. **Their** is the possessive form of the third-person plural pronoun. **There** is usually an adverb, meaning *at that place* or *at that point*:

> They parked their bikes there.

> There is no point arguing.

tortuous, torturous. The adjective **tortuous** means *full of twists and turns* or *circuitous*. **Torturous**, derived from *torture*, means *involving torture* or *excruciating*:

> The graph presented a <u>tortuous</u> curve.

> The interview was a <u>torturous</u> experience for the applicant.

translucent, transparent. A **translucent** substance permits light to pass through, but not enough for a person to see through it; a **transparent** substance permits light to pass unobstructed, so that objects can be seen clearly through it.

try and. This is a feature of conversational English. Use **try to** instead.

turbid, turgid. **Turbid**, with respect to a liquid or colour, means *muddy, not clear*, or (with respect to writing style) *confused*. **Turgid** means *swollen, inflated, or enlarged*, or (again with reference to style) *pompous or bombastic*.

unique. This word, which literally means *of which there is only one*, is both overused and misused. As a synonym of *unparalleled* or *unequalled*, it should not be used in comparisons such as *more unique* or *very unique*.

while. To prevent misreading, use **while** only when you mean *at the same time that*. Do not use **while** as a substitute for *although, whereas*, or *but*:

> ✗ <u>While</u> she's getting fair marks, she'd like to do better.

> ✗ He headed for home, <u>while</u> she decided to stay.

> ✓ He fell asleep <u>while</u> he was reading.

-wise. Avoid using **-wise** as a suffix to form new words that mean *with regard to*, for the tone is too casual for formal writing.

> ✗ <u>Saleswise</u>, the company did better last year.

> ✓ The company's sales have decreased this year.

your, you're. **Your** is a pronominal adjective showing possession; **you're** is a contraction of *you are*:

> <u>You're</u> likely to miss <u>your</u> train.

abbreviation. A short form of a word, often consisting of the word's initial letters and a period; *eng.* is a typical abbreviation of *engineering*.

abscissa. Another name for the horizontal or x-axis on a line graph.

absolute value. The magnitude of a number, often calculated by taking the square root of the square of a number.

abstract. A brief, comprehensive summary (50–200 words) accompanying a formal scientific report or paper and outlining its contents. As an adjective, **abstract** describes something theoretical or intangible rather than concrete.

acronym. A pronounceable word made up of the first letters of the words in a phrase or name: e.g. *SAW* (*surface acoustic wave*). A group of initial letters that are pronounced separately is an **initialism**: e.g. *HDTV*; *UHF*.

active voice. See **voice**.

adjective. A word that modifies or describes a noun or pronoun: e.g. *cloudy*; *new*; *legal*. An **adjective phrase** or **clause** is a group of words modifying a noun or pronoun: e.g. *the results that are expected*.

adverb. A word that modifies or qualifies a verb, adjective, or adverb, often answering a question such as *how? why? when?* or *where?*: e.g. *slowly*; *absolutely*; *soon*; *there*. An **adverb phrase** or **clause** is a group of words functioning like an adverb: e.g. *in the lab*; *if X is valid*. (See also **conjunctive adverb**.)

agreement. Consistency in tense, number, or person between related parts in a sentence: e.g. between subject and verb, or noun and related pronoun.

algorithm. A step-by-step approach to doing something specific; the term is most often used to describe computer procedures.

ambiguity. Vague or equivocal language with meaning that can be taken two or more ways.

analysis. A structured approach to thinking, or the results of thinking in a structured way.

antecedent (or **referent**). The noun for which a following pronoun stands: e.g. *engineers* in *Engineers are experts in their fields.*

appendix. A section added at the end of a work to include material not essential to the main discussion but complementary to it.

appositive. A word or phrase that identifies a preceding noun or pronoun: e.g. *Dr. Lee, my supervisor, is a fine mentor.* The second phrase (*my supervisor*) is said to be **in apposition to** the first (*Dr. Lee*).

article. A word introducing a noun that identifies whether the noun is general or specific, singular or plural. *A* and *an* are called **indefinite articles**; *the* is a **definite article**.

assertion. A positive statement or claim: e.g. *The data are convincing.*

auxiliary verb. A verb used to form the tenses, moods, and voices of other verbs: e.g. *was* in *It was done.* The main auxiliary verbs in English are *be, have,* and *do. Can, could, may, might, must, shall, should, will,* and *would* are called **modal auxiliaries**.

average (mean), median, mode. Three measures used to characterize the centre point of a set of values. The **average** (or **mean**) is calculated by adding a set of values and then dividing the result by the number of values added. **Median** represents the middle number in a set of numbers. **Mode** is the most frequently occurring value.

bibliography. 1. A list of works used or referred to in writing a paper or report. 2. A reference book listing works available on a particular subject.

calibration. The process of preparing a measuring instrument for use, either by calculating an error factor or by eliminating a difference between the expected value and the measured value for some standard.

case. Any of the inflected forms of a personal pronoun (see **inflection**).

> **Subjective case**: *I, we, you, he, she, it, they.*
>
> **Objective case**: *me, us, you, him, her, it, them.*
>
> **Possessive adjective case**: *my, our, your, his, her, its, their.*
>
> **Possessive noun case**: *mine, ours, yours, his, hers, its, theirs.*

centrifugal, centripetal. A **centrifugal** force is directed away from the axis of rotation, where a **centripetal** force is directed toward the axis of rotation.

circumlocution. A roundabout or circuitous expression, often used in a deliberate attempt to be vague or evasive: e.g. using *at this particular point in time* for *now*.

clause. A group of words containing a subject and a predicate. An **independent clause** can stand by itself as a complete sentence: e.g. *The solution remained stable*. A **subordinate** (or **dependent**) **clause** cannot stand by itself but must be connected to an **independent clause**: e.g. <u>*Unless the temperature rises*</u>, *the solution remains stable*.

cliché. A phrase or idea that has lost its impact through overuse: e.g. *beyond the shadow of a doubt; a window of opportunity*.

collective noun. A noun that is singular in form but refers to a group: e.g. *family; team; staff*. It will take a verb that is either singular or plural, depending on whether it refers to the group as a whole or its individual members.

colloquial language. Everyday expressions that are appropriate to speaking. Formal writing avoids **colloquialisms**: e.g. *Let's get the bugs out of the program*.

comma splice. See **run-on sentence**.

complement. A completing word or phrase that usually follows a linking verb to form a **subjective complement**: e.g. (1) *She is <u>my colleague</u>*. (2) *That substance tastes <u>bitter</u>*. When the complement is an adjective, it can be called a **predicate adjective**. An **objective complement** completes the direct object rather than the subject: e.g. *We considered the assessment <u>fair</u>*.

complex sentence. A sentence containing at least one dependent clause in addition to an independent one: e.g. *The estimates were accepted although they were sketchy*.

compound sentence. A sentence containing two or more independent clauses: e.g. <u>*Several solutions exist*</u>, but <u>*only one is viable*</u>. A sentence is called **compound-complex** if it contains a dependent clause as well as two independent clauses: e.g. *Several solutions exist, but only one is viable <u>as long as there are budgetary constraints</u>*.

conclusion. The part of a paper or report in which the findings are pulled together or the implications revealed so that the reader has a sense of closure or completion.

concrete language. Specific language that provides details: e.g. *grey crystalline deposits*; *rusted barbed wire*; *toxic waste*.

conditional verb. The verb form called for in hypothetical situations: e.g. *If the data were recalculated, the results would be different.*

confidence interval. A statistical calculation that yields a range of values instead of a single estimate for some aspect of a population.

conjunction. A word used to link words, phrases, or clauses. A **coordinating conjunction** (*and, nor, but, or, yet*) links two equal (parallel) parts of a sentence (see **correlative conjunctions**). A **subordinating conjunction**, placed at the beginning of a subordinate clause, shows the logical dependence of that clause on another: e.g. (1) *Although the work is complete, it is unsatisfactory.* (2) *They ran several tests after they installed the software.*

conjunctive adverb. A type of adverb that shows the logical relation between the phrase or clause that it modifies and a preceding one: e.g. (1) *Incineration is one alternative; it produces toxic waste, however.* (2) *The battery died; therefore, the car would not start.*

connotation. The range of ideas or meanings suggested by a certain word in addition to its literal meaning. Apparent synonyms, such as *artificial* and *imitation* and *synthetic*, even *counterfeit*, have differing connotations. (See **denotation**.)

context. The setting, background, or foundation for an investigation that helps establish its place in the larger scheme of things.

contraction. A word formed by combining and shortening two or more words: e.g. *isn't* from *is not*; *they'll* from *they will*. Contractions are appropriate in letters and casual messages, not in formal reports or academic writing.

coordinating conjunction. See **conjunction**.

copula verb. See **linking verb**.

copyright. A legal mechanism that authors, illustrators, mapmakers, software developers, and others use to keep people from using their work without permission.

correlative conjunctions. Pairs of coordinating conjunctions that call for **parallel wording**: e.g. *either/or*; *neither/nor*; *not/but*; *not only/but (also)*.

cost benefit analysis. A decision-making process that involves comparing the costs and benefits associated with each option.

critical path method. A project management method that models the activities and events of a project to determine how much time is needed to complete the project.

culture. The values and beliefs shared by a group of people, e.g. members of a profession, organization, or company.

dangling modifier. A modifying word or phrase (often including a participle) that is not grammatically connected to any part of the sentence: e.g. _Examining the results, several discrepancies were noted._

deduction. A research process that tests a _hypothesis_ and draws conclusions based on test results.

demonstrative pronoun. A pronoun that points to something: e.g. (1) _This is the result_; (2) _That looks like the reason_. When used to modify a noun or pronoun, a demonstrative becomes a kind of **adjective**: _this reaction_; _those data_.

denotation. The literal or dictionary meaning of a word. (See **connotation**.)

diction. The choice of words with respect to their tone, degree of formality, or register. Formal diction is the language of speeches and research papers or reports. The informal diction of everyday speech or conversational writing often includes slang.

discourse. Talk, either oral or written. **Direct discourse** (or **direct speech**) cites an actual quotation in its context: e.g. _Edison said, "There is no substitute for hard work."_ In writing, direct discourse is put in quotation marks. **Indirect discourse** (or indirect speech) gives the gist of the quotation rather than a word-for-word citation. Quotation marks are not used, although the reference is documented: e.g. _Edison said that nothing could replace hard work._

ellipsis marks. Three spaced dots indicating an omission from a quoted passage [...].

empirical evidence. Data created by making measurements or doing experiments.

encryption. A process to convert information into code so that it cannot be read by someone who has not been given access, most often to protect information sent over the Internet.

endnote. A citation or note appearing at the end of a paper or a chapter in a book.

entropy. The tendency of all physical systems to move toward disorder.

equilibrium. A state in which opposing forces or actions are in balance.

error bar. A graphical depiction of a confidence interval.

error factor. The difference between the actual value and the measured value as calculated during **calibration**. This factor is used to adjust all subsequent measurements to account for the systematic error created by the measuring instrument.

essay. A composition on any subject. Some essays are descriptive or narrative; in an academic setting, most are expository (explanatory) or argumentative.

euphemism. A word or phrase used to avoid some other wording that might be considered offensive or harsh: e.g. *custodian* for *janitor*; *underperform* for *fail*.

expletive. A word or phrase used primarily for grammatical purposes, usually followed by a form of the verb *be*: e.g. *It is raining*; *there are several puddles*.

exploratory writing. Informal writing done to help generate ideas before formal planning begins.

fair dealing. The limited right of researchers and others to borrow small amounts of a copyrighted work without official permission, yet with documentation.

fault trees. A structured process used to identify and assess potential causes of system failure before the failures actually occur. Analysts begin by selecting a top-level event, like a critical safety issue, and then work down to evaluate all the contributing events that may ultimately lead to the occurrence of that top-level event. The resulting fault tree diagram is a graphical representation of the chain of events in the system, and it includes all the information needed to estimate the probability of the top-level event.

fission. A reaction in which the atomic nucleus is split and energy is released. This reaction is the key process within both the atomic bomb and nuclear power generators.

flowchart. A graphical representation of a process.

footnote. A citation or note appearing at the bottom of the page in a paper or article.

fused sentence. A sentence combining two independent clauses without punctuation. (See **run-on sentence**.)

fusion. A reaction in which several atomic nuclei combine and energy is released. This process takes place continuously in the sun and stars.

general language. Language that lacks specific details; abstract language.

gerund. A **verbal** marked by its -*ing* ending and functioning as a noun in a sentence: e.g. *We look forward to* interviewing *the candidate.*

grammar. The study of the forms and relations of words and of the rules governing their use in speech and writing.

Greek alphabet. The alphabet used to represent variables and constants in equations. By convention, some of the characters are regularly used to represent a specific variable or constant: e.g. *pi* (π) represents the commonly used irrational number 3.1415+.

hypothesis. A testable statement that indicates what an experimenter expects to find through his or her work.

hypothetical instance. An imagined occurrence, generally indicated by a clause beginning with *if*. (See **conditional verb**.)

idiom. A phrase that has no explanation for its structure other than that it "sounds right": e.g. *This* makes sense.

independent clause. See **clause**.

indirect discourse (or **indirect speech**). See **discourse**.

induction. A research process in which investigators come to a conclusion based on what they have observed.

inertia. The tendency of a body to resist acceleration.

infinitive. A verb form made up of the root form of a verb usually introduced by the marker *to*: e.g. *to evaluate*. The base infinitive omits the *to*: e.g. *evaluate*.

inflection. The change in form of a word to indicate number, person, case, tense, or degree: e.g. *Boys* run *fast. That boy* ran faster.

initialism. See **acronym**.

intensifier (or **qualifier**). A word that modifies and adds emphasis to another word or phrase: e.g. *very* slowly; *quite* important. Avoid adding such words to absolutes like *major* or *empty* or *complete*.

interjection. A strong expression or exclamation, usually followed by a comma or exclamation mark: e.g. *Well*, that's important. *Ouch!*

interrogative sentence. A sentence that asks a question and that concludes with a question mark: e.g. *How much time elapsed? Did the link work?*

interrogative words. Question words used in direct queries or in noun clauses: e.g. *what, who, how*, etc.

intransitive verb. A verb that does not take a direct object: e.g. *fall, sleep, happen*.

introduction. A section at the start of a report or paper that tells the reader what will be discussed—and why.

italics. Slanting type represented in handwriting or typescript by underlining.

jargon. Technical terms when used unnecessarily or in inappropriate places: e.g. *resource recovery facility* for *incinerator*.

linking verb (or **copula verb**). A verb such as *be, seem*, or *feel* used to join subject to complement: e.g. *The strategy is complex.*

literal meaning. The primary, or denotative, meaning of a word.

logarithm. The power to which a base must be raised to produce a given number. The common logarithm's base is 10, the natural logarithm's base is e, and the binary logarithm's base is 2. For example, the common logarithm of 100 is 2, the natural logarithm of e is 1, and the binary logarithm of 8 is 3.

matrix. The mathematical representation in which data and equations are organized into rectangular arrays of numbers and variables.

mean, median, mode. See **average**.

misplaced modifier. A word or group of words that can cause confusion by not being placed next to the element it modifies: e.g. *We nearly examined twenty sources.* [Revised: *We examined nearly twenty sources.*]

modifier. A word or group of words that describes or limits the context of another element in the sentence.

mood. 1. As a grammatical term, the form that shows a verb's purpose:

Indicative mood: *She is working hard.*

Imperative mood: *Work hard!*

Interrogative mood: *Is she working hard?*

Subjunctive mood: *It is essential that she work hard.*

2. When applied to literature generally, the atmosphere or tone created by the author.

negatives. Words or constructions that carry a negative meaning: e.g. *no, not, never, none, nobody, nothing.*

non-restrictive modifier. See **restrictive modifier.**

noun. An inflected part of speech naming a person, place, thing, idea, or feeling—and usually serving as subject, object, or complement. A **common noun** is a general term: e.g. *day, school, automobile.* A **proper noun** is a specific name: e.g. *Wednesday, Queen's University, Toyota.*

number. Generally, a distinction between singular (1) and plural (>1). **Cardinal numbers** represent how many of something there are (*one, two, three,* etc.), while **ordinal numbers** represent a ranking or position (*first, second, third,* etc.)

object. 1. A noun or pronoun (called the **direct object**) that completes the action of the verb: e.g. *He asked a question.* An **indirect object** is the person or thing receiving the direct object: e.g. *He asked her* [indirect object] *a question* [direct object].
2. The noun or pronoun in a group of words beginning with a preposition: e.g. *between them; in the corner.*

objective complement. See **complement.**

objectivity. A position or stance taken without bias or prejudice. (Compare **subjectivity.**)

optimization. Mathematical techniques used to make a decision, a system, or a design as effective or as functional as possible.

ordinate. Another name for the vertical or y-axis on a line graph.

outline. With regard to a paper or report, a brief sketch of the main parts, to help in organizing them; a written plan.

paragraph. A set of sentences arranged logically to explain or describe an idea, event, or object; the start of a paragraph is usually marked by an indentation or double spacing.

parallel wording. Wording in which a series of items has a similar grammatical form: e.g. *The Babylonians, the Egyptians, and even the Bible note the existence of pi*.

parameters. Constants whose values characterize aspects of a system when the system's behaviour is represented as a set of equations.

paraphrase. Restate in different words.

parentheses. Curved lines enclosing and setting off a passage; not to be confused with square brackets.

parenthetical element. A word or phrase inserted as an explanation or afterthought into a passage that is grammatically complete without it: e.g. *Fuzzy logic, in more than one sense, resembles human decision making.*

participle. A verbal that functions as a modifier. Participles can be either **present**, marked by an *-ing* ending (e.g. *being* or *having* or *taking*), or **past** (e.g. *taken*); they also exist in the **passive**: e.g. *being taken* or *having been taken*.

part of speech. Each of the major categories into which words are sorted according to grammatical function. Some grammars consider only function words (nouns, verbs, adjectives, and adverbs); others include prepositions, pronouns, conjunctions, and interjections.

passive voice. See **voice**.

past participle. See **participle**.

patent. A legal mechanism by which a person or company who owns a patent can sue others who make, use, or sell the product or process without the permission of the patent owner.

periodic sentence. A sentence in which the normal order is inverted or in which an essential element is suspended until the very end: e.g. *Not until the early twentieth century, with the development of reinforced concrete, was it possible to build a skyscraper.*

person. In grammar, the three classes of personal pronouns referring to the person speaking (**first person**: *I*), the person(s) spoken to (**second person**: *you*), and the distant person(s) spoken about (**third person**: *he, she, it*)

personal pronouns. See **pronoun**.

phrase. A set of words lacking a subject–predicate combination, typically forming part of a clause. The most common type is the **prepositional phrase**—
a unit consisting of a preposition and an object: e.g. *Experiments were divided
into three stages*.

plagiarism. The deliberate use of someone else's work or ideas without acknowledgement.

plural. Indicating two or more, specifically with numbers. Nouns, pronouns,
and verbs all have plural forms.

possessive case. See **case**.

precision. The number of significant digits to which a value has been measured.

prefix. An element placed in front of the root form of a word to make a new
word: e.g. *pro-*; *in-*; *sub-*; *anti-*. (Compare **suffix**.)

preposition. A short structure word or phrase heading a group of words repre-
senting an object; together, a preposition and its object form a **prepositional
phrase**: e.g. *under* the time limit; *because of* the constraints.

process. A series of actions or operations leading to a particular and usually
desirable result.

pronoun. A word that stands in as a noun. A personal pronoun stands for the
name of a person: *I, you, she, he, it, we, they*.

public domain. A term applied to work that lacks copyright protection; permission for copying is not required, although everything should still be documented.

punctuation. A conventional system of signs and symbols (e.g. comma, period,
semicolon) used to indicate stops or divisions in a sentence.

qualitative data. Data that is satisfactorily described not by numbers but by
words.

quantitative data. Data that is measurable or enumerable.

quotation. The recording or repeating of something someone has said or written.

random error. Variations observed in a data set but not explicable in a
study.

range. A measure of the variability of scores in a sample. It tells how closely a set of scores cluster around the mean, and it is equal to the difference between the highest and lowest observed values in a data set.

redundancy. Unnecessary or ineffectual repetition: e.g. *join together*; *first and foremost*.

reference works. Sources consulted when preparing a paper or report.

referent. See **antecedent**.

reflexive (intensive) pronoun. A pronoun ending with *-self* or *-selves* to echo or emphasize a preceding noun or pronoun: e.g. *The researchers congratulated themselves*.

register. The degree of formality in word choice and sentence structure.

relative clause. A clause introduced by a relative pronoun: e.g. *The approach that was taken was the most cost effective*.

relative pronoun. *Who, which, that*, or their compounds, used to introduce an adjective clause: e.g. *the approach that was taken*.

request for proposal (RFP). A formal invitation describing project require-ments. The appropriate response to an RFP is a formal proposal outlining both how the respondent plans to meet the project requirements and the expected compensation for completing the project.

restrictive modifier. A phrase or clause that identifies or is essential to the meaning of a term: e.g. *They read the article that their professor had recom-mended*. It should not be set off by commas. A **non-restrictive modifier** is not needed for identification and is usually set off parenthetically with com-mas: e.g. *They read Jennings' article, which their professor had recommended*.

rhetorical question. A question posed and answered by a writer or speaker to draw attention to a point; no response is expected on the part of the audi-ence: e.g. *How important are these findings? Indeed, they are significant for sev-eral reasons*.

risk management. Actions taken to understand, control, and limit the possi-bility of adverse consequences.

run-on sentence. A sentence that goes beyond the point where it should have stopped. The term covers both the **comma splice** (two sentences incorrectly joined by a comma) and the **fused sentence** (two sentences incorrectly joined without any punctuation).

scientific method. A structured approach to research that requires the formulation of a hypothesis based on a systematic and objective collection and review of existing data followed by the experimental testing of that hypothesis.

scientific notation. A convention in which a real number is expressed as the product of a real number and a base (usually 10) raised to a power: e.g. 3.257×10^5 represents 325,700.

sentence. A grammatical unit that includes both a subject and a predicate. The end of a sentence is marked by a period.

sentence fragment. A group of words lacking either a subject or a complete predicate; an incomplete sentence punctuated as a sentence.

significant digits. The number of decimal places to which a result can be meaningfully reported when the result is expressed according to scientific notation: e.g. 3.257×10^5 has four significant digits.

simple sentence. A sentence made up of only one clause: e.g. *Data fusion is a popular information processing technique.*

slang. Colloquial speech inappropriate for academic or professional writing, often used in a special sense by a limited group: e.g. *clicks* for *kilometres per hour*; *ace* for *succeed*.

squinting modifier. A kind of misplaced modifier that could be connected to elements on either side, producing ambiguity: e.g. *Students who study often do well on exams.*

standard deviation. A measure of the variability of scores in a sample, showing the average distance of a set of scores from the mean.

standard English. The English currently spoken or written by literate people and widely accepted as the correct and conventional form.

statistics. A term referring to both (1) the set of techniques for estimating the characteristics of a population based on the characteristics of a sample drawn from that population, and (2) the estimates created using these techniques.

stochastic process. A variable that changes in a way that depends, at least partially, on chance. Such variables are measured and studied using probability and statistics.

subject. In grammar, the noun or noun equivalent with which the verb agrees and about which the rest of the clause is predicated: e.g. *Research is a challenge, but many people thrive on it.*

subjective complement. See **complement**.

subjectivity. A personal stance that is based on feelings or opinions and is not impartial or disinterested. (Compare **objectivity**.)

subjunctive. See **conditional verb** and **mood**.

suboptimization. Optimization of a subsystem. The principle states that suboptimization does not always lead to global optimization.

subordinate clause. See **clause**.

subordinating conjunction. See **conjunction**.

subordination. Making one clause dependent upon another (see **clause**).

suffix. An element added to the end of a word to form a derivative: e.g. *prepare, preparation; sign, signify*. (Compare **prefix**.)

synonym. A word with the same dictionary meaning as another word: e.g. *begin* and *start*.

syntax. Sentence construction; the grammatical relationship of words and phrases.

synthesis. A process in which separate elements combine to create a coherent whole.

tense. A set of inflected forms taken by a verb to indicate time (i.e. past, present, future).

theme. A recurring or dominant idea.

theory. A set of general statements or abstract principles created to explain a set of facts or phenomena.

thesis statement. A one-sentence assertion that presents the central argument of a paper.

topic sentence. The sentence in a paragraph that expresses the main or controlling idea.

transition. A word or phrase that shows the logical relation between sentences or parts of a sentence and thus helps to signal the change from one idea to another: e.g. *therefore*; *however*; *for example*.

transitive verb. A verb that takes an object: e.g. *heat*; *bring*; *finalize*. (Compare **intransitive verb**.)

transitivity. An aspect of a relationship between objects. Equality is **transitive** because $a = b$ and $b = c$ implies that $a = c$.

true value. The real value researchers strive to obtain when measuring a characteristic of a system or a descriptor of a population.

usage. The way in which a word or phrase is normally and correctly used; accepted practice.

variable. An element that can represent any one of a set of values. In an experiment, the **independent variable** is the one manipulated by the experimenter; the **dependent variable** is what the experimenter predicts will be affected by manipulations of the independent variable.

variance. A measure of the variability of scores in a sample, telling how closely a set of scores cluster around the mean.

verb. That part of the predicate expressing an action, process, state, or condition, telling what the subject is or does. Verbs are inflected to show tense (time). The principal parts of a verb are the basic forms from which all tenses are made: the *base infinitive*, the *past tense*, and the *past participle*.

verbal. A word that resembles a verb in form but does not function as one: a **participle**, a **gerund**, or an **infinitive**.

voice. The form of a verb that shows whether the subject acted (**active voice**) or was acted upon (**passive voice**): e.g. *They presented the award* (active). *The award was presented by them* (passive). Only transitive verbs (verbs taking objects) can be made passive.

WEIGHTS, MEASURES, AND NOTATION

The conversion factors are not exact unless so marked. They are given only to the accuracy likely to be needed in everyday calculations.

1. IMPERIAL AND AMERICAN, WITH METRIC EQUIVALENTS

Linear measure

1 inch	= 25.4 millimetres exactly
1 foot = 12 inches	= 0.3048 metre exactly
1 yard = 3 feet	= 0.9144 metre exactly
1 (statute) mile = 1,760 yards	= 1.609 kilometres
1 int. nautical mile	
= 1.150779 miles	= 1.852 km exactly

Square measure

1 square inch	= 6.45 sq. centimetres
1 square foot = 144 sq. in.	= 9.29 sq. decimetres
1 square yard = 9 sq. ft.	= 0.836 sq. metre
1 acre = 4,840 sq. yd.	= 0.405 hectare
1 square mile = 640 acres	= 259 hectares

Cubic measure

1 cubic inch	= 16.4 cu. centimetres
1 cubic foot = 1,728 cu. in.	= 0.0283 cu. metre
1 cubic yard = 27 cu. ft.	= 0.765 cu. metre

Capacity measure

Name	System	Equal to	Metric
fluid oz.	imperial	1/20 imp. pint	28.41 ml
	US (liquid)	1/16 US pint	29.57 ml
gill	imperial	1/4 pint	142.07 ml
	US (liquid)	1/4 pint	118.29 ml
pint	imperial	20 fl.oz.(imp.)	568.26 ml
	US (liquid)	16 fl.oz.(US)	473.18 ml
	US (dry)	1/2 quart	550.61 ml
quart	imperial	2 pints	1.1365 litres
	US (liquid)	2 pints	0.9464 litre
	US (dry)	2 pints	1.1012 litres
gallon	imperial	4 quarts	4.546 litres
	US (liquid)	4 quarts	3.785 litres
peck	imperial	2 gallons	9.092 litres
	US (dry)	8 quarts	8.810 litres
bushel	imperial	4 pecks	36.369 litres
	US (dry)	4 pecks	35.239 litres

Avoirdupois weight

1 grain	= 0.065 gram
1 dram	= 1.772 grams
1 ounce = 16 drams	= 28.35 grams
1 pound = 16 ounces	
= 7,000 grains	= 0.45359237 kilogram exactly
1 stone = 14 pounds	= 6.35 kilograms
1 quarter = 2 stones	= 12.70 kilograms
1 hundredweight = 4 quarters	
= 112 lb.	= 50.80 kilograms
1 (long) ton = 20 cwt. = 2,240 lb.	= 1.016 tonnes
1 short ton = 2,000 pounds	= 0.907 tonne

2. METRIC, WITH IMPERIAL EQUIVALENTS

Linear measure

1 millimetre	= 0.039 inch
1 centimetre = 10 mm	= 0.394 inch
1 decimetre = 10 cm	= 3.94 inches
1 metre = 100 cm	= 1.094 yards
1 decametre = 10 m	= 10.94 yards
1 hectometre = 100 m	= 109.4 yards
1 kilometre = 1000 m	= 0.6214 mile

Square measure

1 square centimetre	= 0.155 sq. inch
1 square metre = 10 000 sq. cm	= 1.196 sq. yards
1 are = 100 sq. metres	= 119.6 sq. yards
1 hectare = 100 ares	= 2.471 acres
1 square kilometre = 100 ha	= 0.386 sq. mile

Cubic measure

1 cubic centimetre	= 0.061 cu. inch
1 cubic metre = one million cu. cm	= 1.308 cu. yards

Capacity measure

1 millilitre	= 0.002 pint (imperial)
1 centilitre = 10 ml	= 0.018 pint
1 decilitre = 100 ml	= 0.176 pint
1 litre = 1000 ml	= 1.76 pints
1 decalitre = 10 l	= 2.20 gallons (imperial)
1 hectolitre = 100 l	= 2.75 bushels (imperial)

Weight

1 milligram	= 0.015 grain
1 centigram = 10 mg	= 0.154 grain
1 decigram = 100 mg	= 1.543 grain
1 gram = 1000 mg	= 15.43 grain
1 decagram = 10 g	= 5.64 drams
1 hectogram = 100 g	= 3.527 ounces
1 kilogram = 1000 g	= 2.205 pounds
1 tonne (metric ton) = 1000 kg	= 0.984 (long) ton

3. SI UNITS

Base units

Physical quantity	Name	Abbr. or symbol
length	metre	m
mass	kilogram	kg
time	second	s
electric current	ampere	A
temperature	kelvin	K
amount of substance	mole	mol
luminous intensity	candela	cd

Supplementary units

Physical quantity	Name	Abbr. or symbol
plane angle	radian	rad
solid angle	steradian	sr

Derived units with special names

Physical quantity	Name	Abbr. or symbol
frequency	hertz	Hz
energy	joule	J
force	newton	N
power	watt	W
pressure	pascal	Pa
electric charge	coulomb	C
electromotive force	volt	V
electric resistance	ohm	Ω
electric conductance	siemens	S
electric capacitance	farad	F
magnetic flux	weber	Wb
inductance	henry	H
magnetic flux density	tesla	T
luminous flux	lumen	lm
illumination	lux	lx

4. TEMPERATURE

Celsius (or Centigrade): Water boils (under standard conditions) at 100° and freezes at 0°

Fahrenheit: Water boils at 212° and freezes at 32°

Kelvin: Water boils at 373.15 kelvins and freezes at 273.15 kelvins.

Celsius	Fahrenheit
-17.8°	0°
-10°	14°
0°	32°
10°	50°
20°	68°
30°	86°
40°	104°
50°	122°
60°	140°
70°	158°
80°	176°
90°	194°
100°	212°

To convert Celsius into Fahrenheit: multiply by 9, divide by 5, and add 32.

To convert Fahrenheit to Celsius: subtract 32, multiply by 5, and divide by 9.

5. METRIC PREFIXES

	Abbr. or symbol	Factor
deca-	da	10
hecto-	h	10^2
kilo-	k	10^3
mega-	M	10^6
giga-	G	10^9
tera-	T	10^{12}
peta-	P	10^{15}
exa-	E	10^{18}
deci-	d	10^{-1}
centi-	c	10^{-2}
milli-	m	10^{-3}
micro-	m	10^{-6}
nano-	n	10^{-9}
pico-	p	10^{-12}
femto-	f	10^{-15}
atto-	a	10^{-18}

These prefixes may be applied to any units of the metric system: hectogram (abbr. hg) = 100 grams; kilowatt (abbr. kW) = 1000 watts; megahertz (MHz) = 1 million hertz; centimetre (cm) = $^1/_{100}$ metre; microvolt (μV) = one millionth of a volt; picofarad (pF) = 10^{-12} farad, and are sometimes applied to other units (megabit).

6. POWER NOTATION

This expresses concisely any power of ten (any number that is composed of factors of 10). 10^2 or ten squared = $10 \times 10 = 100$; 10^3 or ten cubed = $10 \times 10 \times 10 = 1,000$. Similarly, $10^4 = 10,000$ and $10^{10} = 1$ followed by ten zeros = 10,000,000,000. Proceeding in the opposite direction, dividing by ten and subtracting one from the index, we have $10^2 = 100$, $10^1 = 10$, $10^0 = 1$, $10^{-1} = ^1/_{10}$, $10^{-2} = ^1/_{100}$, and so on; $10^{-10} = 1/10,000,000,000$.

7. BINARY SYSTEM

Only two units (O and 1) are used, and the position of each unit indicates a power of two.

One to ten written in binary form:

	eights (2^3)	fours (2^2)	twos (2^1)	one
1				1
2			1	0
3			1	1
4	1	0	0	
5		1	0	1
6		1	1	0
7		1	1	1
8	1	0	0	0
9	1	0	0	1
10	1	0	1	0

i.e. ten is written as 1010 ($2^3 + 0 + 2^1 + 0$); one hundred is written as 1100100 ($2^6 + 2^5 + 0 + 0 + 2^2 + 0 + 0$).

INDEX

THE MAKING SENSE SERIES

Margot Northey
MAKING SENSE:
A Student's Guide to Research and Writing
Fourth Updated Edition

Margot Northey and David B. Knight
MAKING SENSE IN GEOGRAPHY AND ENVIRONMENTAL SCIENCES:
A Student's Guide to Research and Writing
Second Updated Edition

Margot Northey, Lorne Tepperman, and James Russell
MAKING SENSE IN THE SOCIAL SCIENCES:
A Student's Guide to Research and Writing
Second Updated Edition

Margot Northey and Brian Timney
MAKING SENSE IN PSYCHOLOGY AND THE LIFE SCIENCES:
A Student's Guide to Research and Writing
Third Updated Edition

Margot Northey and Judi Jewinski
MAKING SENSE IN ENGINEERING AND THE TECHNICAL SCIENCES:
A Student's Guide to Research and Writing